W9-ACZ-920

LONGMAN LINGUISTICS LIBRARY
Title no 13
STRUCTURAL ASPECTS OF LANGUAGE CHANGE

LONGMAN LINGUISTICS LIBRARY

Title no:

Structural Aspects
of Language Change

James M. Anderson

Associate Professor of Linguistics
University of Calgary

LONGMAN

for S.S.C.S.

Preface

The history of linguistics is primarily a chronicle of events that have moulded linguistic thinking from the early classical period through the Middle Ages and the very productive nineteenth century to the present. Historical linguistics is mainly concerned with changes in language through time. It seeks to examine underlying principles of change, whether they are motivated by structural relationships inherent in a language design, by external forces in the environment of the speakers, or by variations in cognitive capacities innate in the human species. Language change is an inexorable property of language itself and investigations of sources, processes, inhibitors and results of change are paramount to our understanding of language phenomena.

The main concern here is to bring together under one cover the major approaches that have characterized the study of language change. The text is designed primarily as an introduction to principles and methods of historical linguistics but some attention is given to people and events that were instrumental in formulating the basic tenets of our discipline. Besides a treatment of various approaches to the study of language change, related material that has helped to substantiate linguistic conclusions on particular topics has been included.

For advanced students concerned with this aspect of linguistics, further insight into any part of the subject matter can be gained by following up the references cited.

The author would like to acknowledge a debt of gratitude to Dr Bynon, Dr Spence and George W. Patterson for careful reading and helpful suggestions. In a more general way the work has also profited from discussions with Dr Romeo, Dr Rochet and Professor Creore. Special thanks are due to my former teacher of Romance and historical linguistics, Dr E. Dorfman. For helpful editorial suggestions I should also like to thank Mrs E. L. Wittig; Miss Strange for conscientious typing of the manuscript; and Robert Byers for assistance in indexing. My wife's contribution to this book is incalculable. Her persistence and patience in reading and typing the manuscript over many months while attending to a rather energetic family greatly helped accelerate the entire project.

Preparation of the manuscript was assisted by financial support extended by The University of Alberta and by The University of Calgary.

University of Calgary   J M A
January 1973

Contents

10 Linguistic models

Figures

Acknowledgements

We are grateful to the following for permission to reproduce copyright material:

The University of Chicago Press for an extract from *Language Change and Linguistic Reconstruction* by H. H. Hoenigswald, © 1960 by The University of Chicago.

Chapter 1

Introduction

The general objectives of historical linguistics

An object such as a plant can be described with reference to its structure or composition. Similarly, its function in the universe can be stated in a general way. However, we are still confronted with the question – why and how does the organism work (or grow, as the case may be)? We are forced to turn away from the object itself and seek the answer among the factors present in the environment such as light, heat, and energy. These components then become part of the description which is no longer simply structural and functional.

A description of linguistic structure and an analysis of the function of linguistic components do not fully explain language change. Additional information must be sought in such diverse areas as psychology (cognitive factors), anthropology (social and cultural factors), and biology (anatomical, neurological, and physiological factors). Data from these areas must be eventually incorporated into a general theory of language change.

Historical linguistic studies may begin by a description of the structure of several stages of a language and the function of the units under consideration. The modifications that have occurred between the several stages are formulated into general statements of correspondences which are then ideally explained by a hypothesis independent of the empirical data. The hypothesis may account for the data (*ie*, the changes) on the basis of certain features in man's psychological or cultural make-up, on the basis of linguistic design inherent in human language, or by genetic modifications among various speech communities. Whatever hypothesis is formulated, it should invite invalidation. A good hypothesis is formulated in such a way as to be subject to experimental and statistical methods for disproof.

Most of the notions in historical linguistics are not yet sufficiently well formulated to invite methods of testing. They appear in the guise of explanation of change but are still in the infant stage. This should not deter our investigations, however, since hypotheses do not spring from a vacuum. An idea comes first, suggested by the historical facts. Much of the difficulty in testing historical explanations of change is in the time factor itself. The exact conditions under which a change has occurred cannot be reduplicated. Even in periods of recorded history too many unknown variables of a sociological and psychological nature prevent an all-inclusive reconstruction of the causes of language change. In historical linguistics there are large numbers of labels which are sometimes taken as explanations although they merely denote a situation or a process. Terms such as substratum, superstratum, adstratum are simply words for certain social conditions under which language change takes place. Other terms – assimilation, dissimilation, split, merger, etc – must be understood in relation to the system in which they occur. These relationships may revolve around syntagmatic (distributional) considerations, paradigmatic (oppositional) considerations, or both. A major goal of the discipline is to relate processes of change to the specific linguistic environment, *ie*, to determine the conditions under which changes occur, to relate the environments to the general or overall linguistic structure and determine the motivations of change by reference to the interaction of linguistic (structural) and extra-linguistic variables.

The study of change in a particular language is part of the broader framework of historical linguistics and makes up the general data for historical studies. Historical linguistics, however, is not limited to the study of the history of one or several related languages, but, rather, it inquires into the nature of change itself. In so doing, a model is sought that will represent and explain language modification universally, both in accordance with language as a natural phenomenon and as a cultural entity. The processes by which changes occur and a determination of motivating forces behind them, form the abstract basis of historical linguistics.

The role of explanation in language change

There are several views with regard to the role of explanation in language change. One lists the sound changes and to some extent generalizes them to include classes of sounds, but maintains that . . . ' if the facts have been fully stated, it is perverse or childish to demand an explanation into the bargain.' According to this view the facts speak for themselves and any attempt to explain them is gratuitous and results in obfuscation.[1] A similar and slightly more elaborate view has recently been put forth in the statement,

> While of interest, accounting for changes in meaning is not the historical linguist's first concern. As in historical phonology, our procedure is not to explain why we say *father*, rather than *pater*, but rather to relate the two . . .

and, 'A linguist establishes the facts of change, leaving its explanation to the anthropologist.'[2]

An alternative view seeks explanation of change and appeals to external information to account for the facts by attempting to establish the nature and degree of influence of one or more languages on another. Thus the primary concern is with various types of linguistic borrowings and linguistic interference when two or more languages occupy the same geographical area. A specific type of influence in this connection has been termed substratum influence which deals with the social aspects of languages in contact and the modifications resulting from this contact.[3] A recent and further consideration of language change attempts to account for modification by recourse to internal linguistic factors, that is, by reference to the linguistic system as a whole, and by the manner in which individual parts of the system (in relation to one another) affect the entire linguistic design. Emphasis is placed on the paradigmatic aspect of change. This approach leads to explanatory structural hypotheses of change. Underlying these structural hypotheses are the paradigmatic relations of structural units to each other in the system or sub-systems of the language, their function in the paradigm, and the assumption that all languages tend towards a symmetrical phonological configuration.[4] Another approach concerns attempts to integrate social and structural aspects into language change. This appeals to the social environment in which change takes place, as well as to psychological attitudes of the speakers relating to the social factors. The interaction of these forces (social and psychological) with the particular structure of the linguistic system under consideration is examined in an attempt to account for language change within a broad perspective.[5]

The last view mentioned here concerns the generative-transformational theory of language. The transformational approach revolves around rule-governed changes in which – as in other methods – relative chronology is a primary concern. This allows rules to be derived from chronologically earlier rules in the order of events. The output of one rule is often seen as the input of the next. The relationship of these rules of change to synchronic rules of structure, *eg*, distributional and redundancy rules, and to universals of language design can constitute explanation for change in the sense that general laws can be stated from these relationships. If it can be demonstrated, for instance, that under certain conditions Rule A was added to the language and at a subsequent period Rule B was added, and that the addition of the latter was in some way a consequence of the former, Rule B is accounted for by Rule A.

In spite of a number of pronouncements arbitrarily limiting the study of language change to a narrow and somewhat sterile and mechanical field of inquiry, the historical linguist may be considered primarily a rational descriptivist who imposes upon the data hypotheses to account for the facts. As the tools of historical studies are refined and brought into line with empirical data from descriptive linguistics, the historian must also substantiate old hypotheses or dismiss them by examining the facts in conformity with these data. The above-mentioned views concerning the role of explanation in language change can be seen in a scientific perspective by comparing them with the following quotation:

The work of collecting and classifying facts is the scientific activity of description, and in some sciences it is almost the only objective at the moment, not because the workers in those fields would not like to do other things but because they are still laying an observational foundation. Parts of biology and archaeology are cases in point. The search for reasons goes behind the facts to relationships between facts and the general laws which can be derived from those relationships, and the discovery of these things constitutes scientific *explanation*, which can be defined briefly as accounting for particular events by reference to general laws, together with the actual conditions under which those laws act, or accounting for laws by reference to principles still more general. For instance, in classical mechanics the falling of heavy bodies might be explained by reference to the law of terrestrial gravitation, and this law in turn might be explained by reference to Newton's more general principle of universal gravitation. Finally, the attempt to anticipate, and therefore control, events relies on the ability of science to *predict*, that is, to obtain knowledge of future events. We may therefore summarize three aspects of scientific activity as leading to three objectives: classification which leads to description, explanation which leads to understanding, and prediction which leads to control.[6]

Some researchers in historical linguistics are concerned with the observational foundations, while others seek explanation in the form of general principles to account for observations already recorded. There is a vast amount of information in synchronic studies concerning the types of structures that occur in language including the kinds and nature of variation found on all levels of language, *ie*, phonological, morphological, syntactic, and semantic. Synchronic data give the linguist a good idea of what to expect in language. If postulated changes in the history of a language deviate from these expectations, the changes are suspect in that the data may have been misinterpreted by the linguist or they are inadequate on some other grounds. Based upon observations of a number of languages with recorded histories and deriving certain expectations from descriptive analysis of languages, historical linguistics is reaching the point at which, given certain conditions, the type of change that may occur can be relegated to a few alternatives. Whether or not the change will occur, however, is another matter. Prediction of language change appears to be a long way in the future. To be sure, there is a great deal to be done in collecting and classifying facts. In historical linguistics, many of the world's languages remain untouched. Many of them will never be analysed in any detail due to lack of recorded history, or their extinction. In no field of inquiry is there such a thing as all the facts. There is no non-arbitrary cut-off to stop describing and begin explaining. Historical linguistics is no exception.

The historical approaches that go beyond the data in their attempt to account for change by reference to general principles are set out in more detail in later chapters.

Synchronic and diachronic considerations

It is not possible to isolate a particular linguistic modification and to assign to it certain causes and effects which will give complete information concerning the change. This is necessarily true, since there is no given base period from which to proceed, or end point by which to judge the effects. For convenience, arbitrarily determined periods in the history of a language are examined: the changes that have occurred between two or more periods are then related to the language structure and to external forces operating on that structure. Relevant to the analysis are the main influences carried over from an earlier period but not necessarily the origin of these influences.

Synchronic analysis is generally kept quite independent of historical linguistics: de Saussure seems to have been the first to make this distinction clear and to insist on a dichotomy between historical and descriptive studies. Following this lead, Bloomfield stated that historical information can only distort descriptive analysis. This is a reaction to a good deal of confusion in the nineteenth century between these two areas. Statements of this sort should not be confused with a dynamic picture of a synchronic state in which the description encompasses elements entering the language as well as those on their way out. This non-static functional representation is essential for synchronic analysis underlying historical linguistics.

Throughout recorded history man has been aware of the mystery of language. His interpretation of what language was has had a direct bearing on his view of language change. Curiosity about their language stimulated linguistic enquiries among the peoples of antiquity. The early Jews, for example, devoted some interest to etymologies and to a theological explanation of language, maintaining that language was a gift to man from Jehovah – placing man above all other animals. The animals were then given names by man. Linguistic unity was shattered, however, by the fateful construction of the Tower of Babel. The ancient Greeks placed more emphasis on the abstract problems of language such as the natural or conventional relationships between words and the things they stood for.

Prompted primarily by rhetorical refinements, the Sophists attempted to subject language to empirical considerations through measurements of clause and sentence length. They distinguished sentence types, gender and tense, and gave names to common processes of their language such as analogy, allegory, assonance, metaphor and puns. The Stoics concerned themselves with problems of language acquisition, sounds, etymologies, origin of language, to mention a few, while the Alexandrians were divided over regularity in language (and the lack of it), *ie*, analogy versus anomaly. These issues, which were carried to Rome and continued there, represent early attempts to understand language in a structural framework and to some extent to account for the discrepancies between different stages of the language as manifested in the written texts.

In India, the desire to preserve the ancient and sacred writings resulted in a grammar and a phonological description of Sanskrit as early as the fifth century BC. Indian scholars recognized language change as something detrimental to the holy writings and channelled their efforts toward inhibiting this erosion of the language. The Indian and Graeco-Roman linguistic endeavours were independent of each other although there were areas of similarity: both were concerned with the natural or conventional status of words and both compiled glossaries and commentaries to explain and preserve linguistic forms. In the analysis of word structure and phonetics, the Indian scholars (*eg*, Pāṇini) were well ahead of their western counterparts.[7]

Latin grammars and speculative-philosophical notions about language occupied the attention of grammarians throughout most of the middle ages when views of language were primarily derived from the earlier Jewish and Graeco-Roman traditions. The dominant religious view of language, derived from the early Jews concerning linguistic differentiation, obviated the need for much inquiry into language change. There was also interest in language in other parts of the world, for example, in the Far East and in the Arab civilization, but there seems to be little direct relationship between these linguistic endeavours and the western traditions.

From the fifteenth century on, grammars of modern languages were written in Europe beginning with a Castilian grammar by Antonio de Nebrija. The sixteenth century saw several French grammars (those of Meigret, Estienne, Bèze, for example) and the first Portuguese grammar by Fernad de Oliveira. In the seventeenth century appeared the grammar of the Port-Royal scholars Lancelot and Arnaud. The concentration on Latin receded as emphasis was placed on the study of the contemporary languages.[8]

A concentrated historical approach to language began in the eighteenth century when efforts were made to compare and examine languages from the point of view of their origins. During this period, language came to be seen as an historical line of development in which constant modification occurred resulting in different and more recent stages. These endeavours were intensified in the nineteenth century and with a somewhat different orientation. Languages were studied and compared in order to discern earlier stages, but less emphasis was placed on discovering the origins of language which had occupied much of the philosophical thought about language during the previous century. During the latter part of the eighteenth century and the first half of the nineteenth, many of the ideas still current in modern linguistic thought were established. In this period, comparative philology was firmly implemented as a discipline.

The discovery during the latter part of the eighteenth century that Sanskrit was related generically to Latin and Greek led to intensive comparative study of these and other Indo-European languages resulting in classification, examination of the history of phonological, morphological and lexical forms, studies of geographical distribution of the members of the Indo-European family, and attempts at reconstruction of the common language from which they were descended.[9]

This formative period of linguistics was not entirely a matter of historical-comparative research and classification of languages and processes of change, nor was it only concerned with the common ancestor of language or language families. Some sound theoretical notions were put forth that remain today as important linguistic considerations. These notions go back to philosophical views such as those expressed by von Humboldt who thought of language as a continuing activity and not as substance of a finished work. He also considered each language to be a picture of the original aptitude for language in that, more than merely a cultural phenomenon, it is the outgrowth of cognitive function specific to man. As a forerunner of structuralism, von Humboldt viewed each language and dialect as an organic whole, each different from the others. Insofar as he felt each language to be symbolic of the character of its speakers, he anticipated some of the ideas underlying later aspects of the relation between language and culture. He opposed a universal grammar of deduction but wanted an inductive general grammar based on comparisons of the different ways in which the same grammatical notion was used in different languages. Last, but not least, he felt that language changed under the mental power of its speakers. This posi-

tion has recently been taken up again to explain some socially motivated changes in language.

Nineteenth-century scholars saw separate languages as the result
of divergence from an earlier and often unknown common source.[10]
Their early endeavours were first applied to Indo-European languages and resulted in the view that language change is regular and
systematic. This gave rise to a structural view of language in which
linguistic units (sounds, morphemes) were seen to participate in a
network of interlocking relationships. Each language had a linguistic
structure that could be identified and analysed. Further study of
speech sounds introduced the notions of phonetics and eventually
phonemics. Language sounds were then seen as both continuous
(since they merge uninterruptedly into one another in a speech
event) and as discrete units (since they are represented on a higher
and abstract level by phonemes). From the point of view of historical
linguistics, the infinite variety of phonetic values of speech sounds
seemed to be contradictory to concepts revolving around regularity
of language change until it was established that sounds cluster
around a norm; these norms, then, were the discrete units of language
and change could be explained by shifts in norms.[11] The structure of
phonemes in conjunction with their role in the phonological paradigm of languages has more recently led to attempts to explain language change within a paradigmatic framework. The qualities of
related entities are determined by their interrelationships. A change
in the condition of any one component of a system entails a modification throughout the entire system affecting all components in some
manner.

In English, for example, the structure of the phoneme /p/ is
determined by its relationship to other phonemes in the phonological system. Opposed to /t/ it is labial, opposed to /b/ it is voiceless
and opposed to /f/ it is occlusive. In a language that displayed the
consonant system,

```
p   t   k
[ ]  d   g
f   s   x
```

the phoneme /p/ would be regarded as consisting of the distinctive
features labial and occlusive since the feature voiceless is not needed
to distinguish it. Each phoneme performs a function: /p/ in English
distinguishes a large number of words from /b/, cf : *pin*/*bin*, *pat*/*bat*,

pan/ban, *nap/nab*, etc. The phoneme /ž/ on the other hand appears less frequently in the English lexicon, and in more restricted positions distinguishing few words, *cf : pleasure, measure, rouge*.

Every phonological system is in a constant state of flux. The function of the phonemes has a bearing on their degree of stability within the system. If a change occurs such as loss of a phoneme, the structural relationships are changed and a new system results. This paradigmatic or functional-structural view of language change has had more appeal to students in Europe than in the United States. In Europe this approach to language change was established on the foundations of philological endeavours and can be considered as an extension of philological activity with a shift in emphasis from the utilization of language as a tool to delve into the racial and cultural histories of civilizations, to an examination of the tool itself. Students of language in the United States, on the other hand, became primarily concerned with descriptive analysis of the numerous and largely unknown American Indian languages. In this connection, historical considerations were often set aside while descriptive techniques and classification of rapidly disappearing languages became paramount. The long-standing philological tradition is reflected in the association between linguistics and anthropology in the United States which has embodied the fundamental notion that language is a part of culture and can be viewed within this framework. This has resulted in attempts to reconstruct earlier civilizations and cultural continuity and in endeavours to explicate the relationship between verbal expression and social attitudes on the one hand and linguistic structures and universal outlook on the other.[12]

Bloomfield's view of language has had an undeniable impact on American linguistics. His influence on aspects of historical linguistics is perhaps more difficult to judge. There is no doubt that his consideration of language change as an unobservable phenomenon[13] which has been defined only in terms of assumptions[14] hindered the development of historical studies. The emphasis on empirical foundations in linguistics did not, then, extend to language change. This situation has not been helped by the lack of formal precision and empirical considerations still found today in some historical linguistic methodology.[15]

Viewed within a generative-transformational framework, language change is a direct outgrowth of synchronic theoretical notions about language. This linguistic theory revolves around an ideal speaker-listener situation which reflects the language of the speech community. Within this framework, diversity among speakers (idiolects) is theoretically irrelevant. The linguistic competence of this idealized speaker-listener underscores the homogeneous aspect of the language group and everything else is linguistic performance. Language change reflects a modification in competence brought about by the addition or re-ordering of rules and occurs within the relationship between speaker-listener and parent-model.[16] The child restructures its grammar from the data provided by the parent's speech. In this sense language change is discrete just as the generation gap between parent and child is discrete.

A counter view maintains that linguistic theory must incorporate the heterogeneous nature of language and that deviations from a homogeneous system are coded and must form part of the theory of linguistic competence. This is a non-discrete view of change in which a continuous process of transfer occurs among children, especially from slightly older to younger children. They derive their language input from many sources and constantly restructure the grammar.[17] Any comprehensive theory of language change must ultimately deal with such social, structural, and cognitive motivations as well as constraints deriving from these factors.

Data for historical linguistics

Historical linguistics is chiefly concerned with how and why language changes. The linguist must utilize current linguistic theories in descriptive studies of language in order to analyse change within an accepted framework of what language is, and to describe and account for change within an acceptable network of linguistic relationships that are universally valid. It would be a risky business indeed to posit a type of change in an earlier stage of a language which would not appear to be feasible among present-day languages.

From a general theoretical aspect, historical studies are primarily concerned with characteristics of change which are common to language and thus relate to universals of language change. Many changes are specific to the particular language in question. For example, the consonant cluster combination /kt/ in Latin *octo* became Italian /tt/, *otto*. There is nothing inherent in language itself which may account for this precise modification. Assimilation of one sound to a neighbouring sound, however, may be a language universal of change inasmuch as all languages undergo assimilatory processes. To arrive at universals the histories of individual languages must be investigated.[18] When written records are not available for such purposes, the study must take the form of reconstruction based on the techniques discussed in Chapter 4.

Written records go back in time to about four thousand BC but then only in limited cultural and geographical areas of the Middle East. Writing in most other areas of the world did not begin until much later and for many cultures it has not yet begun. Historical stages of language, based on inferences from language reconstruction, can extend the horizons beyond the written period, but no important facts emerge that help explain the origins or early evolution of language.

There is a rather extensive body of literature in language studies – written mainly in the eighteenth and nineteenth centuries, but still revitalized today by laymen – concerning the obscure period of history in which language emerged. Most of these essays have one thing in common – they invent situations which have no known precedents to account for the appearance of language. It is not the purpose here to review the numerous hypotheses which have been concerned with the origin of language. Questions revolving around this aspect of linguistic studies can only be ultimately answered in a biological context in which the capacity for and the emergence of language are viewed as species-specific behaviour related to life processes and set in the framework of evolution.

Language change can be viewed from at least three different perspectives. In a young child language unfolds, stimulated by the external environment, as physiological and neurological prerequisites for language mature. This type of ontogenetic modification presents a number of interesting problems concerning the relationship between developing physiological structures and the accompanying expansion and restructuring of the child's linguistic system. Studies of language acquisition in the developing child may, to some extent, offer insight into the evolutionary changes that shaped man's linguistic propensity. The type of broad change associated with the biological notion of phylogenetic change may in part be reconstructed from ontogenetic change, if it can be demonstrated that the latter in some way recapitulates the former. The traditional domain of historical linguistics is associated with another kind of language change, namely, changes that occur in languages independently of any biological modification or maturation processes in man. This is the kind of change that causes language divergence within the species while comparable innate linguistic parameters are associated with its individual members.

Synchronic studies clearly point up the similarities between languages resulting from the same innate structure and capacity of human beings for language. Differences among languages are somewhat superficial and simply reflect various sounds and arrangements selected from a common pool inherent in the species. All languages have organizational properties involving phonological, syntactic, and semantic rules. There is presumably a finite number of such rules and their overlap among languages is great. Most languages, for instance, would be expected to contain rules that allow for commands, negation and tense. All known human languages have vowels and consonants on the phonological level and no known languages exist without polysemy in their semantic organization.

All languages are constantly changing. Change in structure also reflects a commonality among languages indicating a similarity in the ways in which they can modify and diversify. A change from /p/ to /n/ would be extremely rare if it ever occurred or from /o/ to /k/, while /t/ to /d/ or /e/ to /i/ is well within the bounds of phonological modification. There are limited numbers of possible types of structural change further underscoring the similarities between languages as systems of communication.

The languages of the world so far examined are subject to the same general array of linguistic modifications. They have selected out of a common pool different changes or changes in a different order. This appears to have occurred through processes of change or transformations applied to an underlying or common structure. The search for a common denominator in language is reflected in the recent interest in linguistic universals and their relationship to cognitive characteristics of organization among human beings.

Written records constitute the most valuable source of information for the diachronic stages of a language. Writing, as manifested in the various systems throughout the world, has special importance for language historians.

The oldest known systems of writing are the Egyptian hieroglyphics, the Sumerian cuneiform inscriptions, and the Chinese script. Systems of writing also arose in other areas of the world, as in Central America among the Mayas and Aztecs.

Writing seems to have developed in a parallel manner in the various cultures which first used it – pictures or drawings pertaining to features of the environment gradually took on narrative value and became more abstract in formulation. At the same time they became highly conventionalized so that they could be regarded as symbols and not merely as pictures. Such narrative drawings or pictograms were used extensively by some North American Indian tribes. A single composite picture might, for example, have three suns to represent three days, a turtle for luck, and several canoes and men carrying spears signifying travel and battle. The number of horizontal lines on the gravestones in some Indian cultures represented campaigns and the vertical lines stood for the number of wounds received in battle.[19] These conventional markings are independent of language. It is not necessary to know the language of the scribe in order to determine the meaning, although some cultural information is necessary since not all cultures will represent pictorially the same things in the same way. Between the written form and the meaning, however, there was no phonetic link. Pictograms can be read, then, with varying choice of words in any language.

Writing may be independent of language in two fundamental ways: the pictographic systems could be read in any language with equal facility if one understood the cultural code in cases where the representations had become too abstract to be self-evident. Systems of writing are independent of language in another way; for example, an alphabetic system can be superimposed on any number of unrelated languages as a general orthographic convention since, unlike pictograms, the alphabetic symbols have no meaning in themselves. A determination of semantic content presupposes a knowledge of the language. In a pictographic system the symbols had meaning apart from the spoken language; in alphabetic systems the meanings of the symbols are related to the language that uses them through a phonetic link. It is generally assumed that the step from narrative picture writing to a system based upon phonetic representations of a particular language took place through the rebus method; that is, the visual representation was transferred to the pronunciation of the picture and the picture writing then came to represent sounds. In this manner sequences of pictures could take on certain meanings when pronounced as a unit; for example, a picture of an eye in conjunction with another picture meaning *sea*, might come to mean *icy*, or a bee plus a leaf might signify *belief*,[20] etc. The use of homophones may have been instrumental in forging the phonetic link between sign and meaning.

Once pictograms became subject to the spoken language to convey their meaning, they formed a new kind of writing based on phonograms. This transition did not occur all at once, however, but lasted for a long period in which both pictograms and phonograms were used in the same system. American Indian cultures range from no writing at all to this type of mixed system. The Aztecs were embarking on the phonogram stage before their civilization was disrupted by the westward movement of technologically more sophisticated peoples. The Aztec situation is of interest because it may represent the manner common to all languages in which pictograms became phonograms. They took the sign for *deer* which in Aztec was *mazatl* and placed it above the sign for *teeth*, Aztec *tlantli*. Only the first part of each word of the individual signs was pronounced and came to mean *mazatlan*. This composite phonogram represents a site in Mexico. The sign for *snake* placed over the sign for *hill* in Aztec relating to the words *coatl* and *tepec* recpectively, gave *coatepec*, which is also the name of a town in Mexico. In this way pictograms were arranged to correspond to the Aztec words taking on phonetic value in the process.[21] Early writing systems in the Old World were modified by the introduction of the syllabary, where each syllable is represented by a phonetic symbol, for example Sanskrit *ka* क *ta* त *pa* प. There have been, and still are, many such writing systems in use. Japanese hiragana and katagana systems are syllabaries as were the Babylonian cuneiform and Linear B from the island of Crete. In theory the syllabary is less economical than alphabetic systems since more symbols are required, *cf : ka ta pa ak at ap* which would need six symbols in a syllabary and four in an alphabet. They may also require symbols in the writing system that do not correspond to the spoken language. In Cyprus, the Greek word for city, *ptolin*, was written in the syllabary as *po-to-li-ne*.[22]

The alphabetic system ideally has one symbol for each vowel and consonant. Present-day alphabets show a number of exceptions to this one-to-one correspondence. On the one hand, a written symbol may represent two or more sounds as, for example, English *th* which represents [θ] and [ð] *cf : thing* and *that*. On the other hand, one sound may have multiple graphic representations as, for example, the sound [š] in *mission, ssi; sugar, s; nation, ti; she, sh*, etc.[23] The English vocalic symbols fare no better, *eg, oo =* [ʌ] as in *blood*, [u] as in *good* and [uw] as in *food*. Other languages have similar situations in the writing systems, *eg*, French *c* corresponds to both [k] in *comment* and [s] in *cent*. These conditions are due to the effect of sound change where the orthography remained fixed. The spoken language, over relatively short periods of time changes sometimes rapidly, sometimes more slowly, but the writing system generally lags behind these changes and can only be brought into line through orthographic reform.

We would be little aware of language change if it were not for written records that go back hundreds of years in the history of a language and point to entirely different linguistic systems, *eg*, Latin and Modern French. Where records are available, the investigator can examine the differences in a language between any two points in time. Since writing systems are often a poor reflection of the spoken language, the investigator must proceed with caution, determining the pronunciation of a sign in certain positions through the use of rhyme, commentaries of earlier writers on their language, and misspellings by semi-literate people who more faithfully reproduced the spoken language by recourse to phonetic writing. Latin writers, for example, have left direct evidence for various forms of Latin. Popular speech is recorded in the works of Plautus (254–184 BC). The much later *Appendix Probi* attempted to teach 'correct' Latin to the less educated by pointing out their errors and contrasting these with the 'proper' form, *eg*, *frigida non fricda*. Various graffiti have been preserved (as, for example, at Pompeii) which depict attempts by semi-literate people to record an expression on the outhouse wall, as well as on grave markers. Many inscriptions have been compiled in the *Corpus Inscriptionum Latinarum*. Documentation of this kind is found in most languages with a long written tradition.

There are still a number of undeciphered writing systems in existence ranging geographically from the ancient inscriptions of Spain to the writing preserved on wooden tablets of Easter Island. Other ancient orthographic systems are in a state of partial decipherment such as the Mayan writing system, the Sinaitic script, and Etruscan. The eventual understanding of these and other largely unknown forms of writing, *eg*, Linear A of Crete and the Carian script of southwestern Asia Minor, will help clear up some problems in linguistic typology and illuminate historical and cultural periods that are still considered prehistory. The value of such work has been amply demonstrated by the decipherment of Linear B and the Hittite cuneiform in recent decades.[24]

The long history of alphabetic writing has greatly facilitated the advancement of historical linguistics in the western world. Except for some specific scribal devices mostly in the form of diacritics and recombinations of certain letters to represent new sounds (*eg*, Spanish *ñ* and Portuguese *nh* refer to a palatal nasal) – the Latin alphabet has changed very little in two thousand years. The Latin system is only a stage in a much older tradition of writing dating back through the Greek, Phoenician, and the Sinai scripts, with the earliest antecedents buried in the obscure past. However, some scholars consider the Egyptian pictographs to be the ultimate source of the Graeco-Roman alphabet.[25]

Writing systems do not constitute the only source of information for language change, however. The concept of data in historical studies must take into account empirical principles and their relationship to the observability of change. This is an important consideration which offers the opportunity of formulating a theory of change based upon modifications occurring in present-day speech communities. Detailed yet broad studies of changes in progress allow a determination of the relationship between linguistic conditions and possible changes. Linguistic conditions are themselves embedded in a linguistic structure which is in turn embedded in a larger context of social structure. An evaluation of the various linguistic and social factors and their relative influences under known conditions will establish the constraints imposed upon change. Overriding social factors are man's inherent biological properties which govern possible changes in linguistic structure through physiological and perceptual constraints. Problems concerning onset or initiation of change and their subsequent spread from speaker to speaker or from one speech community to another often neglect the interaction between these areas.[26]

Regularity of sound change

Sound change has loomed as the dominant factor in language change: since the neo-grammarians, emphasis has been placed on its regularity which, in their doctrinaire view of language, permitted no exceptions. Opponents of the view that sound change is always regular have labelled as sporadic, occurrence or non-occurrence of sound changes which do not show up as regular correspondences between divergent languages. For the proponents of regularity in change, the notion of sporadic modification implied unscientific or mentalistic concepts which denied the very foundations upon which the major nineteenth-century contributions to linguistics were founded.[27]

What appear to be exceptions to regular rules of phonological change
do arise. For example there are systematic correspondences between
Spanish, French, and Italian. Latin /k-/ before a front vowel became
/θ/, /s/ and /č/ respectively.

Latin	>	*Spanish*	*French*	*Italian*	
centum		ciento	cent	cento	one hundred
		/θiénto/	/sã/	/čénto/	
caelum		cielo	ciel	cielo	sky
		/θiélo/	/syεl/	/čiélo/	
cervum		ciervo	cerf	cervo	stag
		/θiérvo/	/sεɹ/	/čérvo/	

There are some phonological rules, however, that do not extend
beyond one example, *eg*,

arbor	>	arbol	arbre	albero	tree

In such cases Latin *-or* > Spanish *-ol*, but *ar-* > Italian *al-* etc. These
seemingly aberrant changes have been considered sporadic or irregular. The regularity principle adopted by nineteenth-century scholars
as a fundamental principle of language change and still often considered today as a primary tenet of change is simply that under the
same conditions the same sounds behave in the same way within a
particular span of time and within a particular language or dialect.
More or less explicit in this assessment of phonological change is the
notion that lexical items containing identical environments will behave alike with respect to modifications in those environments, *eg*,
French /k-/ preceding /a/ > /š/,

cantāre	>	chanter /šãte/
cārum	>	cher /šεɹ/
canem	>	chien /šyɛ̃/

irrespective of morphological, syntactic, or semantic characteristics
of the lexical items. These lexical forms (and others) fall into a class
based upon their environmental similarities with respect to the
modification of /k-/ to /š-/. Spanish diverges from French among
these lexical forms by regularly not modifying /k-/ before /a/, *cf* :

cantar /kantár/
caro /káro/
can /kan/ (perro)

The reflexes of Latin *arbor* can be considered regular developments in these languages insomuch as the modification in each language reflects a class of lexical forms consisting in this case of one member.

Phonetic change may affect certain sounds in specific environments, or it may affect the same sounds in all environments. Latin [k] became French [s] under some conditions, but [š] under others, as in the examples above *centum > cent* and *cārum > cher*. There are many cases in language, however, in which sounds or groups of sounds simply shift to new articulations, *ie*, change without split. In English (with a few exceptions) long [ī] and long [ū] became [ay] and [aw] respectively. In French, free stressed [u] became [ü] under all environmental conditions. The phonetic environments are not responsible for these unrestricted changes. To explain context-free phonetic change, external linguistic phenomena such as substratum influence have often been proposed. For example, Celtic speech habits in Gaul have sometimes been credited for the modification of French [u] > [ü]. When what would otherwise have been regular change has been disrupted through failure to occur where expected, *eg*, Latin [pl-] > Spanish [λ-] (*ll*), *plōrāre > llorar*, but *cf* Latin *planta* and Spanish *planta*, recourse to external linguistic factors must be sought. In this case the discrepancy between [pl-] and [λ-] is explained by the fact that *planta* was incorporated into the language as a learned word after the change in question was complete. Language borrowings, dialect mixture, phonetic symbolism, taboo forms – all appear to have varying degrees of influence on language change. Whether these and similar considerations will remain simply marginal to a theory of change (*ie*, as some sort of ancillary explanation of irregularity) or whether they are dynamic features of all languages and thereby contain vital forces that often disrupt regular change, has yet to be determined.

Some phonetic changes are restricted or inhibited in their diffusion throughout the lexicon and do not occur in phonetic environments where they would be expected to operate. In Spanish, for example, morpheme-final /-e/ was lost after /l/ *cf* Vulgar Latin *sále > sal* 'salt', and *cóle > col* 'cabbage'. The loss of /-e/ after /l/ does not occur, however, among verbs in the third person singular, *cf* Spanish *sale* 'he departs'. In standard Yiddish final unaccented *e* (phonetically [ə]) has been lost, *eg*, *tage > teg* 'days', *erde > erd* 'earth', *gibe > gib* 'I give', except when *e* is an adjective inflectional

ending, *eg, di groyse shtot* 'the big city', *dos alte land* 'the old country'.[28] To account for this type of restricted phonetic change recourse
to higher level linguistic structure has yielded a number of interesting observations concerning morphological and semantic inhibiting
influences.

Contrary to the behaviouristic or anti-mentalistic views of recent
generations of linguists, attempts to account for some aspects of
phonetic change have been concerned with the identification of inherent perceptual and psychological characteristics in man, relating
to general phonological structure itself. The perceptual 'need'
among speakers and listeners to maintain a certain degree of phonological space between sounds and the psychological 'pressure' towards symmetry and equipollence in the phonological paradigm are
but two examples of the types of considerations to emerge from this
approach.

Within the generative-transformational view, language is regarded as an internalized system of rules. A sound change is not a
change in the sounds alone but rather a change in a rule. A rule
change necessarily affects all the linguistic elements (*eg*, morphemes)
that pertained to the rule before the modification occurred. Phonetic
changes are motivated or inhibited by the phonetic environment,
by morphological and semantic constraints and by the abstract
(systematic phonemic) level of language. Grammatical prerequisites
concerning change may at times override the phonetic environment
in some portions of the lexicon leading to diverse residue and to
seeming irregularity. Similarly, the abstract or underlying phonological representations also appear to assert influence on the surface
or phonetic level leading to non-phonetic change. The often quoted
Lachman's Law will serve as an example of phonetic change motivated by a more abstract level of phonology: Latin displayed alternations in vocalic quantities *cf :*

    agō   āctum
    regō   rēctum

but long and short alternation was not present in

    faciō   factum
    capiō   captum

The underlying forms of *actum* and *rectum* are considered to have been

/agtum/ /regtum/

Based partially on the [g] in *agō* and *regō*, Lachman's Law states that vowels became long in the environment of voiced obstruents followed by voiceless obstruents, *ie :*

$$v \rightarrow [+\text{long}] \; / \underline{\quad\quad} \begin{bmatrix} +\text{obstr} \\ +\text{voice} \end{bmatrix} \begin{bmatrix} +\text{obstr} \\ -\text{voice} \end{bmatrix}$$

(where /——— = in the environment of). If vowel lengthening occurred after the assimilation rule that changed [gt] to [kt] the forms *factum* and *captum* would also have been affected, yet the assimilation rule is an old rule in Indo-European, occurring in Latin, Sanskrit, and Greek. The vowel lengthening rule is considered, then, to have been added in Latin, not at the phonetic level but at the underlying level of representation, *ie*, /agtum/, which need not be thought of in diachronic terms but simply as an abstract representation mapped into *actum* [āktum] by synchronic rules of Latin grammar.[29] The psychological reality of underlying forms is, however, a controversial issue.

Notes

1 Joos, *p* v, where he also states, '. . . why borrow trouble by explaining the invisible?' In all fields of human endeavour, however, from physics to linguistics, from atoms to laryngeals (see Chapter 2) the invisible has been explained with astonishing results by its effect on observable data. According to Joos the above was also the view of language of Bloomfield who Joos refers to as the Newton of linguistics. Newton, however, did not restrict his view of the universe to the visible of which there is actually very little compared to the invisible forces at work.

2 Lehmann (1962), *p* 200. These statements are primarily directed towards semantic change. Not all semantic change, however, is directly relatable to cultural changes.

3 For a comprehensive study of substratum influences, see Jungemann. There have been no suggestions that I am aware of simply to leave this area of human behaviour to be accounted for by sociologists or psychologists.

4 See Martinet (1955).

5 See Labov for the application of these notions to language change.

6 Caws, *p* 91. See also Chapter 11.

7 See Lyons (1969), *pp* 19–20.

8 For a detailed account of the events and trends in language studies of these early periods, see Dinneen, Robins, and Mattoso Cámara.

9 For an account of this activity, see Jespersen (1922), Pedersen, and Dinneen.

10 Most of the early fruitful and lasting work in historical linguistics is derived from German philologists of the nineteenth century. Some of their major contribu-

tions are discussed in Chapter 2. They were not the only scholars, however, nor the first to become aware of problems historical in nature. The following comment is relevant here and is quoted in full from Weinreich, Labov and Herzog, p 104:

> For obvious reasons, awareness and discussion of language change developed first in the Romance world. The interest of Dante in this question is well known, that of his compatriot Tolomei less so (Claudio Tolomei, *II Cesano, ca* 1530). J. Chr. Kraus (1787) was already sophisticated enough to stress the opportunities offered to·culture history by the greater conservatism of grammar over vocabulary. Many other examples could be cited. Therefore, Hockett (1965, 185), like the authorities on which he bases himself, oversimplifies the matter in attributing the 'genetic hypothesis' to Jones, Gyármathi, Rask, Grimm, and Bopp. The plain enumeration of these names is an oversimplification in another sense, too: the writers named differed greatly in their ability to draw inferences from the fact of change. For Grimm, temporal seriation of attested stages of Germanic languages was fundamental, but then he set himself no reconstructive tasks; Rask, on the other hand – although perhaps the boldest and most clear-headed thinker of the group – was slow in coming to terms with the facts of change; in his 1818 masterpiece he was still asking what *attested* languages Old Norse may have originated from.

11 See Hockett (1965). This view, however, has now been challenged, see Postal, p 307.

12 See Boas and Whorf.

13 Bloomfield, p 347.

14 *Ibid*, p 364, and Labov (1966), pp 10–11.

15 See for example Weinreich, Labov and Herzog, p 169.

16 Halle (1962).

17 These two views of homogeneity and heterogeneity as part of linguistic theory and their effect on linguistic views of change have been amply discussed and documented, see Weinreich, Labov and Herzog.

18 The investigation of specific languages is a necessary but not sufficient condition for determining universals of change. Some changes may conceivably be unique or occur only under very limited circumstances.

19 For further examples and drawings, see Gelb.

20 Hughes, p 123, and Moorhouse, p 18.

21 Moorhouse, pp 81–83.

22 *Ibid*, p 52.

23 Baugh, p 15, gives fourteen signs for the sound /š/.

24 For examples of ancient and undeciphered scripts, as well as accounts of decipherments, see Friedrich, Doblehofer and Tovar.

25 The historic evolution of letter shapes may be found in Moorhouse and Gelb. A schematic presentation of the chronology of Near Eastern writing systems and dates are found in Gelb, p x. The beginning of writing in China and Tibet are discussed in de Lacouperie.

26 See Weinreich, Labov and Herzog.

27 See Bloomfield, p 355.

28 See King (1969), p 123.

29 See Kiparsky (1965) and King, *op cit, pp* 43 *ff.*

Chapter 2

Indo-European languages

Origins and distribution

The foundations of historical linguistics were laid in the nineteenth century through intensive comparative and historical research on Indo-European languages. The term Indo-European refers to all those languages which represent the descendants of an earlier stage (much as Latin represents an earlier stage of the Romance languages) which has been designated Proto-Indo-European (PIE). There is no fixed time or locus in which to place PIE: the similarities and systematic divergences of Indo-European languages indicate this earlier form which simply reflects a period in a continuum that recedes in time to the emergence of language itself in at least one species of the genus Homo.

During the nineteenth century, as Indo-European languages were examined and compared, relationships emerged based upon phonological correspondences and grammatical similarities. The methodology employed in these investigations has been referred to as the comparative method (see Chapter 3). Comparative Indo-European studies resulted in a hierarchy of language relationships which indicate their genetic or family affiliations.

In its main outlines, the Indo-European family of languages has been traditionally divided into two major groups – centum and satəm. These two groups are named according to their treatment of *$/k/$ in the word for 'hundred'. The centum languages preserve $/k/$, cf Latin *centum*, Greek *he-katón*, Old Irish *cēt*, Tocharian *känt;* while the satəm languages, named after the Avestan word for hundred, modify $/k/$ to $/š/$. Compare Sanskrit *çatam*, Lithuanian *sziñtas* or *šimtas* and Old Slavic *sŭto*. These examples are customarily cited in general treatments of the subject as having derived from an earlier common form of PIE.

The dichotomy centum-satəm was commonly regarded as a division between western and eastern Indo-European. Even before the discovery of Tocharian,[1] a centum-type language uncovered in Chinese Turkestan Buddhist writings of the sixth–eighth centuries, the dichotomy was not very satisfactory. Greek, for example, is not only cut off from other centum languages by Albanian, but it also shows more affinities with the satəm group. Notions concerning early dialectal unity of centum and satəm languages appear to have been a convenient fiction and it is one that historical linguistics is still saddled with.

The major sub-groupings of the Indo-European languages are as follows:

Proto-Indo-European (for Hittite see Chapter 3)
  Centum languages :
    Celtic, Italic, Germanic, Hellenic, Tocharian
  Satəm languages :
    Balto-Slavic, Indo-Iranian, Armenian, Albanian

Within the framework of Indo-European membership exact relationships have not been clearly established. There are enormous difficulties involved, for example, in determining with certitude the hierarchical arrangements of even the major members of the Indo-European family of languages. The scarcity of written documentation for this early period leaves the burden of establishing relationships to linguistic reconstruction. Even when documentation is available, a hierarchical determination of language relationships is not an easy task. A detailed comparison of the languages in question is, to begin with, a major undertaking and the investigator is always faced with the fact that some dialects that would have ordinarily fitted into the hierarchical scheme, have disappeared. The descendant languages from one node on the Indo-European tree – Latin – serve to illustrate hierarchical groupings (*Fig* 1).

Any historical representation of even such well-known languages as the Romance group is, at best, controversial. Some Romance specialists place Catalan with Iberian-Romance, others prefer to show closer affinities between Italian and Romanian, etc. One misleading aspect of all such hierarchical arrangements of language

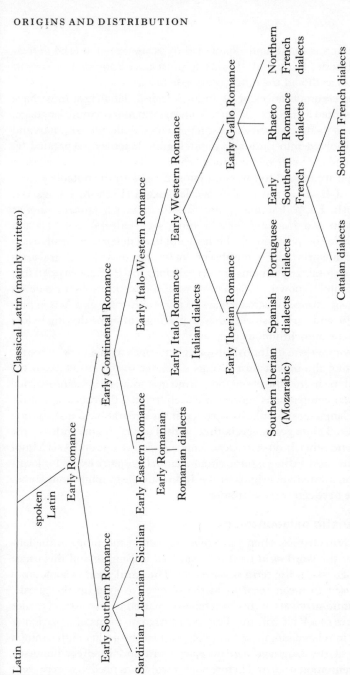

Fig 1: Romance languages. See Hall (1950) for the original but slightly different arrangement of that shown above.

derivation is that linguistic uniformity is suggested at each derivational node. Early Italo-Romance must have consisted of various
dialects as did all the other intermediate stages.

The common ancestor of Indo-European languages must have
represented a dialectal offshoot from an even more remote language,
much as its descendants at first represented dialectal variations and
later evolved into mutually unintelligible languages separated by
thousands of years of continuous change. Most of the languages of
Europe are related to this common source, with the notable exceptions of Basque, the Ural-Altaic languages (Finnish, Hungarian,
Turkish, Lapp, Estonian), and various extinct languages such as
Etruscan and Iberian.[2] The location, size, cultural make-up and
linguistic composition of P I E have not been determined with exac-
titude due primarily to the absence of written records, cultural artefacts, or fossilized remains known to belong to a P I E society. All that
is definitely known is that speakers of a once more homogeneous
language group appeared in various parts of Europe and Asia in prehistoric and early historic times, replacing, ruling or driving before
them the autochthonous peoples.

A comparison of Indo-European languages with a view to recon-
structing the parent form brings us closer to the structure of the
prototype in that the phonological and grammatical systems reached
by such comparisons represent closely related dialects and not diverse languages. Similarly, a glance at the geographical distribution
of these languages suggests that, with Tocharian and Indic in the
east, and other Indo-European languages in Europe and Asia Minor
(Hittite, now extinct), some circumstantial evidence exists for locat-
ing the immediate origins of the Indo-European migrations somewhere between these extremes.

Linguistic palaeontology

Semantic changes often leave relics of former meanings in the language: the word *meat* used to mean *food* in English and this usage
still persists in the term *sweet-meats*. The word *ghost* is sometimes
still used to mean *spirit* as in the phrase 'to give up the ghost'.
Semantic survivals of this kind have been used to reconstruct earlier
features of a P I E culture. The lack of cognate forms of a particular
word in related languages may suggest that the earlier and common
stage of the language had no such word and in effect linguistic
differentiation occurred before such a word was needed to represent

a cultural entity. There are, for example, no words for *silver*, *gold*, or *iron* common to the Indo-European family of languages, thus P I E probably had no such terms. It has been concluded from this that knowledge of these metals came about in the various cultures independently and at different times. The general term for metal found in Latin *aes*, Sanskrit *ayas* and Old English *ār* (Modern English *ore*) suggests that the break-up of the common language took place at the end of the Neolithic period (during the last centuries of the third millennium B C). Conclusions concerning the origin of the Indo-European people based on cognate forms such as those for *birch* and *beech* have suggested to some observers that their homeland was in the vicinity of these trees. Deductions of this kind are risky, however, for at least three reasons: there is no assurance that these words formed part of the vocabulary of Indo-European speakers during the period in which the homeland is sought; lexical items are easily borrowed and these words may have originated in one branch of the Indo-European languages and at an early time spread to the others; in deductions of this sort one must also consider the climatic factor – the geographical limitations of these trees may not now correspond to their position of five or six thousand years ago.

Semantic considerations have also a role in inferences of this nature. Lexical items change in meaning, making it difficult to determine if a particular name referred to the same physical object in prehistoric times as it does now. Furthermore, various dialects may contain the same lexical item with different meanings. A case in point is the term *robin* used in the United States to refer to a member of the thrush family and in England to a member of the warbler family.

Even riskier conclusions beguile the linguistic palaeontologist who attempts inferences about the social organization, religion, and race of such prehistoric peoples from cognate sources. A reconstruction of the social organization of the Roman people, for example, based upon cognates in the Romance languages such as those for *bishop*, *beer, war*, and *horse*, would suggest that the Romans were beer-drinking Christians who fought on horseback – all of which is false.[3]

Archaeological considerations for Proto-Indo-European

Archaeological investigations have been instrumental in determining the chronology of Indo-European dispersions through cultural relationships and in casting some light on conditions encountered by these people in their wanderings.

Indo-European speakers appeared in various geographical areas – at first in small numbers except perhaps in India – and gradually spread their influence throughout new regions. They migrated from their homelands for unknown reasons, possibly pushed by hordes moving in from the east, or perhaps they were simply seeking more living space. The result of these migrations was geographical isolation (a prime factor for internal language modification) and new external factors, *eg*, substratum and adstratum influences, both of which led to profound modifications in the individual Indo-European languages. (For an explanation of these terms, see Chapter 5.)

The working of copper, bronze, and iron brought Europe out of the Stone Age, the knowledge of metallurgy having reached there by way of culturally superior newcomers who seem to have arrived in small groups and assumed the position of an aristocracy. Many of the carriers of this more advanced culture were Indo-European speakers who filtered into neolithic Italy some time before the second millennium BC. They entered Italy by small incursions from central Europe and through cultural dominance and prestige gained control over the neolithic tribes. The latter learned the language of the invaders just as the Celts of western Europe in a later period learned the language of a vastly inferior number of Romans who invaded their lands but who brought with them a more prestigious culture.

Coinciding with the Copper and early Bronze Age in Italy were the palafitte structures erected in or on the edges of lakes and with which an entirely new funeral rite – cremation – is associated. These dwellings correspond to the first half of the second millennium BC and may have been connected culturally with similar dwellings in Austria and Switzerland. In the second half of the millennium occurred a Bronze Age civilization also characterized by palafitte and known as terramare (a local patois expression which means 'fat earth'). In both cases they appear to have their origins in central Europe. The Iron Age brought with it other cultures into northern Italy, the most important of which for linguistic history is the Villanovan. Since the newcomers appear to have come from the same area as the terramare peoples, that is, from the Danubian lands, they may also have brought with them an Indo-European language. In fact, these three cultures may well have been the carriers of Indo-European languages into Italy via the Alps or in

some cases across the Adriatic. Cultural innovations in Italy, however, came by two routes: ironworking, for example, is thought to
have originated in the Near East, possibly among the Hittites, and
to have spread westward, entering Italy by the northern route
carried by Indo-Europeans, and by a southern route carried by
Mediterranean peoples who inhumed their dead and did not speak
Indo-European.

There is a long period between the first indication of Indo-European dialects in Italy and the first extant written records. Nor are
written records likely to turn up for this period since the skill of
writing was learned from the Etruscans in Italy, and the Etruscans
themselves were relative latecomers to the peninsula.

The establishment of Rome as the primary political and cultural
centre of Italy eventually led to further Romanization through conquest of the entire peninsula and of most of Europe. In this way
Latin, an Indo-European language, was spread throughout the
Roman domain. Latin was not the only Indo-European representative of these early migrations, however. Another Indo-European
dialect, Oscan, was the chief language of central Italy until Roman
subjugation and remained in use in official documents until the social
wars of 90–89 BC. Closely related to Oscan is the language known as
Umbrian. The only extensive document is the Tabulae Iguvinse,
which consists of nine bronze tablets. These are written partly in
Latin and partly in Umbrian whose alphabet, like Oscan, was derived from a western Greek alphabet through Etruscan intermediacy.
These, plus a host of minor dialects, show varying degrees of relationship to Latin, but scanty documentation leaves the details of the
relationships obscure[4] (*Fig* 2).

The Venetic language and culture appears to relate to Illyrian and
to have extended to Liguria. It shows some points of agreement with
Latin, *eg*, /bh/ and /dh/ > /f-/, /-b-/, /-d-/ in both languages.[5] Ligurian once extended to the Po river, south to Etruria and perhaps beyond. It is as yet not clear whether this is an Indo-European language or the language of one of the neolithic tribes inhabiting the
region. Ligurian does appear to show some slight affinity with Sicel
and the latter has been related to Latin, but by very limited linguistic and cultural evidence; for example, the Siculi and the Latins are
known to have come together during the gatherings at Mount Alban
and both languages show some striking similarities in the verbal
form 'to be', *cf* Sicel *esti*, Latin *est*. How much of the suspected

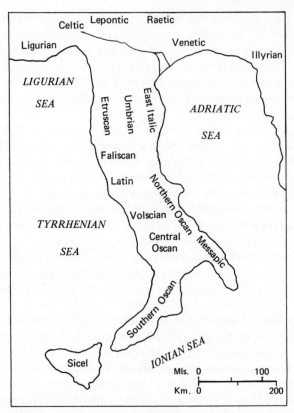

Fig 2: Languages and dialects of Italy *c* fifth century BC

linguistic affiliations between these and other Italic tongues is due
to genetic relationship or borrowings will only be determined
through the discovery of more documentation. Siculi and Ligurians
may have been in contact in remote times when both occupied
considerably more territory than they did by the fifth century BC.
Linguistic borrowing probably accounts for such forms as Latin
blatea 'swamp' and Illyrian *balta*. The Etruscans' arrival in Italy
during the eighth century BC and their gradual extension of power
throughout much of the central part of the peninsula must have
acted as a disruptive force on the Indo-European and neolithic inhabitants by cutting a wide swath through the languages and dialects
of the period, and by reducing the frontiers of languages with an
earlier greater geographical extension.

Very little is known about the language situation in Italy before about 600 BC. The subsequent replacement of the Italic languages by Latin, and its diffusion throughout a large part of Europe (and eventually to many other parts of the world – primarily through colonization) presents a dramatic example of language spread and displacement. From humble beginnings as a dialect of the Italic branch of Indo-European, Latin steadily encroached upon neighbouring dialects eventually absorbing both Indo-European languages and non-Indo-European languages in Italy and western and eastern Europe.[6]

Archaeological evidence in Greece points to a period of Indo-Europeanization in the form of migrations from the north and roughly corresponds in time to the Indo-European incursions into Italy. Linguistic differentiation among Indo-Europeans in Greece resulted in a number of languages and dialects (see *Fig* 3). It has been stated that:

> Whether the Greek invasions began about 2000 BC corresponding to the break between the Early and Middle Helladic periods, or some centuries later, is disputed. But it is reasonably clear and now pretty generally admitted that at least from the beginning of the Late Helladic, that is, the Mycenaean period (*ca* 1600–1200 BC), the dominant element of the population was Greek.[7]

The Doric invasion of the Balkans occurring around the twelfth century BC was considered the last of several prehistoric waves of Greek invasion. It was preceded by several centuries of Greek occupation. From the time of the earliest records, Greek appears in numerous dialects. The differentiation of the larger dialect groups was then presumed to have occurred at a period long before the Greeks entered their present homeland.[8] This idea has recently been modified by new research and it now seems more likely that the break-up of the dialects began only after the entry of the Greeks into the Balkan peninsula. This has been equated with the archaeological break between the Early and Middle Bronze Age cultures.[9]

Recorded Greek history used to be seen as beginning in the eighth century BC when the Phoenician alphabet was introduced. The prior period was known primarily from archaeological artefacts and from legend. Pre-Hellenic archaeology distinguishes three phases of the Bronze Age: early (2800 to 1900), middle (1900 to 1600) and late (1600–1200) – the figures vary a little with different writers. The

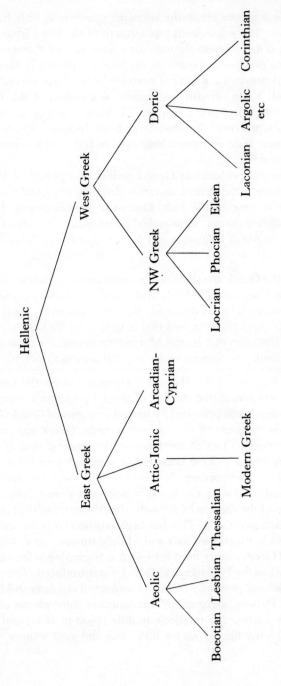

Fig 3: Greek languages

first flowering of civilization that occurred in Crete in the Middle Bronze period ended violently in about 1400 BC. On the mainland it began with the late Bronze or late Helladic period and lasted until about the twelfth century BC when the more important centres of civilization were sacked and left in ruins.

The history through written documentation in this part of the world has recently been extended back in time into the Late Bronze period (sometimes referred to as Mycenaean) through the decipherment of Linear B, an ancient syllabary found in Crete and on the mainland.[10] Linear B turned out to represent an early form of Greek. Linear A, another ancient Minoan script seems to be the older and at present still offers a number of problems in decipherment.

Archaeological and linguistic facts suggest that Mycenaean power and language extended from the Peloponnese through Crete and up to Rhodes and Cos in the Dodecanese. These areas fell under invasions of the Dorians who occupied them in historical times. The movement may have caused the collapse of Mycenaean power and the destruction of Knossos on Crete[11] (*Fig 4*). An isolated dialect of the central Peloponnese – Arcadian – closely resembled the dialect of Cyprus. Archaeological evidence has shown that Cyprus was colonized by people speaking a Mycenaean dialect used all over the pre-Dorian area, hence Cypriot and Arcadian appear to be the remains of a Mycenaean dialect. These important archaeological and linguistic discoveries served as inferential controls on the direction the decipherment of Linear B would take.

Early Greeks also settled on the coasts of Asia Minor which put them in contact with the ancient cultures of the East. These contacts were important as a channel of communication which helped extend cultural innovations such as metallurgy, agriculture and animal domestication from the East into the Balkans and eventually to Europe.

Indo-European speakers are believed to have entered Scandinavia or at least to have penetrated Jutland in about 2100–2000 BC and to have conquered the entire peninsula during the subsequent two or three centuries.[12] Their language is sometimes referred to as Teutonic and their culture was characterized by the use of separate graves and the use of battle axes, which gave them some advantage over the autochthonous neolithic tribes. Very little is known about prehistoric Germanic migrations. The Goths, whose language is generally described as East Germanic, are thought to have migrated

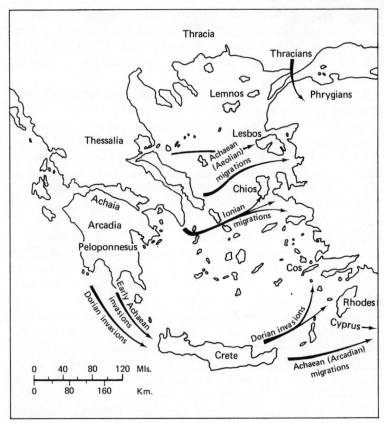

Fig 4: Early Greek migrations

to eastern Europe from Scandinavia, subsequently moving westward into Italy and Spain. South of the Baltic were other German
speakers whose language appears to have been the ancestor of West
Germanic and its many languages and dialects. A schematic representation of the general outlines of Germanic relationships is as
follows (*Fig* 5).

Celtic speakers of the Indo-European group of languages spread
over the British Isles at about the beginning of the Bronze Age.
The second half of the first millennium BC, however, witnessed a
substantial Celtic expansion into Spain, Italy, and Asia Minor as far
as Ankara. By the fifth century AD, Celtic speech on the continent
had all but disappeared, leaving little documentary information. It

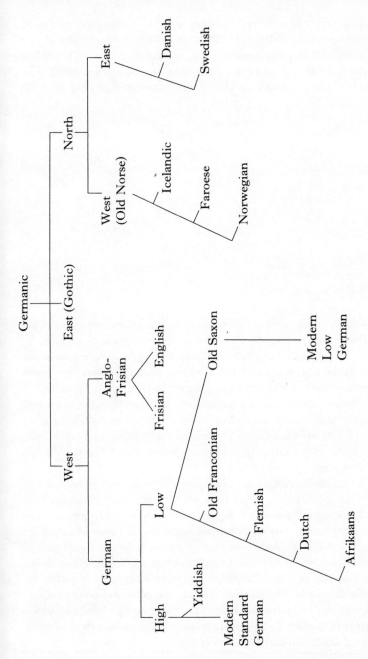

Fig 5: Germanic languages

was generally replaced by Germanic and Latin languages except in areas of the British Isles and in Brittany. Celtic and Latin show close linguistic affinities but questions concerning their exact relationship and their time and place of separation are far from settled. The various Celtic languages can be roughly diagrammed (*Fig* 6).

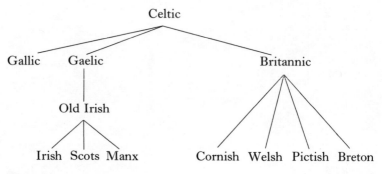

Fig 6: Celtic languages

As with most linguistic classifications there are some very perplexing questions concerning the Celtic languages and their dispersion. In Spain, for example, evidence of Indo-European people appears as early as the eighth century BC. It seems probable that these Indo-Europeans were Celts whose language was later partly preserved in inscriptions (mostly proper names) written in an alphabet borrowed from the Iberians. It is not clear, however, whether the Celts (or so-called Celtiberians) in Spain migrated there from the British Isles or whether they represent an independent offshoot which settled in Spain at a very remote time.

The Baltic languages were once spoken as far east as Moscow as place-names indicate. They have many features in common with the Slavic languages which expanded greatly in the fourth century from their historically more remote homeland in eastern Europe. In the south Baltic speakers were subdued by invaders of Asiatic origin, the Bulgars, who established the Bulgarian state. The Bulgars originally spoke an Altaic language but were eventually absorbed by the Slavic people. The Balto-Slavic languages have an ancient affiliation with the Indo-Iranian languages. Both groups have a common heritage in the first Indo-European palatal change which resulted in the centum-satəm dichotomy (*Fig* 7).

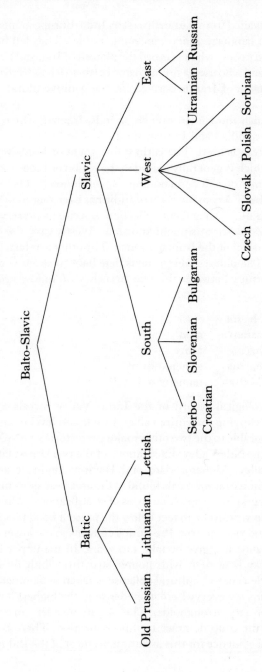

Fig 7: Balto-Slavic languages

India was invaded from the northwest by Indo-European speakers, known in their language as *árya*, meaning 'noble'. They left behind them a kindred people who occupied the plateau of Iran and tracts of Central Asia, and who used a similar name for themselves from which the modern name of Iran is derived, *ie*, the genitive plural of the word *airya*.

To distinguish the Indian branch of Indo-Iranian, which comprises both the Indian and Iranian speakers of Indo-European, the term Indo-Aryan is used. The earliest document of Indo-Aryan is the Rigveda which is generally placed in the region of 1200–1000 BC. From this time on, documentation is continuous. The actual period of the Indo-Aryan invasion of India has been placed between 1700 and 1400 BC.[13] An ancient collection of writings preserved by adherents to Zoroastrianism and known as Avesta, gave rise to the name of one dialect of the Iranian branch. The other is referred to as Old Persian. The oldest Avestan texts date back to about 600 BC.

The similarities between the two branches of Indo-Aryan are easily seen:

Sanskrit	*Avesta*	
híraṇya-	zaranya-	gold
sénā	haēnā	army
sóma-	haoma-	a sacred drink
Mitrá-	Miθra-	name of a deity[14]

The archaeological record of the Indus Valley reveals a large civilization occupying the entire valley. In size and level of civilization it is comparable to the two other major prehistoric sites – Mesopotamia and the Nile Valley. Excavations of the two largest cities of the Indus Valley, Mohenjo-daro and Harappa, indicate zealous municipal administration. Seals found in the area bear short inscriptions in a pictographic script. The levels of stratification at Mohenjo-daro extend downward to 39 feet below the present flood plain. The adjacent mound rises 30 feet. Pre-Indus cultures in the lower strata date back to 2600 BC, give or take 140 years. In the upper levels, economic decay is evident with poorer structures built on richer ones. No single cause of cultural collapse is taken as axiomatic but skeletal remains are everywhere in evidence in the highest levels of some of these city strongholds. The Aryan invaders may have administered the coup de grâce to this civilization. There is some circumstantial evidence for this assumption: most of the Indus sites were forts and Indra, the Aryan God of war, is sometimes referred to as *purmadara* 'fort-destroyer'. It is possible, but far from certain, that Harappa may correspond to Hari-Yupuya, mentioned in the Rigveda as the scene of the defeat of the non-Aryan inhabitants of northern India. Many skeletal remains show death by violence and their owners appear to have been fleeing from an enemy. These remains have been dated to around 1700 BC.[15]

A few of the many Indo-European languages of the Indo-Iranian group are shown in *Fig* 8.

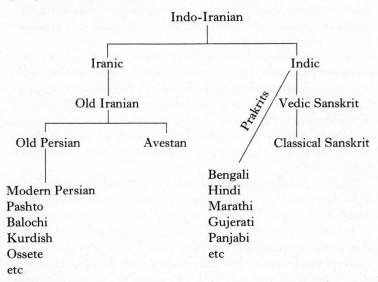

Fig 8: Indo-Iranian languages

Indo-European names inscribed upon cuneiform tablets in the Middle East appear to be the oldest linguistic information available concerning early contacts between Indo-Europeans and other language communities. Precursors of Indo-European invaders are found among the Kassites, who established a dynasty at Babylon in about 1760 BC. The Kassites were not Indo-European but in the names of their kings, elements occur similar to the names of Indo-Iranian deities (shown below in the second column):

šuriaš	surya
Indaš	Indra
Maruttaš	Marutaḥ

An Indo-European dynasty appears to have ruled over the people of Mitanni on the upper Euphrates. The princes had Indo-European names, *eg*, *šutarna*, and paid homage to Indo-Iranian deities. In 1360 BC the Mitanni and Hittite kings signed a treaty in which four of the gods invoked as witnesses are familiar from the Indian Vedas: Indra, Varuna, Mitra, and Násatyá.

There is some evidence, then, that there were Indo-Europeans in Syria by the upper half of the second millennium BC who shared linguistic affinities with Indo-Iranian (satəm) languages. Equally startling was the subsequent discovery (revealed by cuneiform documents of the same epoch) that the Hittite language of Cappadocia was also Indo-European.

Excavations begun in 1906 by Hugo Winckler at Boğazköy, ninety miles east of Ankara, uncovered the ancient site of Hattusas which was the capital of the Hittite empire from about 1700–1200 BC. Tablets recovered here belonged to the royal archives and contained the law code, royal decrees, treaties, prayers, letters, records of omens and mythological legends. One group of texts of unique interest refers to the training of race horses and contains a number of Indic words.

The Hittite language was not indigenous in Asia Minor but is an Indo-European language superimposed upon the earlier peoples by invaders. During this early period, other Indo-European languages or dialects established themselves in various parts of Anatolia (Luvian, Palaic, Lycian, etc). The land settled by these Indo-European speakers was known by the indigenous people as Hatti. Documentary evidence suggests that the Hittites were established in the land before 1900 BC. In 1915 B. Hrozny discovered the affinities between Hittite and Indo-European (see Chapter 3 for Hittite languages) and the connection is now accepted. The relationship is perhaps most obvious in the noun inflections containing six cases and similar in form to Latin and Greek. The enclitic personal pronouns -*mu* 'to me', -*ta* 'to thee', -*ši* 'to him' are much like Latin *me*, *te*, *se*. The active verb conjugation is very much like the conjugation of the -*mi* verbs in Greek.[16] Much of the vocabulary, however, appears to be non-Indo-European in origin, but compare Hittite *kwis*, Latin *quis*; and Hittite *genu*, Latin *genu*; Hittite *akw-anzi* 'they drink' and Latin *aqua*. By about 1000 BC the Indo-European names had all but disappeared, swallowed up by the local languages[17] (*Fig* 9).

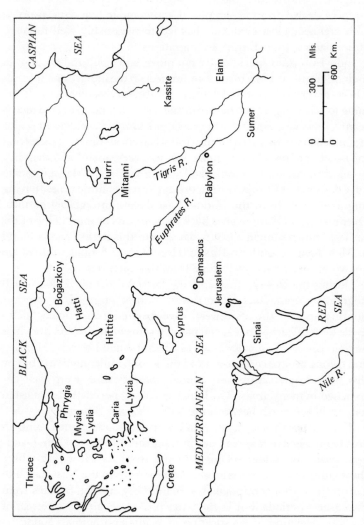

Fig 9: The Ancient Eastern Mediterranean

Conclusion

Linguistic information based on written records and linguistic inferences drawn from geographical and comparative data, coupled with archaeological evidence, has led to reasonably well-founded notions about Indo-European migrations.

Indo-European speakers did not move into a cultural vacuum in their migrations. They made some impact on the indigenous cultures wherever they encountered them, permitting archaeologists to determine to some degree the nature of the contact. Concrete evidence is scanty, however, especially in northern Europe. Estimates of population density in this area for pre-Indo-European times suggests that the number of people per square mile was very small[18] and that they primarily consisted of hunting and fishing cultures.[19] Man appears to have dominated Europe during the upper palaeolithic times, having migrated there from the Middle East during interglacial periods. His presence in Europe goes back 40,000 years or more. One of the earliest known human shelters dates from this period and is found in Molodova in southern Russia. Hunting and fishing cultures are known in many parts of Europe from this early date.

During the closing phases of the last (Würm) glaciation, small migratory populations in northwest Europe engaged in reindeer hunting and, in the southwest, cave-dwellers constructed finely-made tools of barbed bone, and painted somewhat abstract drawings on their cave walls at places such as Altamiras and Lascaux. Hunting and fishing groups continued until the second millennium B C, but by this period agriculture and animal domestication were well entrenched in many areas. The hunting–fishing populations persisted longest in the north between the Baltic Sea and Siberia.[20]

The first traces of agriculture in Europe are found in the Danubian area from whence it spread out into northern Europe. (The Danubian Basin was under strong influence from the Near East where these cultural innovations arose. Migrations from the Near East into Europe had been continuous via Spain, Italy and the Balkans from the earliest periods, but in the latter phases, *ie*, after the retreat of the last glaciation, domestication of plants and animals found its way into the Danubian Valley and on into Europe.)[21] Archaeological artefacts link the Balkans, the Danubian Plain and the Hungarian Plain, and as far north as Slovakia, as western outposts of Near Eastern societies.[22] Radiating from the Near East these influences must have come into contact with Indo-European speakers who helped carry them to more distant areas. Indo-Europeans appear to have gained a knowledge of metallurgy from Near Eastern sources, and carried it into Italy and other areas of Europe.[23]

There is no evidence – linguistic or archaeological – to indicate that the early Danubian culture (Danubian I) was Indo-European speaking. Some facts, however, suggest that later dwellers in the Danubian area were Indo-European. Cremation rites appear in the bronze period which, as mentioned earlier, also appeared in northern Italy in the region of the Po Valley by terramare. Cremation appeared in India among the early invaders, replacing the inhumation rites of the indigenous people, as well as in other areas associated with Indo-European. The fact remains, however, that cremation was not restricted to Indo-Europeans.

In spite of a number of theories concerning the Indo-European homeland, varying from Asia to Scandinavia, none are satisfactory from all points of view. The general area just north of the Black Sea, however, seems to offer the best possibilities in the light of present knowledge. Many imported copper relics, along with stone implements and weapons, were found in grave sites in southern Russia. The metal artefacts attest to Mesopotamian origins.[24] These communities of copper-using agriculturalists date back to about 2500 B C. Some similarities between these communities, in the form of burial rites and sacrifices, have been found with cultures in Anatolia and Mycenaea.[25] The latter are both known to have been Indo-European speaking cultures, giving rise to the speculation that the copper-using communities of southern Russia were also Indo-European. As such, they must reflect the earliest use of metal-working among Indo-European speakers in Europe and subsequently spread their craft and language into the Danube basin and surrounding areas – eventually branching out in all directions. Initial differentiation of Indo-European languages must have occurred much earlier, in the third, fourth, or fifth millennium B C. Linguistic considerations alone cannot answer the question of the homeland or period of dispersion of these early peoples, nor will such considerations fare any better with the great flood of questions that will arise once the problems involving the homeland and dispersion have been satisfactorily answered. Archaeological studies accompanied by linguistic evidence, however, have led to a good deal of information concerning these facets of Proto-Indo-European.

Once the pieces concerning the origin and dispersal of Indo-

Europeans have been put together, there will be even earlier homelands, migrations, and linguistic affinities to seek out, not to mention
the considerations revolving around the racial make-up and cultural
homogeneity of these early people. Historical linguistic methods
can in part determine the structure of the P I E language by reference
to the extant languages and written records and thereby provide a
basis for further comparison with other language groups.

Notes

1 For discussions concerning Tocharian chronology, morphology and historical
   changes, as well as the significance of Tocharian for Indo-European linguistics,
   see Arndt.
     Recent investigations of the problems concerning Indo-European relation-
   ships are presented in a collection of papers by Birnbaum and Puhvel. See also
   Pedersen.
2 The hypothesis that the Finno-Ugric languages (Hungarian, Lappish, Finnish,
   etc) are related to Altaic languages (Turkish, Mongol, etc) results in the common
   name Ural-Altaic.
3 The northern part of Central Europe has been localized as the home of P I E based
   upon the prehistoric geographical distribution of the beech, the turtle, and the
   salmon. For some of the examples used here as well as others, and for further
   criticism and references see Pulgram, p 147. Lehmann (1962), pp 207–209, presents a more sympathetic point of view. See also Baugh, pp 42–48, for comments
   and bibliography.
4 For the story of archaeology in Italy, see MacKendrick. For a linguistic account
   of the archaeological facts, see Pulgram. For an historical and comparative view
   of Latin, see Palmer and Buck.
5 See Palmer, p 41.
6 For more detail concerning the early Italic languages, as well as some of the
   cultural similarities between these linguistic groups, see Palmer, pp 33–73, and
   Polome, pp 59–76.
7 Buck, p 16.
8 *Ibid.*
9 Chadwick, p 10.
10 See Chadwick.
11 Other possibilities exist, *eg*, the Dorians may have moved into a political vacuum
   caused by the destruction of Mycenaean power by some external force, see Chadwick, pp 10–11.
12 See Sommerfelt (1962), pp 252–255, for a brief account of the Indo-Europeanization of Denmark.
13 See Burrow, p 31.
14 For further examples, see Burrow.
15 For an archaeological account of the excavation of the Indus Valley, see Wheeler.
16 For a review of Hittite grammar see Sturtevant (1964). For a more definitive
   description, see Friedrich. Hittite customs, art, economy, religion, etc are well
   portrayed by Gurney.

17 See Childe, *pp* 18–19 and *p* 30.

18 Clark, *p* 127.

19 *Ibid*, *p* 124. Clark finds no indication that the Maglemose culture of Northern Europe during the Mesolithic period practised agriculture or domestication of animals.

20 See Piggott, *p* 29.

21 Clark, *p* 216. ˙

22 Piggott, *p* 44.

23 Other factors relate to a fairly sophisticated form of civilization in the Near East at a very early period, *eg*, evidence of animal domestication is found in northern Iraq dating from about 9000 B C. It may be somewhat older in other nearby areas. The town of Jericho was a permanent site with high defensive towers (30 feet high) before 7000 B C.

24 See Childe, *p* 185.

25 In Mycenaea the burial shafts and in Anatolia the royal tombs at Alaca Hüyuk. See Piggott, *p* 123.

Chapter 3

The comparative method

Lexical items in two or more languages that display similarities in sound and meaning and which appear frequently enough to exclude accidental similarities and borrowings (although the latter could be quite extensive) indicate that these languages are genetically related, *ie*, have a common origin. Such lexical forms are referred to as cognates. Once a list of proposed cognates has been drawn up, the investigator attempts to establish systematic relationships between them. These relationships take the form of regular phonological correspondences. Correspondences offer the surest proof that languages are genetically related and reach their highest degree of validity when the phonological characteristics of one or more languages can be predicted from the information contained in one member of the group.

Nineteenth-century scholars examining Indo-European languages understood that phonological correspondences among cognate forms were possible because phonological change was systematic. Compare the following examples:

Spanish	*Portuguese*	*Italian*	*French*	
/kábra/	/kábra/	/kápra/	/šɛvɣə/	goat
/káro/	/káru/	/káro/	/šɛɣ/	expensive, dear
/kása/	/káza/	/káza/	/šɛ/	house
/kábo/	/kábu/	/kápo/	/šɛf/	chief
–	/kãũ/	/káne/	/šiɛ̃/	dog

The most obvious correspondences among these limited examples appear as follows:

consonants	k˜k˜k˜š
	b˜b˜p˜v/f
	r˜r˜r˜ɽ
	s˜z˜z˜ø
stressed vowels	a˜a˜a˜ɛ
	ã˜a˜ɛ̃

Further regular correspondences would be discovered if we add to the list. That certain historical events may interfere with the correspondences and hence our predictions, is clear from the fact that Spanish has *perro* where we would expect something like /káne/. In fact further information would reveal that the missing form ought to be /kan/ since /-e/ is lost after /n/ in Spanish, *cf* Latin *pāne* > Spanish *pan*. Often, as in this case, a search through dialectal or archaic usages of a word may reveal that it existed but is no longer widespread.

Evaluating these correspondences, we would expect /š/, /ɽ/, and /ɛ/ to be derivative and /k/, /r/, and /a/ to represent earlier phonological stages. We would not expect /š/, for example, to become /k/ in three languages and remain in one of them although this is conceivable especially if an initial split occurred between Spanish, Portuguese and Italian on the one hand and French on the other. Further correspondences confirm our suspicion, at least with regard to /k/, *cf*

/kúra/	/kúra/	/kúra/	/küre/	curate, priest
/kuérpo/	/kórpu/	/kórpo/	/koɽ/	body
/kórto/	/kórtu/	/kórto/	/kuɽ/	short
/kolór/	/kor/	/kolóre/	/kulöɽ/	colour

In these examples we find the alternation /k˜k˜k˜k/ indicating that /k/ > /š/ only in some cases, as in the environment immediately preceding /a/.

One language may show a change not found among one or more of the related languages, however, as in the case of Latin *thēsaurum* which became French *trésor* and Spanish *tesoro*. The change in this lexical form in French has no counterpart in the corresponding Spanish lexical item. Some seemingly limited phonological changes appear to disrupt regular change and obscure the phonological correspondences between related languages.

Unlike Latin, the prototype for the Romance languages, the proto-language for Indo-European is unknown. Linguistic correspondences between the individual members of this language family are the only reality that the historical linguist has at his disposal.

Proto-Indo-European consonants

Consonantal comparisons of major Indo-European languages such as Latin, Sanskrit, and Greek, based upon cognate forms, lead to a formulation of correspondences and a proto-design:

PIE	p	t	k	k^w
Latin	pater	trēs	centum	quis
Sanskrit	pitā́	tráyas	çatám	kás (nom masc)
Greek	patḗr	treîs	he-katón	tís
	father	three	hundred	who

PIE	b	d	g	g^w
Latin	dē-bilis[1]	decem	genus	ueniō[2]
Sanskrit	bálam	dáça	jánas	gam
Greek	beltíōn	déka	génos	baínō
		ten	kin	come

PIE	bh	dh	gh	g^wh
Latin	ferō	fūmus	ānser (*hanser)	fōrmus
Sanskrit	bhárāmi	dhūmás	haṁsás	gharmás
Greek	phérō	thūmós	khēn	thermós
	bear	smoke	goose	warm

Early attempts to establish the consonant inventory of PIE included the following:

```
p    t    k̂    k    kʷ
b    d    ĝ    g    gʷ
ph   th   k̂h   kh   kʷh
bh   dh   ĝh   gh   gʷh
```

The palatal order, represented by /k̂/, /ĝ/, /k̂h/ and /ĝh/ were posited to account for the palatal sounds in the *satəm* group of languages. These palatals were considered a frontal articulation of the velar order as found, for example, among the variants of /k/ in the English words *keep* and *cool*. The palatals were thought to have become /č/, /ǧ/

and /š/ in Sanskrit lexical forms such as *ca* /ča/, *janas* /ǧánas/ and *çatam* /šatám/. The centum languages were supposed to have retained the velar articulation of these sounds shown in the chart as /k/, /g/, /kh/, /gh/. In short, the parent language was thought to contain both types of /k/ articulations.

The voiceless aspirate series /ph/, /th/, /kh/, /kʷh/ was established to cover the infrequent cases in which Sanskrit /ph/, /th/, etc are found instead of the usual /bh/ /dh/, *cf* Sanskrit *sphal-*, *sthā-*.[3] Greek also displays voiceless aspirates, *cf* : *phérō* 'to bear', but these were shown to have been derived from the voiced aspirate series which is maintained in Sanskrit, *cf*: *bhárāmi*, but which has become /f/ in Latin, *cf*: *ferō*.

As the influence of environmental factors on language change in Indo-European became clearer, scholars were able to discard palatal sounds and voiceless aspirates in the proto-language; they were able to show that these sounds were derived from other proto-consonants within the evolution of the individual languages that contain them. It was demonstrated that Latin had labiovelars, *quis*, *quod*, but that these were not present in the other languages, *cf*: *quis*, Greek *tís*, Sanskrit *kás*. The labiovelar /gʷ/ appeared in Latin as /w/, *ueniō*, but in Greek as /b/, *baínō*, and Sanskrit as /g/, *gam-*. /gʷh/ became /f/ in Latin, *formus*, /th/ in Greek, *thermós* and /gh/ in Sanskrit, *gharmás*. The labiovelars /kʷ/ and /gʷ/ were presumed to have existed in the proto-language and to have been modified completely in Greek and Sanskrit. The reflexes of the labiovelars in Latin, Greek, and Sanskrit appear somewhat complicated since environmental (syntagmatic) influences in each language gave rise to several different sounds. In general, the changes were as follows:

PIE	Latin	Greek	Sanskrit
kʷ	kʷ	p, t, k	k
gʷ	w, gʷ	b, d, g	g
gʷh	f, w, gʷ	ph, th, kh	gh, h

In Latin, /kʷ/ remains in most environments but /gʷ/ is retained only after a nasal as in *unguen*, otherwise the occlusive element is lost leaving /w/ as in *veniō*. /gʷh/ also retains /gʷ/, after a nasal, *cf*: *ninguit*, but becomes /f/ or /w/ elsewhere.

The influence of a following vowel is primarily responsible for the various modifications in Greek. In the environment of a high back vowel, *eg*, /u/, the velar element is retained and the labial element is lost, *eg*, $k^w + u > k$. The vowels /a/ and /o/ have the opposite effect in that the labial element is retained, *eg*, $k^w + a$, o (or consonant) $> p$. Before front vowels, *eg*, /e/ or /i/, the labiovelars lose the labial component and are articulated in a more frontal position in accordance with the frontal articulation of the vowel. In short, they assimilate to the vowel position, $k^w + e, i > t$.[4]

The consonantal structure of the proto-language can now be thought of as consisting of four orders and three series,

$$
\begin{array}{llll}
p & t & k & k^w \\
b & d & g & g^w \\
bh & dh & gh & g^wh^5
\end{array}
$$

The parent language also contained the sibilant /s/ which occurs in Latin *septem*, Sanskrit *saptá* ; in Greek /s-/ + vowel > /h/, *eg*, *heptá*, but it is retained in other positions. From the foregoing discussion the main outlines of the Classical Greek and the Classical Latin consonantal systems can be derived from the reconstructed PIE system. However, some additional information is needed for Sanskrit.

Classical Greek					*Classical Latin*			
p	t	k			p	t	k	k^w
b	d	g			b	d	g	g^w
ph	th	kh^6			f	s	h	
s								

The discovery of Sanskrit as an Indo-European language in the later eighteenth century had a great impact on language studies during the nineteenth century.[7] By broadening the perspective of language relationships it gave real impetus to the study of comparative philology. Some of the ideas of earlier periods, for example that Hebrew was the original language from which all others came, began to drop away.

The symmetry of the Sanskrit system seemed to reflect a more perfect arrangement of phonological unity than either Greek or Latin, hence it was felt that Sanskrit represented an older stage of the other two. They were considered simply deviant and corrupt forms of Sanskrit. Later scholarship has shown this assumption to be misguided and it is now accepted that Sanskrit is an independent modification of PIE as are the other Indo-European languages.

The Sanskrit consonantal pattern can be schematically presented as follows:

Classical Sanskrit

p	t	ṭ	č	k
b	d	ḍ	ǧ	g
ph	th	ṭh	čh	kh
bh	dh	ḍh	ǧh	gh
v	s	ṣ	š	h

There have been several important palatalization movements in the Indo-European languages which have led to differentiation among the members of the family. These changes can be characterized as the first palatalization (which occurred within the closely associated dialects of PIE and separated the Indo-Iranian and Balto-Slavic branches from the others), and the second palatalization (which occurred within the Indo-Iranian dialects further differentiating them from the Balto-Slavic). These movements can be inferred from comparative studies and took place in prehistoric periods. No absolute dates can be established for these changes, but the comparative method reveals the chronological order in which they occurred. A third major palatalization took place in historical times, that is, as attested by documentation in Latin, and shaped the consonantal design of the Romance languages. This will be discussed in Chapter 7.

Phonetic basis of palatalization

Front vowels, *eg*, /i/, /e/, /æ/, /y/, often have an assimilatory effect on preceding consonants by modifying the consonantal place of articulation in accordance with the vowel. This is essentially an anticipatory process in which the front mass of the tongue is moved forward and upward into the palatal region simultaneously with the articulation of the consonant. Velar and dental or alveolar sounds, and less frequently, labials, are palatalized in this manner. If the palatalization process is carried through to its ultimate conclusion, these sounds become palatals and distinct from palatalized sounds, *eg*,

ke > k^{y}e > če or će
te > t^{y}e > če or će

First palatalization

The first palatalization represents an early dialectal difference in
P I E. If we restrict our attention to one feature – the palatalization
of P I E */k/ – the dialectal situation can be envisaged as something
similar to that shown in *Fig* 10.

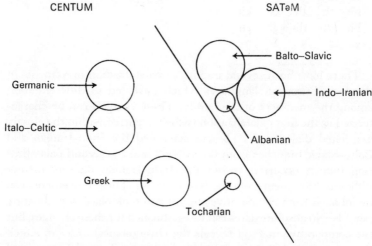

Fig 10: Early dialectal variations in Proto-Indo-European

The palatalization of */k/ must have occurred among contiguous
P I E dialects before widespread migrations took place, since it is
found in these languages with little variation in the conditions under
which it occurs. The phonological process can be shown in the
following schematic representation:

p   t   [č] ← k   ← kʷ
b   d   [ǧ] ← g   ← gʷ
bh   dh   [ǧh] ← gh ← gʷh

At first the palatal sounds must have been allophonic variants of the
velar conditioned by front vowels (1). The reduction of the labiovelars (2) would establish a new phonemic opposition between
palatals and velars by opposing them in the same environments
before front vowels (3), thus

(1)	(2)	(3)
/k/ [tš] i, e	kʷi > ki	/k/ [tš] i, e > /č/
[k] a, o, u	kʷe > ke	/kʷ/ i, e > /k/
	etc	

The voiceless palatal /č/ (phonetically [tš]) subsequently lost its occlusive element, resulting in /š/, the sound in Sanskrit *çatám* 'hundred', (not to be confused with *satəm* the Avestan word for hundred), and *dáça* 'ten'. Note that Sanskrit /a/ is a reflex of earlier */e/, *cf* Latin *centum*, *decem*. Similarly the voiced palatals /ǧ/ and /ǧh/ became /ž/ and /žh/ respectively.

The early consonantal system common to the satəm languages must have appeared as follows:

```
p    t    š    k
b    d    ž    g
bh   dh   žh   gh
```

Second palatalization

The effect of the second palatalization is clearly seen by comparing Latin, Greek and Sanskrit. The Sanskrit phoneme /a/ often corresponds to Latin and Greek /e/ and /o/:

	Greek	Latin	Sanskrit
	estí	est	ásti
/e/			
	génos	genus	jánas
	ostéon	os	ásthi
/o/			
	dómos	domus	dámas

These and many other similar correspondences suggest that Sanskrit /e/ and /o/ had both merged with /a/. Note that Sanskrit /a/ after /č/ corresponds to Latin and Greek /e/ in the related forms *que*, *te* and *ča*. This suggests that Sanskrit /e/ became /a/ after the palatalization of /k/ to /č/. If the vocalic modification had occurred first, consonantal palatalization would not have taken place. The second palatal shift can be schematically represented as follows:

```
p    t    š    č  ← k
b    d    ž    ǧ  ← g
bh   dh   žh   ǧh ← gh
```

For a time during the second palatal change /k/ and /č/ must have been allophonic variants in mutually exclusive environments, *ie*

```
        [k] + a, o, u
/k/
        [tš] + i, e
```

With the subsequent merger in Sanskrit of /e/, /o/ and /a/ the allophone [tš] came to oppose the allophone [k] in identical environments and became a voiceless palatal phoneme, *ie*

$$[k] + o \quad /k/ + a$$
$$>$$
$$[tš] + e \quad /č/ + a$$

The reflexes of the two palatal shifts appear only among the voiceless palatals /š/ and /č/. The sonants /ž/ and /ǧ/, /žh/ and /ǧh/ derived from the same palatal processes fell together and appear in Sanskrit as /ǧ/ and /ǧh/. These events together with several other modifications (*eg*, *-s > -h*) resulted in the Sanskrit consonantal pattern described earlier. This system comprising five orders and five series, is primarily the result of palatal changes, the introduction of a voiceless aspirated series, and the development of a cacuminal or retroflex order (*ie*, *ṭ*, *ḍ*, *ṭh*, etc).

First Germanic sound shift

An early demonstration of the usefulness of the comparative method is found in the works of Rask and Grimm.[8] Rask laid much of the groundwork for comparative Indo-European philology and Grimm, while adding to this information, was also able to synthesize many phonological correspondences into a formula thereafter known as Grimm's Law. These correspondences reflect the consonantal shift manifest in the Germanic branch of the Indo-European language family, *ie*

voiceless occlusive > voiceless fricative
voiced occlusive   > voiceless occlusive
voiced aspirate   > voiced occlusive

Known as the First Germanic Sound Shift, this modification occurred early in the history of the diverging Indo-European languages, effectively differentiating the Germanic branch from the others.[9] Compare the examples shown opposite of Latin and Sanskrit on the one hand and English on the other. (Note that the rare P I E */b/ does not lend itself to well-defined cognates.)

The modifications represent unconditioned sound change since environmental circumstances do not account for them. The few contextual limitations operating on this shift, *ie*, the exceptions, are easily stated.

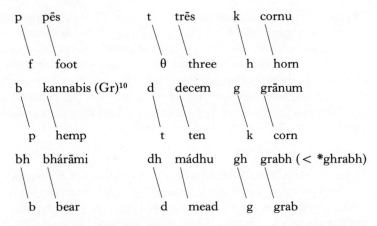

p	pēs	t	trēs	k	cornu
f	foot	θ	three	h	horn
b	kannabis (Gr)[10]	d	decem	g	grānum
p	hemp	t	ten	k	corn
bh	bhárāmi	dh	mádhu	gh	grabh (< *ghrabh)
b	bear	d	mead	g	grab

Given several divergent languages, simply to consider the statistically more frequent occurrence of a sound as the earliest or protosound is not always reliable, *cf*

Sanskrit	bhárāmi	bh-	*Armenian*	berem	b-
Greek	phérō	ph-	*Gothic*	baíra	b-
			English	bear	b-

By way of illustration, let us assume that all of the initial sounds in the above list are possible proto-sounds. The predominance of /b-/ suggests that it is a better choice for the original sound than /bh-/ or /ph-/. On the other hand, assuming that the simplest description of change is the best one and that phonological changes take place one step at a time, we can establish the following relationships:

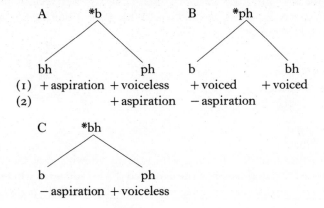

A   *b

	bh	ph
(1)	+ aspiration	+ voiceless
(2)		+ aspiration

B   *ph

	b	bh
(1)	+ voiced	+ voiced
(2)	− aspiration	

C   *bh

	b	ph
	− aspiration	+ voiceless

Change C requires only one step for each derivative sound to differentiate them from*/bh/. Changes A and B require two changes in at
least one of their reflexes. The logical candidate for the proto-sound
is then */bh/. A little more information would soon reveal that Gothic
and English are more closely related to each other than they are to
the other languages and that they reflect a common stage containing
/b-/. The predominance of /b-/ in three out of five languages is then
somewhat deceptive in terms of comparative reconstruction.

Grassmann's Law
Grimm's formula represented a notable breakthrough in linguistic
studies. However, he did allow a number of errors to creep into his
scheme which later was modified by other scholars. Grimm posited
the change /p t k/ became /f θ h/ – but compare Latin *est*, Greek
estí, Sanskrit *ásti*, with Gothic *ist*, and English *is*. In these environments /t/ does not correspond to /θ/. Grimm had not counted on
environmental restrictions. He also overlooked in his generalizations
the fact that Germanic /b/ may correspond to Sanskrit /b/, *cf* Sanskrit *bōdha*, Gothic *biudan*, and not Sanskrit /bh/.

Grassmann observed these deficiencies in Grimm's formulations,
ie, that after voiceless fricatives Germanic voiceless occlusives did
not become fricatives. Grassmann further formulated the 'law of the
aspirates' which does not permit two aspirates to stand in the same
syllable: the first is always reduced to its non-aspirated counterpart.
Thus the earlier form of *bōdha* was *bhōdha*. Where this modification had occurred in Sanskrit, the German /b/ corresponded to
Sanskrit /b/. In Greek, however, the voiced aspirates became voiceless before de-aspiration. In short, Germanic /b/ corresponds to
Indo-European (*eg*, Sanskrit and Greek) /b/ and /p/, but it corresponds to P I E */bh/. *Cf*

P I E	*bheudh-
Sanskrit	bŏdha-
Greek	peuθo-
Gothic	*beuda-

Verner's Law
Verner further modified Grimm's formula by showing that Ger-
manic voiced /b d g/ (instead of the expected /f θ h/) appeared where
Sanskrit and Greek had an unaccented vowel preceding /p t k/.

PIE *$/t/$ then appeared as Germanic $/d/$ or $/ð/$ instead of $/θ/$ in a particular environment. Compare, for example,

Sanskrit	pitár-
Greek	patér
Gothic	fadar
Old English	fɛder[11]

This insight into different reflexes, based on a difference of accent in the proto-language, helped to account for such seemingly aberrant forms as German *ziehen/gezogen* and *sieden/gesotten* and Old English *séoðan/soden* and *céosan/coren* ($s > r$ via z).[12]

Verner's observation suggests that initial syllables in PIE behaved in the same manner as medial unstressed syllables where $/p > f/$, $/t > θ/$, etc. Consonants in accented syllable onset position became voiced. A few examples will suffice to show this influence.[13]

Sanskrit	*Gothic*
pitár-	fadar
saptá	sibun (with loss of $/t/$)
bhráta	bróðar ($ð < $*$θ$)

In the various Germanic languages the effects of the changes stated by Verner have been obscured by subsequent modifications particular to each language.[14] The accent in Germanic later became generally fixed on the first syllable of the word.

The Neo-grammarians Leskien, Osthoff, Brugmann, and others found a good deal of support in these modifications to Grimm's Law, which served to substantiate their point of view that sound laws operate without exception and that apparent exceptions are actually laws in themselves.[15]

Second Germanic sound shift

Comparison of cognates within the Germanic branch itself reveals another shift in consonantal sounds which further separated High German from the other Germanic dialects (see table overleaf).

A large number of phonological contexts inhibit or in other ways modify these changes: for example, $/t/$ does not correspond to $/ts/$ in High German if followed by $/r/$, and compare English *tread* with High German *treten*. The standardization of certain dialectal features in High German also disrupted regular phonological developments.

English	Low German	High German	
pound	pund	Pfund	p~pf
ten	tein	zehn	t~ts
cat	katte	Katze	k~k
bed	bed	Bett	b~b
day	dag	Tag	d~t
good	gôd	gut	g~g
foot	fôt	Fuss	f~f
thin	dünn	dünn	θ~d
help	helpen	helfen	h~h

Vowels, diphthongs and semi-vowels

Proto-Indo-European is commonly thought to have contained five long and five short vowels of the type /i e a o u/ plus the reduced vowel /ə/. Indo-European /e/ and /o/, both long and short, are represented in Sanskrit by /ă̆/, cf Latin *decem*, Sanskrit *daça* ; and Latin *novus*, Sanskrit *návas*. It was once thought that the proto-language had only /a/ long and short (as reflected in Sanskrit), which split into /ĕ/, /ŏ/ and /ă/ in the other Indo-European languages. It is now certain, however, that a merger occurred in Sanskrit in which the mid-vowels coalesced in /ă̆/. Compare the following examples containing short vowels:

	Latin	Greek	Sanskrit
i	quid	tí	kím
u	jugum	zugón	yugám
e	est	estí	ásti
o	os	ostéon	ásthi
a	ager	agrós	ájras

It has been customary to posit */ə/ in Proto-Indo-European to account for differences such as /i/ in Sanskrit *pitắr* on the one hand and /a/ in Latin *pater* and Greek *patér* on the other hand. The symbol *ə* was not meant to have any precise phonetic value but was simply used to set up a proto-sound for /a/ and /i/. There are of course other possibilities that may account for the difference between *pitắr* and *pater*, etc (other Indo-European languages have /a/) without introducing an indeterminate vowel into the proto-system. The Sanskrit form may in fact represent early morphological variation in the parent language in which a stem *p*V (where V = vowel) plus

-itar, an attested variant suffix, became *pitár* through loss of the stem vowel.[16] The diphthongs /ei, eu, ai, au, oi, ou/ attributed to the parent language were sometimes thought to have had long counterparts since long diphthongs appear in some Indo-European languages (as for example the Greek dative singular *grāi* 'old woman' and *nēi* 'ship'). The six diphthongs are preserved in Greek but are partially monophthongized in Latin, becoming long vowels (see Chapter 7). In Sanskrit the coalescence of /e/ and /o/ with /a/ affected the onset of the diphthongs, resulting simply in /ai/ and /au/. These two diphthongs were subsequently modified to /ē/ and /ō/.[17]

Syllabic liquids and nasals in Proto-Indo-European have been posited as /l̥ r̥ m̥ n̥/. Phonetically these would be equivalent to the syllabic sounds in English in the final syllables of the words *able*, *runner, bottom* and *hidden*. These semi-consonants gave rise to different reflexes in the various languages, *eg*, PIE *dekm̥*, Greek *déka*, Latin *decem*, Sanskrit *dáça*, Gothic *taihun*, Lithuanian *dešimt*, etc. Long counterparts for the syllabics have also been reconstructed. Justification for these Proto-Indo-European sounds and phonological patterns has been found in one language or another. Many of the above sounds were posited by Brugmann, but Indo-Europeanists have since disagreed and the controversy still continues.[18] Some Indo-Europeanists, for example, leave out the diphthongs and account for Indo-European developments with a much simpler system, including laryngeals, and vowels in combination with /w/ and /y/. The distribution of long vowels, the distribution and number of unaccented vowels (reduced vowels) and the existence of long diphthongs are debatable for PIE.

Ablaut

The comparative method was responsible for techniques worked out to account for vowel differences in Indo-European languages. The notion of vowel gradation, or ablaut, a term used by Grimm, purports to explain the vocalic differences within a particular Indo-European language as well as the vocalic differences within the family of Indo-European languages. Vowel variation includes differences in vowel quality and differences in vowel quantity.

quantitative alternation: apophony
qualitative alternation: metaphony

The main cause for this vowel gradation was variation in the kind and amount of stress. Groups of vowels in ablaut relationship are called series and each vowel in a series belongs to a particular grade, *eg*, full grade, secondary grade, reduced grade, and zero grade. Of an /e/ and /o/ series, for example, /e/ may belong to the full grade being fully accented, /o/ to the secondary grade, carrying secondary accent, while further reduction in stress results in /ə/ or reduced grade, and finally the loss of the vowel altogether results in zero grade. For example, in English [kæn] alternates with [kən] as variants of style and stress, but if in the course of time these two forms came to mean different things, where say, [kæn] came to mean the present tense and [kən] came to express the future, then the sound /æ/, stressed, would correspond to full grade and /ə/ would correspond to secondary grade in an /æ/–/ə/ series. Lengthened grade resulted from lengthening the vowel of the first or second grade.

In Indo-European languages we find such evidences of ablaut in the following forms:

Metaphony

GREEK	pétomai	e		LATIN	tegō	e
	póte	o			toga	o
	eptómai	ø				

Apophony

SANSKRIT

normal grade	*extended or strengthened grade*	*zero or weakened grade*
/a/	/ā/	ø
pád 'foot'	pādam	upabdá 'trampling'
(genitive singular)	(accusative singular)	(upa + pad-a
(guṇa)	(vṛddhi)	*p* becomes *b* via assimilation)[19]

This vocalic relationship of /a/ (Indo-European /a e o/) was recognized by Indian grammarians who gave the name *vṛddhi* to the strengthened grade and *guṇa* to the normal grade. Zero grade was used as the point of departure to construct the other two. European philologists however treated *guṇa* as the normal grade and derived the *vṛddhi* and zero grades by the opposite processes of strengthening and weakening. The same gradation applies to suffixes, *cf* stem *rajan-* 'king', normal grade in vocative *rájan*, zero grade in genitive singular *rájñas*, extended grade in accusative singular *rájānam*.

Laryngeal theory

Before the discovery of Hittite there existed in Indo-European studies a theory based upon laryngeals. Among other things, they were supposed to account for many of the long vowels in Indo-European languages.[20] In some instances the laryngeals disappeared without a trace but in others their effects survived. The long vowel in Latin *plānus* was supposed to be derived from a combination of short vowel plus a laryngeal (henceforth H). The loss of the laryngeal gave rise to compensatory vowel lengthening and in some cases may have been responsible for ablaut relationships. Documentary evidence for laryngeals appeared in Hittite: compare for example Hittite *paHHur* and Greek *pŭr* 'fire'; Hittite *palHi-* and Latin *plānus* */plaH-/. With confirmation from Hittite the laryngeal theory is generally accepted today although there is no universal agreement concerning all particular aspects of it. One view, briefly stated, proposes three laryngeals H_1 H_2 H_3[21] and that the long vowels of Proto-Indo-European were the result of a combination of a single vowel /e/ plus one of the laryngeals, *cf* Sanskrit,

dhē	*dheH$_1$	put
stā (> sthā)	*steH$_2$	stand
dō	*deH$_3$	give

The three different vowels, /e/, /a and /o/ developed in accordance with the 'colouring' of the three laryngeals.

Another view maintains that in the case of Sanskrit *sthā* the original root consisted of *st* followed by a vowel, followed by H. In some inflectional forms, however, the root vowel was lost resulting in *stH* and this was analogically spread throughout the entire verb. In this way an attempt is made to link the Sanskrit voiceless aspirates /ph/, /th/ and /kh/ with laryngeals instead of with Proto-Indo-European voiceless or voiced aspirates. Long vowels that did not arise from ablaut were assumed to be due to short vowels becoming long upon loss of laryngeal. Hittite preserves some laryngeals, however, where the vowel in Indo-European languages is short.[22] In Hittite there is only one laryngeal – not the three demanded by the theory. Nor does it always appear in Hittite where it should, as demanded by the theory. Nevertheless, the discovery of a laryngeal in a language that is related to P I E, or perhaps is an earlier form of P I E, stands as a monument to the rigorous endeavours of those who anticipated such a sound through the comparative method.[23]

The laryngeal associated with Hittite but lost in other Indo-European languages has led some scholars to conclude that Hittite branched off from the parent language at an earlier stage than the general breakup of the other Indo-European languages. It has been suggested that Hittite on the one hand and Proto-Indo-European on the other hand are both descended from an earlier common ancestor sometimes referred to as Proto-Indo-Hittite.

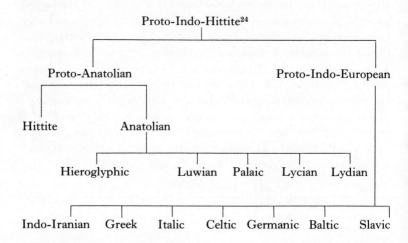

Conclusion

The comparative method is possible because languages change within a framework of universal principles. Many of these principles relate to phonological change which is an instrumental factor in language modification. The regular and systematic course along which phonological change proceeds is often disrupted, however, by other linguistic and non-linguistic forces which play an important role in language change. These will be considered in subsequent chapters.

The last century saw a good deal of linguistic activity, some of which has been sketched here. The advent of structural concepts, implicit in works such as Grimm's formulations and those of following generations of scholars, has changed the emphasis of comparative philological studies. Comparative linguistics, thus termed more in accordance with the procedures and goals of contemporary linguistic thought, delves into the nature of language with a view to understanding language as the proposed net result.

The primary concern of this chapter has been to highlight some of the results of the comparative method in its application to some of the Indo-European languages and P I E rather than to investigate in depth the tremendous volume of literature dealing with these languages. Many notable achievements have thus been omitted.

Notes

1 The sound /b/ has a low frequency of occurrence in Indo-European. No adequate cognate forms are available, but in the examples above, the Greek word *beltion* 'better', and Latin *de* 'from' + *-bilis* 'strength' (*ie*, 'weakness'), appear to be related to Sanskrit *balam* 'strength'.

2 Latin *bos* represents a dialectal borrowing of a modification of /u/ to /b/ since the cognate form with Greek *boûs* and Sanskrit *gāuh* would have been *uōs*. See Hudson-Williams, *p* 27.

3 See Buck, *p* 117.

4 For an enumeration of these and more specific environments and examples and exceptions, see Buck, *p* 126, Palmer *pp* 226–227 and *p* 229 for Latin /h/, and Meillet (1922) *pp* 91–92.

5 For an account of the research that led to these discoveries, see Jespersen (1922).

6 Greek also contained *ps*, *dz*, *ks*.

7 The Jesuit missionary Coeurdoux, as early as 1767, ascertained similarities between Sanskrit and Latin but the information was not widely known. In 1786, Sir William Jones brought to the attention of the scholarly world the position of Sanskrit vis-à-vis other Indo-European languages.

8 Franz Bopp is generally considered the father of comparative philology; working independently of Rask and Grimm, his work appearing in 1816 was concerned with the origin of grammatical forms and marks the birth of comparative grammar. The following years, 1818–1819, saw the publications of Rask and Grimm. Grimm's sound law appeared in 1822.

9 See Jespersen (1922), *p* 44 for details of Grimm's initial formulation.

10 See Bloomfield, *p* 348.

11 See Lehmann (1962), *p* 95.

12 See Pedersen, *p*. 282.

13 'Every internal /θ/ became /ð/ unless the change was opposed by the placing of the accent on the preceding vowel.' De Saussure, *p* 146, maintains that /θ/ tended to sonorize in Germanic, as in Latin, spontaneously within the word but only the placement of accent prevented it. The older view gave the accent the dominant role. Here the accent is regarded as an inhibitory factor.

14 The /d/ in Gothic *fadar* was a voiced fricative (see Lehmann, 1955, *p* 2). In this case, Gothic /ð/ shows up in West Germanic as /d/, Old English *faeder*. The /d/ in this form became /ð/ by analogy with *brother* where the /θ/ > /ð/ in English in

intervocalic position and independent of Verner's Law. This was still occurring as late as the sixteenth century. Thus Indo-European $-t'->$ Germanic $-\theta'->$ Gothic $-\eth'-$, but West Germanic $-d-$.

The question of the phonetic changes and their relative chronology in Verner's Law is not settled, however. Several opposing views have been put forth in which, (a) the accent shift followed the voicing change, (b) the accent shift preceded the voicing change, and (c) both changes occurred together. See Bennett (1968). For bibliographical references concerning the first Germanic consonantal changes and a treatment of their ordered relationships, see Voyles.

15 See Bloomfield, p 357. For a treatment of the Neo-grammarians and their influence upon linguistic scholarship, see Jankowsky.

16 See Lockwood, p 94.

17 See Whitney.

18 See Lehmann (1955). For early comprehensive treatments of this subject, see Brugmann, Delbrück and Meillet (1922).

19 For vowel gradation, see Buck, pp 106–117.

20 In another aspect of the laryngeal theory, Indo-European schwa was involved. There were essentially two theories concerning the nature of laryngeals: de Saussure conceived of them as sonants, having both vocalic and consonantal variants. P I E schwa was considered to be the vocalic allophone of the sonant standing between consonants in zero grade of the root. Herman Möller and Jerzy Kurylowicz advanced the contrary opinion that the laryngeals were always non-syllabic and that P I E schwa resulted from a reduced vowel in contact with a laryngeal consonant. This is the view elaborated by Sturtevant and others that is predominant today. For an account of these views, see Prosman.

21 The notation is that of Burrow, p 87.

22 For examples of Hittite and correspondences in Indo-European languages, see Lehmann (1955), p 25.

23 Further examples of laryngeals in Hittite are:

Hittite	Sanskrit	Greek	Latin	
ešHer	ásṛk	éar	aser	blood
Haštai	ásthi	ostéon	os	bone
Hant	ánti	antí	ante	front

See Burrow, pp 84–88.

For a review of laryngeal studies, some new insights, and bibliographical references, see Lehmann (1955) pp 80–97. The origin of Sanskrit voiceless aspirates appears to reflect a voiceless stop plus a laryngeal as seen in cognate forms, cf Greek estēn, Sanskrit tiṣṭhati. In Greek, the voiceless stops are followed by a long vowel. The reconstructed form is thus *steH. The view that voiceless aspirates in Indo-Iranian are the result of laryngeal sounds presupposes that laryngeals were phonemic in P I E and not simply reflexes of an even older period of the language, thus contradicting the theory of an Indo-Hittite origin.

24 Sturtevant (1964), p 9.

Chapter 4

Language reconstruction

As in the case of Indo-European languages, the comparative method of reconstruction has been actively applied to other groups of languages with varying degrees of success. Many of the world's languages can now be assigned to several major families such as the Afro-Asiatic (Hamito-Semitic), Sino-Tibetan, Altaic, Dravidian, Austro-Asiatic, Finno-Ugric, Malayo-Polynesian, and various American Indian families. There are many languages, however, that have not been successfully assigned to a particular family. This is not necessarily for lack of descriptive information, but because the great time depth separating them from other languages has obscured any salient features of relationship.

Intermediate links in the diachronic hierarchy of languages are often lost, further compounding the difficulties in comparative reconstruction. If, for example, Latin and Sanskrit had not been written languages preserving their similarities in documented form, the Romance and Indic languages would appear to be unrelated. Comparative studies of the Romance languages, on the one hand, and Indic languages on the other, would reveal some relevant structural information concerning the linguistic design of Proto-Romance

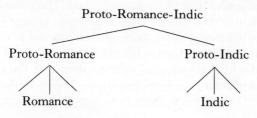

and Proto-Indic, but conclusions about their common heritage based on comparative reconstruction of the two proto-languages would be on very shaky ground indeed.

A comprehensive comparison of all the Romance dialects presently spoken would not lead to anything like the detailed information we have about Latin from the written records. Most of the noun inflections, some of the verb tenses, and some of the phonology could not be reconstructed at all.

A number of language families, such as Indo-European and Hamito-Semitic, cover enormous geographical areas as the result of continuous expansion from earlier periods. As they broadened their territorial limits, other language families were forced to recede and, as often happened, gradually died out. The colonization of the North American continent by predominantly English-speaking representatives of the Germanic branch of Indo-European has all but obliterated the indigenous Indian languages, which in their day corresponded to several major stocks covering large areas. This process of linguistic replacement must have occurred many times during the long history of mankind, effectively erasing from the scene many languages and language families.

The general replacement process, at least in part, parallels technological advances which allow one linguistic group to subdue another who have not undergone the cultural changes necessary to resist the steady encroachment of their territory by the stronger people. Often, however, pockets of the former inhabitants survive, especially in isolated areas which have not been penetrated by the superior forces of the advancing civilization, or for other reasons relating to cultural tenacity on the part of the diminishing people, who refuse to be absorbed into the new culture.

In Europe such a linguistic enclave is found in Brittany where the remnants of Celtic speakers have not been completely absorbed by French speakers around them. Basque represents another such hold-out against Indo-European encroachment in the form of earlier Celtic and Latin, and later Spanish and French. The former extension of Basque appears in place-names to be found in large portions of the Iberian peninsula, as far south as Granada and as far north into France as Bordeaux. Ancient inscriptions on coins and various artefacts lend additional support to the notion that the Basques covered a much larger area in ancient times. This is further borne out by medieval reference to them from non-Basque sources[1] and from language contacts between Basque and adjacent peoples such as the West Cantabrian inhabitants – the ancestors of the Castilians. Today, Basque culture and language are almost visibly shrinking away from areas, such as Bilbao, which a few decades ago were almost exclusively Basque but are now almost entirely Spanish.

Speculations concerning the origins of the Basque people and their language have been about as varied as the points on the compass. However, three main considerations stand out among the many, based primarily on linguistic evidence: (1) the Basque dialects are related to the languages of the Mediterranean which once formed a common linguistic entity; (2) they are related to the languages of the Caucasus; and (3) they are linked to the languages of North Africa. Basque, then, is one of the languages whose historical antecedents are unknown. The scarcity of written records for Basque before the twelfth century, while a definite obstacle for comparative work, does not appear to be the crucial point. While Basque resembles other Mediterranean languages in a very limited way, *eg*

Basque	*Berber*	
izar	izeren	star
izen	isem	name
aker	iker	buck
anai	ana	brother
ama	imma	mother

no convincing phonological correspondences have been formulated to account for an historical relationship. The possibilities exist that words such as these may have been borrowed by one language from the other or that both languages borrowed them from a third source.

The main deterrent, however, to finding languages with a common ancestry with Basque appears to be the time depth that separates Basque from other Mediterranean languages, and the loss of intermediate linguistic links that might have connected Basque historically with a neighbouring language. That there were a number of languages spoken along the shores of the Mediterranean is not in dispute – ample evidence from inscriptions and from early Roman writers confirms this – but whether they had any connection with Basque cannot be determined at present. More light may be shed on this perplexing question when the ancient Iberian inscriptions, dating back to about 600 BC, are eventually deciphered (they have been transliterated) and when more written records are exposed through archaeological excavation around the Mediterranean.

In North Africa the distribution of the Berber languages (which belong to the Hamitic family) indicates a once widespread territorial coverage that was gradually diminished by the incursions of Arabic speakers. Berber territory stretched from the Atlantic coast across North Africa to the Red Sea which is now dominated by the Arabic language. Pockets of Berber speakers exist, however, throughout

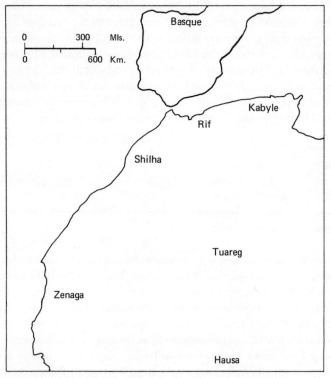

Fig 11: The distribution of Western Berber languages

this entire area with the largest concentration (*ie* the Tuareg languages) in the southern and most inaccessible regions. Both Basque and Berber, then, are now confined to small enclaves but were once spoken over a much wider and contiguous area separated only by the narrow strait of Gibraltar.[2] (*Fig* 11.) Their ancient geographical proximity at least suggests the possibility of linguistic affiliations and a place to begin comparative studies.

There are certain inherent dangers in the comparative method of reconstruction that can easily lead to false premises. Accidental similarities in form and meaning occur among all languages. The word for *eye* in Modern Greek is [máti] and in Malay [mata].[3] If these languages were once related in the remote past, in the sense that all languages appear to stem from a common source, they have diverged to such an extent that there is no longer a reconstructable relationship. The word for *eye* is an accidental convergence. Only a little imagination is necessary to invent phonological rules and a semantic shift in order to suggest that English and Berber languages may be related:

eat	(Rif)	eš	
foot	(Zenaga)	a-fus	hand
goat	(Shilha)	a-ɣad	
star	(Shilha)	i-tri	
black	(Hausa)	bak'l	

The insignificance of such examples becomes apparent in comparison to the Romance and Germanic languages, for example, where lists of cognates can be drawn up that pervade the vocabulary to such an extent that their relatedness is beyond question.

Lexical similarities or lack of them between languages may in part be due to lexical borrowings. Words are often borrowed from language to language, to a greater or lesser degree, depending on the type and amount of contact between them. Even linguistic communities with fairly close-knit cultural ties often find it expedient to incorporate foreign words into their language. The Basques, for example, have not been readily assimilated by their surroundings and maintain strong local traditions; nevertheless, Indo-European lexical items in Basque are not uncommon, having been introduced from Celtic, Latin, and later from Spanish and French. Upon their incorporation into Basque, these words underwent modifications which reflect specific phonological processes. Before any effective comparisons can be made between two or more languages, loan words must be sorted out. In the case of Basque, the source of the loans is often known and their modifications in conformity to the phonological structure can be analysed.[4]

Basque treats loan words in a specific manner. Prothesis (addition

of initial vowel before certain consonants), voicing, avoidance of
certain clusters, substitution of labial fricatives by labial occlusives,
palatalization, loss of medial vowels, as well as several other processes are evident from the following borrowings from Latin
origins:[5]

Latin	Basque	Latin	Basque
rege	errege	festa	besta
schola	eskola	voluntate	borondate
corpus	gorputz	caelu	zeru
causa	gauza	asinu	asto
libru	liburu	anima	arima
astru	asturu	senora	serora
ecclesia	eliza	sensu	zentsu
fronte	boronte	ansere	antzar[6]

Phonological processes, as seen in the behaviour of borrowed
words, indicate to the investigator the kinds of phonological constraints that are operative in the language. Some historical information can thus be derived from the manner in which loan words are
incorporated into a language. A likely source of voiceless palatals,
for example, would be voiceless velars or alveolars. The treatment of
Latin *caelu* in Basque indicates that palatalization before front
vowels readily occurs, *zeru* ($z = \S$ phonetically a dorsoalveolar sibilant).[7] This change is further verified by the alternation between *ze*
and *ki* 'you', the latter used in some of the dialects and appearing
to be the older form. Once loan words are removed from the data
the comparative method can be applied to point up regular and
systematic correspondences between related languages. Its use in
this connection gives the language historian pertinent information
about the relative chronology of changes in particular language
groups, about causes and effects of language change and diversification, as well as information concerning principles and methods to
account for the modifications within a coherent framework or model.
The comparative method can also be applied before languages are
known to be related; that is, as a procedure for discovery. Any two
or more languages can be subjected to comparative analysis in order
to ascertain whether or not they reflect a common heritage.

Several other methods can be brought to bear on problems of
historical relationships and linguistic reconstruction.

The internal method of reconstruction

The primary assumption underlying internal reconstruction is that many events in the history of a language leave discernible traces in its design. An examination of these traces can lead to a reconstruction of linguistic processes of change and thus to a reconstructed form of the language prior to the events which changed it. Morphophonemic alternations reflect historical events. In English, for example, the phonological alternations of the regular plural morpheme are represented as /s/, /z/ and /iz/, cf: cats /kæts/; dogs /dɒgz/; witches /wičiz/. Their distributional regularity in which /s/ follows a voiceless consonant, /z/ a voiced consonant and vowels eg, bees /biyz/, and /iz/ sibilants and affricates, suggests that the plural markers /s/ and /z/ are the result of assimilation in manner of articulation to the final sound of the noun.

The assimilation rule is not a general phonological rule since both /s/ and /z/ may follow a voiced sound such as the vowel /iy/ in seize and cease. It appears to operate on the morphological level among plural allomorphs. If we consider /Vs/ or /Vz/ (where V = vowel) to be the underlying shape from which /s/ and /z/ are derived, some deductions can be made concerning earlier structural characteristics of English. The choice of the underlying form is not arbitrary: some justification for it can be found among other morphological alternations. Differences in forms of the type wife /wayf/, wives /wayvz/; leaf /liyf/, leaves /liyvz/, in which stem final /-f/ alternates with /-v/, indicates earlier voicing of /f/ to /v/. The form /liyf/ + plural (where plural = vowel + consonant) becomes /liyv/ + plural or /f/ > /v/ in the environment vowel___vowel. Nouns such as cat, dog, church and leaf, etc according to the above considerations should have formed their plurals at an earlier period by the addition of a plural marker consisting of a vowel plus /s/ or /z/. The written history of English and comparative studies confirm these conclusions,[8] cf

Old English	Middle English	Modern English
cattas	cattes /kattəs/	cats /kæts/
	leues (leves) /levəs/	leaves /liyvz/
	(singular /lēf/	
	cf Gothic laufs,	
	plural laubōs)	

There are difficulties inherent in the internal method of reconstruction, several of which are evident in the example above. Selection of the underlying form /Vs/ or /Vz/, although in part justified by the distribution of the plural allomorphs and by phonological processes that appear to have brought about their distributional characteristics, nevertheless runs counter to simplicity procedures. To derive /s/ and /z/ from the postulated underlying form involves more steps than the derivation which posits /z/ as the underlying form. Compare the following derivations:

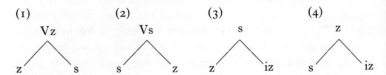

(1)   (2)   (3)   (4)

In derivations (1), (2) and (3), at least two steps are required on the right-hand side to obtain the output, for example, /Vz/ > /s/ through loss of vowel and devoicing. Number (4) on the other hand, requires only one step on each side, devoicing on the left and vowel addition on the right.

From the point of view of descriptive rules of distribution, /z/ appears preferable as the base form from which to derive the other regular plural allomorphs. Diachronically, however, this does not seem to be the best choice inasmuch as certain alternations, eg, /liyf/liyvz/, reflect an earlier vowel + /s/ or /z/ as the underlying form of the plural. The simplest procedure to account for allomorphic variations of the plural morpheme is at odds with another approach that accounts for more facts.

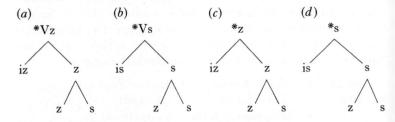

(a)   (b)   (c)   (d)

Letters (a) and (b) are applicable to more facts than (c) and (d) inasmuch as they help to account for stem alternations /f/~/v/. On this basis we may assume that more than one change has occurred in chronological sequence. Implicit in this approach is the notion that phonological change takes place one feature at a time. This may not always be the case. The actual situation in English can be determined from documentary evidence and seems to have been much like the following:

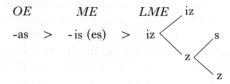

Internal reconstruction may yield erroneous results when chronological sequences of related events are undifferentiated by the method. Underlying forms may only appear to reflect historical reality under such circumstances. Another major obstacle to this type of reconstruction is analogical levelling. For example, the largest single class of Old English nouns was inflected as follows:[9]

	singular	plural
nominative	#	-as
accusative	#	-as
genitive	-es	-a
dative	-e	-um

The nominative and accusative plural of the Old English form for *son* was *suna* > Middle English *sune*. The Late Middle English addition of *-s sones* /sóniz/, presumably by analogy with the regular plural formations shown above, would not be apparent from internal reconstruction. Stages older than the period in which the new analogical formation arose would be subject to error for this lexical form since there would be no means of determining its earlier membership in another class of nouns.

The internal method must rely to a greater or lesser extent (depending on the data) on what was most likely to have occurred. Some phonological changes are more common than others within given phonological circumstances. Voicing between vowels, *eg*, t→d/VpV appears to occur much more readily among known languages than the opposite or devoicing in intervocalic position, *ie*, d→t/V_V. Nasalized vowels are generally the result of influence exerted by a following nasal. Once the influence has been extended to the vowel, the nasal becomes redundant and is lost. The French word *pain* /pɛ̃/ can thus be reconstructed to */pɛN/ (where N = a nasal). The stimulus, then, often disappears after influencing a neighbouring sound.

Recourse to comparative data, if available, may substantiate the reconstruction; for example, */pɛN/ corresponds to Spanish *pan*, Italian *pane* with the nasal consonant intact.

Among languages whose written history is recent or non-existent, internal reconstruction may be the only method of gaining some understanding of their past. Used in conjunction with the comparative method, internal reconstruction may furnish information about events in related languages which reveals the processes by which they diverged. Compare, for example, the reconstruction of canonical shapes in the syllabic patterns in Potawatomi.[10]

paper	/m sən	ʾəkən/	=	C	CVC	CVCVC
				↓ ↑ ↓ ↑ ↓		
my paper	/n məs nəʾ	kən/	= C	CVC	CVC	CVC

Since an endless number of stems in Potawatomi show a comparable variation in shape depending on the presence or absence of inflectional suffixes, the forms can be postulated

paper /məsənəʾ   əkən-/
my   /nə-/

hence: /nəməsənəʾ əkən-/ is a hypothetical base form which contains potential vowels not spoken, *ie*, a form abstracted from actual speech. A rhythmic controlling principle determines which vowels will be heard in actual speech. Potential vowels of alternate syllables are omitted. If the form includes just the stem, the second, fourth and last potential vowels are spoken, *viz*

/məsənəʾ əkən/ > /msən   ʾəkən/

if /n-/ is included, the same rhythmic principle leads to the loss of a different set of potential vowels:

/nəməsənəʾ əkən/ > /nməsnəʾ   kən/

A language related to Potawatomi, Fox, has /mesenahikani/ 'paper' and /nemesenahikani/ 'my paper' where the vowels postulated for Potawatomi occur. Much earlier Potawatomi must have had the potential vowels shown above but lost them through a regular phonological process of reduction.

Internal comparison of linguistic features may divulge a certain order of phonological events by which the underlying forms are connected to the derived forms. In the following examples from

Classical Greek, several processes underlie the correspondences between the nominative and the genitive forms. The genitive examples are more plausible as primary forms from which the nominative is derived and not vice versa. They represent aspects of the language which are more in accordance with its earlier phonological patterns:

	nominative		genitive	
(1)	aíks	goat	aigós	of a goat
(2)	thḗs	serf	thētós	of a serf
(3)	elpís	hope	elpídos	of hope
(4)	órnīs	bird	órnīthos	of a bird
(5)	gígās	giant	gígantos	of a giant

The processes are: (1) shift in stress, (2) syncope, (3) assimilation, (4) consonant cluster reduction, and (5) vowel lengthening. In the first example we find *aigós > aígos > aígs > aíks* in accordance with the first three postulated phonological processes. In the second example, assimilation does not apply (both consonants are voiceless) but cluster reduction occurs, ie, /-ts/ > /-s/. In example (3) the first rule does not apply. Example (5) is the only one with vowel lengthening, that is, rules two, four and five apply.

The examples of internal reconstruction considered so far are subject to confirmation or rejection by further comparative studies or by written historical documentation. This is not always the case, however. The languages of ancient Iberia are only known from inscriptions whose texts are still undeciphered. The following observations concerning several of these texts demonstrate the potential value of the internal method of reconstruction in that conclusions drawn from internal studies may suggest the area most likely to yield fruitful comparative results.

One short document of these inscriptions, the Alcoy Lead Tablet, found near Alcoy in Southern Spain and dating back to the sixth century BC, may serve here to demonstrate the value of internal reconstruction when no other methods can be applied. The text is given in full in transliteration in *Fig* 12.

An analysis of distributional arrangements precedes the quest for a common underlying structure, which, by the application of rules, will account for variation in forms. The situation here, however, is complicated by the fact that the meanings of words are unknown. Even the delineation of morphemes is problematical leaving little to go on except recurring phonological sequences and their seeming variation in response to environmental differences.

> irike or'ti garokan dadula bask buistiner'
> bagarok sss   turlbailura legusegik
> başero keiunbaidaurke başbidirbar'tin
> irike başerokar' tebind belagasikaur
> işbinai aşgandiş tagişgarok binikebin
> salir' kidei gaibigait
>
> ar'nai sakarişker
>
> iunştir' salir'g başirtir şabaridar
> bir'inar gurs boistingisdid şesgersduran
> şeşdirgadedin şeraikala naltinge
> bidudedin ilduniraeni bekor şebagediran[11]

Fig 12: The Alcoy Lead Tablet transliteration

Certain phonological sequences occur as follows:

(1) turl, lura
(2) birinar, binikebin
(3) -gediran, sabaridar
(4) -garok, bekor

Some phonological combinations fail to occur within the word such as occlusives plus *l, r, n,* and *s, eg : tl tr dn* etc; occlusive plus occlusive (with the exception *kb* in *baskbuistiner*); and a number of other combinations among which is *ns.* These clusters appear to be avoided through readjustment of phonological patterns when further morphological elements are added. Corresponding to the distributional patterns of the above forms are the rules:

(1) lur→url/t_
(2) ni →in/Con._
(3) ri →ir/Con._
(4) rok→kor (motivation not clear)

The sequences *ind, din* and *ndi* occur in *tebind, -dedin* and *-gandis.* From an initial assumption that all three are manifestations of a single morpheme, *ie : (d)ni*, they can be derived from the following underlying forms by a single general rule of metathesis.

> *beni
> *deni
> *gani

Justification of the underlying forms will be clear from the following derivational rules.

The addition of -d- leads to the incompatible sequence of consonants -dn- which is resolved by the rule ni→in/con_

    bedni > bedin
    dedni > dedin
    gadni

No further rules are needed to account for -dedin. The rule does not apply to *gadni* where -ş is added since the result of the rule would be -nş, a nonoccurrent cluster, hence, dn→nd

    gadni + ş > gandiş

bedin with the addition of *t*- undergoes several further adjustments avoiding combinations of occlusives and -dn :

    be →eb/con-   tbedin > tebdin
    di →id/con-   tebdin > tebidn
    dn→nd   tebidn > tebind

A general rule can now be formulated that states : *metathesis occurs one place at a time to the left until all phonological sequences are compatible to the system of distribution :*

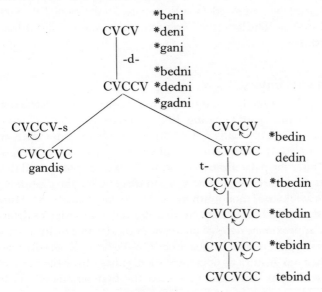

Only the unstarred forms are found in the text.

The phonological sequence *lur* comes under the same general rule:

CVC   (lur)

t-

CCVC   (*tlur > *tulr)

CVCC   (*tulr > turl)

The actual language of this and other ancient Iberian documents has not been successfully related to any other language. The form *tebind*, for example, seems to have no counterpart in other languages that might conceivably be related to ancient Iberian. The underlying form **beni*, however, has at least the possibility of relationship with Rif (a Hamitic language of North Africa) in the word *erbeni* and its dialectal variant *rebeni* 'tomb'. Keeping in mind that words are often borrowed from one language to another, and that accidental similarities are common occurrences in all languages, the underlying form **beni* is only indicative of a potential area of further exploration.

Some inferences can be made about underlying forms from very limited data; their historical validity, however, cannot be ascertained from the data through internal reconstruction. The comparative method must be employed to substantiate results gained through internal studies. The latter may point the way towards fruitful areas of comparison.

Loss in vocabulary

The comparative method and the internal method of reconstruction are limited with regard to dating. Both methods may reveal chronological sequences of events but neither discloses the time when an event occurred. It is clear, for example, that Sanskrit /a e o/ merged with /a/ after the palatalization of /k/ to /č/ (see Chapter 3) and that Old French /k/ became /č/ (later /š/) in *chose* before the diphthong /au/ in *causa* /kausa/ monophthongized to /o/ (see Chapter 7). More precise dating techniques are needed, however, in order to determine the approximate dates of linguistic events leading to divergence (in prehistory) of related languages.[12] This becomes especially relevant when no historical documentation exists. Investigations of American Indian languages promoted the first serious efforts to establish these more precise dating techniques which have become known as glottochronology.[13] Glottochronology uses rate of vocabulary loss or, conversely, the percentage of vocabulary retention to determine linguistic relationships and establish approximate dates for the differentiation of the languages involved in these relationships. Loss of vocabulary often occurs with changes in culture. The technical terms used in astrology, for example, are difficult for modern Europeans to comprehend since astrological observations and pronouncements have little influence upon present-day society.[14] Terms and practices go out of style together.

Because we are out of touch with nature in our city surroundings and influenced by linguistic conformity in science in which 'a set' can refer to any collection of definite distinct objects, certain expressions are gradually disappearing from everyday vocabulary. One seldom hears reference to a 'pride' of lions, a 'clutch' of eggs, a 'raft' of ducks (in the water), a 'brood' of chicks, a 'covey' of quail, etc. The terms 'flock' of geese or 'litter' of puppies are perhaps more firmly entrenched because they are more commonly observed.

Assumptions in glottochronology

Several basic assumptions underlie glottochronology. One is that some items (referred to as the basic core vocabulary) are better maintained than others, eg, the lower numerals, pronouns, words referring to parts of the body, or to natural objects (ie, animals, plants, heavenly bodies, etc).

A second assumption is that the rate of retention of items in the core vocabulary is constant and is approximately the same from language to language. If the percentage of cognates in the core is determined for two related languages, the length of time that they have been separated can be determined. If measured over long periods of time such as a half millennium or more, short-term variations in rate of replacement level out, so that the rate may be treated as a constant.[15]

The Model

If the rate of replacement of basic vocabulary items per thousand years is such that at the end of a millennium, N per cent of the vocabulary will survive, in another thousand years only N per cent of this surviving N per cent will still have resisted replacement. The unreplaced residuum in two millennia will be N^2 per cent. If, however, at a certain time, a parent language splits into two descendants, each will be expected to retain N per cent of the basic vocabulary of the parent, but the items retained in each will be independent of those retained in the other. The percentage of shared vocabulary items, *ie*, cognates, in the two descendants at the end of a thousand years should be once again N^2 per cent.[16]

The underlying notions of glottochronology can perhaps be more clearly seen in the following formulaic presentation:

N = number of words in initial list
K_1 = number of words retained after 1,000 years
r   = rate of retention
t   = number of millennia
K = number of words retained at end of t
k   = proportion of N words of N retained after t periods

$$r = \frac{K_1}{N} \quad \text{and} \quad k = \frac{K}{N}$$

k   can now be defined as $k = r^t$

Difficulties occur with this approach. The notion of a basic core, common to all cultures, is at best dubious. Even if such a core existed, it would most likely be a relative core and not an absolute one. As has been pointed out, change at a given rate is also questionable. It has not been demonstrated that rate of retention is constant from language to language, even statistically. Meillet pointed to a gypsy dialect of Armenian which contained few Armenian lexical items while showing the central structure of the language. The rate of loss in languages such as English, Greek and Lithuanian seems to be much slower than for this Armenian dialect. If different rates of retention must be proposed for each language, the generality of glottochronology is eliminated, and its usefulness greatly diminished.[17]

The rate of loss should apply to those words left in the language after each long period of time. If of a given 100 words 81 per cent remain after 1,000 years, this would equal about 66 per cent cognates in related languages. After the second millennium 81 per cent of the remaining 81 per cent would be retained. After 1,000 years, however, if 19 words are lost, 19 new ones come in. These new words then must enter into the rate of retention or loss. If only the replacements are lost then there is 81 per cent retention during the second millennium. There is a good chance that some of the replacements would be lost in subsequent periods of time. Any single replacement could conceivably be lost over and over. It cannot be shown which words are replacements in one or more of several languages if the proto-language is unknown. Furthermore, a borrowed word may replace a lexical form in several related languages after differentiation. There also seems to be no particular reason for a specific time period such as 1,000 years.[18]

The emphasis placed upon loss in language, however, may well lead to more refined models and principles underlying a statistical approach to language change and reconstruction. The miscalculations in the present approach may turn out to have a positive value.

Dialect geography

Differences in usage among speakers of the same language can be detected even when there are only a few speakers. Variations in usage among speakers of a large language community show degrees of correlations with the social and geographical structure of the society to which they belong. Social stratification and geographical separation are important circumstantial factors in which language diversification occurs. Both allow some form of isolation in which the nature and degree of contact depend on the particular situation.

Whether a society shows social stratification or not, the factor of geographical separation is always operative in contributing to dialectal differentiation. All groups outside of constant linguistic interaction are affected. In a class-structure society at least the lower strata are affected by geographical differences in distribution. In England, for example, the speech habits of the upper classes are more or less uniform throughout the country, while the lower classes show marked dialectal divergence, not only from county to county, but from town to town. Observations of dialectal differences can be placed upon a map in the form of isoglosses which characterize the differences. One can then attempt to draw historical inferences from the geographical distribution of the linguistic forms and usages. This type of activity is necessary for the comparative method if one is to reconstruct the earlier forms of speech of a given language which now consists of a group of dialects.

The result of dialectal investigations is a dialect atlas, crisscrossed by isoglosses which delimit the various dialectal areas. When a number of these lines run together they constitute an important dialectal area. The isoglosses may refer to phonological, morphological or syntactic items and arrangements. An important difference between High and Low German is the phonetic difference exemplified by Low German /makən/ and High German /maxən/ *machen*. A difference between Iberian Spanish dialects is one of phonological distribution of /s/, Castilian /ésta/ *esta*, Andalucian /éta/; but compare *saber* /sabér/ in both.

Conclusions that can be drawn from purely geographical distribution are limited in the extreme and subject to misleading considerations. The age-old hypothesis, for example, assumes that a trait spread over a wider area is older than one spread over a small area. For zoological investigations of animal distribution this hypothesis may be valid, but for language it does not work. This would make Spanish older than Italian or French, and English older than Chinese. An assumption of this sort is meaningless. The difficulty in drawing historical conclusions from geographical distribution of certain characteristics is that both people and their customs can and do move around. People migrate from one area to another and customs are carried with them or diffused throughout adjacent cultures. Human beings and their cultures do not necessarily move in the same direction, at the same time, and at the same rate.

Observations of the present situation between dialects and geography, however, suggest that if we have a large area only a small part of which is broken up into marked dialect differentiation, the large homogeneous area has only recently been settled. For examples one can compare the recently settled and linguistically homogeneous western United States with the east coast of the United States (a smaller area with numerous dialects) or the United States and England. In both cases the more recently settled area shows less dialectal differentiation. Deductions based upon these observations may be applied to other linguistic groups such as Eskimo; this inferentially helps to substantiate the notion that the Eskimos settled recently in the north, as their language is fairly uniform from Alaska to Greenland.

If the variable of migration can be eliminated, more can be done with dialect geography. Western Europe represents a good example of an area where the lower classes have been mostly sedentary for a long time. In sedentary areas the dialect geographer asks if the isogloss is moving (migrating), and if so, in which direction. If no barrier, natural or otherwise, stands in the way, it is fairly certain that the diffusion is still proceeding. Around focal points having some sort of prestige, isoglosses are often found which are moving out. By knowing the rate and direction of diffusion in sedentary areas, the situation at an earlier period can be reconstructed. This method of reconstruction, however, is best used in conjunction with other methods. Dialect geography is of interest to students of historical linguistics by pinpointing areas which, through dialectal cleavage, indicate past linguistic splits, borrowings and internal developments.[19]

Studies of dialectal variations have proved useful for theoretical notions which have special importance for language change. The range and the quality of an allophone for example are determined by the position of the phoneme to which they belong in phonological space. In the German Swiss dialects, where /a/ is flanked by /æ/ it will rarely show front allophones, where flanked by /ɔ/ it will seldom show back allophones. Flanked by both /æ/ and /ɔ/, the phoneme /a/ will have only central allophones.[20]

Implicit in these observations is the assumption that the emergence of allophones is constrained by neighbouring phonemes in the vocalic pattern. Phonological change of the type in which an allophone acquires phonemic status does so in a paradigmatic environment which offers least structural resistance (see Chapter 7). Given several dialects where the phonological system of each is described with reference to phonological space, some tentative calculations can be made as to further divergence, if of course other variables can be isolated.

Considering the multitude of isoglosses going in all directions, territorial dialects have often proved to be fictitious entities, established on the basis of arbitrarily chosen features and by extra-linguistic criteria. This has led some dialectologists to abandon the notion of territorial dialects and others to conclude that the concept is purely relative. Even the consideration only of those isoglosses that have structural importance as dialect boundary markers still leaves arbitrary choices to be made since their number can be very high.

A more recent approach applies the structural view from a different point of departure in placing the focus on the structure of the differentiation. Some dialects will be bounded by a bundle of isoglosses running very close together, while others will show widely spread isoglosses. Once both limits are known, all dialects will fall somewhere in between these limits. Numerical indices can then be established that will reflect the degree of evenness of the isoglosses.[21]

Notes

1 In the Emilian Manuscript written in the tenth century and perhaps representing the most ancient Castilian relic of its kind, are found two glosses or a sort of marginal translation in the Basque language.

2 It is not unknown for two unrelated linguistic groups to settle in immediately adjacent areas. The Etruscans colonized part of Italy after the Indo-Europeans were settled there. The appearance of Etruscan in Italy can also be used as an argument in favour of a similar (but unrelated) incursion of the Basques at a remote time in the past into Iberia from Africa, Eastern Europe, or Asia, thus side-stepping the issue of a common Mediterranean substratum. This has been used in attempts to link Basque with Hungarian, Indo-European, Etruscan, Dravidian, etc. These somewhat romantic endeavours might prove to be more substantial, however, after the adjacent languages (*eg*, Berber) have been thoroughly explored in this connection. For an attempt to show that Basque is an early offshoot of Indo-European languages, see Guisasola. For Basque and Caucasian see R. Lafon.

3 See Bloomfield, *p* 297.

4 It is clear that loan words may undergo changes after they are borrowed and as the borrowing language changes. They may also be borrowed at a period just after profound phonological changes have occurred in the system and not reflect any earlier stage than the one during which they were taken over by the borrowing language. The treatment of loans may nevertheless reflect certain dynamic structural processes which, if considered on a tentative basis, may aid in reconstruction. If it were possible to predict these processes or the structure of loan words from the design of the borrowing language, then their analysis from the point of view of structural processes would be redundant.

5 For a review of phonological processes of change, see Chapter 6.

6 An examination of Basque vocabulary will yield many more such borrowings.

7 See Michelena, *p* 43.

8 English historical documentation shows that the voiced fricatives are derived from voiceless fricatives in intervocalic position (with few exceptions). With no recourse to historical/comparative information it would be feasible to take the view that /z/ was the underlying form and stem final consonants assimilated to the plural allomorph, *ie*, /*liyf/ + /z/ > /liyvz/. This would, however, complicate the assimilation rules, for example,

$$-t + z > t + s$$
$$-f + z > v + z$$

9 See Stevick (1968), *p* 171.

10 See Hockett (1958), *pp* 463–464.

11 The transliteration is that of M. Gomez-Moreno 'Sobre los Iberos y su Lengua', Homenaje a Menéndez-Pidal 3 (1925), *p* 498.

12 Most languages of the world are unwritten and in this sense still belong to 'prehistoric' times.

13 Initial studies along these lines were done by Swadesh. Many others have since taken up the problem, *eg*, see Gudschinsky.

14 See Lehmann (1962), *p* 107.

15 The strong influence exerted by French on English vocabulary during the several centuries after the Norman conquest of England would statistically level out if included in a period of time of a millennium or so.

16 See Hockett (1958), *pp* 529–530.

17 See Lehmann (1962), *p* 110. For a categorical denial of the assumption that the rate of language change is constant, see Fodor.

18 For further detail and elaboration of these concepts, see Chrétien who has demonstrated the defectiveness of the mathematical model. See also Coseriu. For the application of glottochronological techniques to diverse language groups and statements of results during the early period of glottochronology, see *IJAL* Vol xxi No 2 (April 1955). For an early criticism of glottochronology see Hockett (1953).

19 For some of the notions contained here and others, see Hockett (1958) *pp* 471–484.

20 See Moulton.

21 After Weinreich's affirmative answer to his own question 'Is a structural dialectology possible?' there have been a number of important contributions to structural approaches to dialectology. For bibliographical references, as well as for an elaboration of the above material, see Ivić.

Chapter 5

Language divergence

External theories of language change

A fundamental question, how is it that languages change, was first asked by J. H. Bredsdorff. His answer included:

mishearing and misunderstanding
misrecollection
imperfection of organs
indolence
tendency toward analogy
the desire to be distinct
the need of expressing new ideas
foreign influence[1]

These notions revolve around physiological and psychological considerations which, in one form or another, would be used again in attempts to account for sources and determinants underlying language modification. Further explanations of change – some based upon psychological factors, some not – were advanced as the individual and collective histories of languages began to unfold. After F. Diez, the founder of Romance philology,[2] a number of theories of language change centred around the Romance languages. These languages could be more easily assailed historically than most since written records were available for the proto-language, Latin, as well as continuous documentation throughout the Middle Ages. To account for the linguistic diversity of the Romance languages, the following theories have been advanced.

Chronological Theory

According to this view, the individual Romance languages follow the chronology of the conquest, *ie*, they develop from the Latin of the period. The approximate dates of the Roman conquest are: *ca* 250 BC, Sicily, Sardinia, and Corsica; *ca* 200 BC, Spain; *ca* 150 BC, Africa; *ca* 120 BC, Southern Gaul; *ca* 50 BC, Northern Gaul; *ca* 15 BC, Rhaetia; and *ca* AD 100, Dacia. Thus, Italian stems from the Latin prior to the Punic Wars; Sicilian and Sardinian stem from the Latin of 250 BC, etc. This was a popular argument last century but it has few supporters today. There is no record of Latin changing so rapidly from period to period, and the facts do not relate well to the theory. For example, a tendency to drop -*s* after short vowels as in *plenu(s)*, current around 300 to 200 BC, *ie* (during the period of the Sardinian conquest) is not present in Sardinian which keeps -*s*. The theory does not account for the multiplicity of dialects in Italy, nor for the influence of the local populations of the Roman provinces on Latin. Some Romance languages display characteristics that run counter to this view, *eg*, Old French retained a noun declensional system more in accordance with Latin than did Italian. Modern Romanian is more conservative in noun morphology than other Romance languages.

Class Theory

There are references in Classical Latin to different styles of speech – sermo urbanus or eruditus, as distinguished from the sermo plebeius or vulgaris. These are supposed to have been separate languages, mutually incomprehensible. Although the extent to which this is true is questionable, the social differences mirroring a linguistic difference cannot be denied. In all periods of linguistic development, the written language – if one exists – differs from the spoken, except perhaps during that comparatively brief span of time during the process of codification. In Latin, the language of the upper classes resembled the written language except perhaps in the use of certain literary styles. The lower classes spoke a colloquial form of Latin which in many respects differed considerably from the more refined form.[3] The concept of the Class Theory throws some light on the reasons for the radical differences between the Romance languages and Classical Latin (written), since colonization was carried out primarily by the military composed of the common people, but it does not account for the differences between the Romance languages themselves.

Centrifugal Theory

Latin in the provinces was once thought by a few nineteenth-century scholars to present no intrinsic differences, *ie*, no major dialects. Although standardization was not absolute, the differences that occurred were not necessarily those features which became typical of the particular region. Dialects were caused by the tendency of the language in the provinces to break up as the centre of unification broke down. Roman institutions and a good system of communication helped to strengthen the centripetal tendencies of Latin.

The centre of unification began to break down with the fall of the Roman Empire after AD 476. Cut off from the centre, dialects developed. This argument relies on fairly uniform inscriptions throughout the Empire. No break occurs in the Latin of the two periods, *ie*, prior to and after social, economic and military collapse; however, phonological differences must have been taking place which were not recorded in the usual inscriptions since many undoubtedly were restricted to the lower classes. The more conservative written language reflects a more conservative class of people – the upper classes and those who could write. The phonological differences that existed in the Roman Empire must have been somewhat analogous to the situation in the modern English-speaking world where the written language is fairly uniform and does not reflect the numerous dialects of English speakers.[4]

While specifically tailored to the problems involved in the divergence of the Romance languages the notions embodied in these views are, to various degrees, relevant to other linguistically related language groups. The idea of isolation embodied in the Centrifugal Theory may be brought about by migrations, political upheaval or invasions. The factor of isolation is also inherent in the Class Theory in that isolation may be due to social stratification of a society as well as to geographical conditions. The Chronological Theory presupposes isolation of the centre of unity from the outlying areas allowing considerable linguistic diversification before the next period of conquest or migration. This common thread running through these three approaches to the same problem is a strong, factor in language differentiation. The particular effects of isolation in various dialects will be unique to each, however.

In the formulation of these views language divergence has been interpreted as explained by the external facts, social and political, in the Roman world. The relationship between these theories and specific linguistic events has, however, not been made explicit enough to show that they explain language change and hence diversification, although they describe a situation, embodied in a common denominator – isolation – that allows language differentiation to occur. Given the situation, the actual linguistic events must be accounted for by something besides the situation, or the explanation becomes circular.

Substratum Theory

It has been observed many times that some characteristics of a language are carried over into a target language when it is learned by adults. Germans who have learned Spanish, for example, speak it with a decidedly different accent from Englishmen or Frenchmen. One can often determine the national origin of a foreigner speaking English simply by listening to him speak. When a language community learns another language and the new language is modified by the linguistic patterns carried over from the native language we speak of influence of the linguistic substratum.

Just as foreign accents among individuals are structured on the basis of their native language and are not simply the result of random associations, so an entire speech community restructures a new language in a specific manner. Individuals will, of course, approach the new language differently depending on their motivations for learning it (*eg*, social prestige or economic gain). How close one comes to speaking the new language perfectly will depend a good deal on personal desire. The Substratum Theory is concerned with those features that are not well learned (presumably because of interference from the native language) and maintains, for example, that in Spain, Latin was spoken with an Iberian accent and so was modified in a different manner from the Latin spoken in Gaul with a Gaulish accent. Latin was spoken with an Oscan or Umbrian accent in some parts of Italy and in other areas with an Etruscan or Greek accent. In Romania, the Balkan languages and dialects affected the pronunciation of Latin, etc.

The role of substratum influence in language change has been the object of much controversy, mainly because the cases discussed have often been languages for which the possible substratum is obscure. Very little is known about the structure of pre-Roman languages of Europe for example. Even though some of their descendants are extant today, *eg*, Gaelic and Basque, their structural characteristics during the remote period of initial contact with Latin are far from clear. The necessarily speculative character of explanation by substratum influence in such situations has in extreme cases led to a denial of this type of influence altogether. A few examples will suffice to show that the substratum has been alluded to with little investigation of the structures in contact, or has been applied in an *ad hoc* fashion. Nasalized vowels in French have been credited to Celtic influence, but they appear in other Romance languages such as Portuguese – in an area where Celts were rather scarce. The front rounded vowels in French, /ü/ and /ö/, are often attributed to the Celts in Gaul but they appeared also in early Latin, (*decimus* < *decumus* and *libet* < *lubet*) in which /u/ > /i/ via /ü/.[5] Greek also – without the benefit of Celts – has /ü/ which seems to have occurred as a consequence of structural changes from within the language.[6] If no substantial structural reason is readily observable for a modification, the change is too often attributed to 'something' in the substratum. On the other hand, this theory is useful when there is some basis upon which to determine a specific influence. In the following examples Latin /f/ becomes Spanish /h/ and eventually disappears except in the orthography.

farīna	> harina	/arína/
fīlius	> hijo	/íxo/
fābulat	> habla	/ábla/

In these and similar examples the change has been attributed to the influence of Basque speakers in the north of Spain. While in the process of learning the Iberian-Romance language which slowly infringed upon their homeland, Basque speakers are thought to have modified the sound /f/, and this innovation spread throughout Castilian Spanish.

The Basque phonological system appears not to have contained /f/, thereby rendering modification of this sound from the adopted language more probable. There is no evidence, however, that Basque substituted /h/ for /f/; in fact, Basque appears not to have had the sound /h/ in its phonological system until some time later.

Native speakers of one language, on learning another, tend to superimpose their own phonological characteristics on the new language. The phoneme /f/ was labial, voiceless, and fricative within the framework of the Ibero-Romance consonantal system, *eg*

p t ć k
b d ż g
f s

There is no reason to suspect that Basque would have selected a
feature it did not have, namely fricativity, and modified the place of
articulation from labial to laryngeal.

Labiality was distinctive in Basque as in /p^h/ undoubtedly giving
rise to the substitution for labial and voiceless /f/, by the labial and
voiceless /p^h/, ignoring the feature of fricativity, *cf* Basque,

p^h t^h k^h
b d g

/p^h/ would not have modified directly to /h/ but appears to have
passed through a labial spirant stage */ɸ/, *ie*, /f > p^h > ɸ > h/. The
only labial remaining after /ɸ > h/ was /ḅ/ and later Latinisms assume
this sound,

fagum > ḅago   beech tree
festa > ḅesta   fiesta[7]

There is often strong circumstantial evidence in favour of substratum influence on a language. The appearance of the so-called
cerebrals or cacuminal sounds, *eg*, /ṭ, ṭh, ḍ, ḍh, ṇ, ṣ/, introduces an
innovation in Sanskrit not found to this extent in any other Indo-
European languages. These sounds are phonetically retroflex and
are characteristically Indian in that they seem to have been acquired
by the Indo-Aryans after their entry into India. They are found
abundantly in the Dravidian languages, however, and appear to be
ancient in that family.

Since it is only in India and the immediate vicinity that an Indo-
European language has developed such a series of sounds, and since
it may be safely assumed that an early form of Dravidian possessing
such sounds was spoken over large portions of India prior to the
advent of the Aryans, the influence of Dravidian may be suspected
to be responsible for their emergence in Sanskrit. This suspected
development should not form the basis of an explanation of the
emergence of the Indo-Aryan cerebrals, however, without significant evidence relating to the nature of the modification, especially
since the emergence of these sounds can be largely accounted for by

combinatory changes that affected certain consonant groups within the Indo-Aryan system itself.[8] For example, dental /t/ and /th/ preceded by /ṣ/ became /ṭ/ and /ṭh/. The /ṣ/ in this position may be a reflex of Indo-European /s/ which in Sanskrit was replaced by the cerebral /ṣ/ after /k r ṛ i u/. In each case there are good assimilatory phonetic reasons for the change. In cases where the retroflex sounds are not environmentally predictable, distributional changes must be sought which have altered the conditioning factor. Neither of the two views nor a combination of both has been substantiated.

Substratum presence can be readily seen in a large number of present-day situations. The Guaraní Indian language of Paraguay has influenced Spanish spoken in the area as a substratum language. Here Spanish has taken on nasalized vowels, intervocalic /i̯/ has become /ž/ and initial voiced occlusives are pronounced as fricatives. Spanish dental occlusives, /t/, /d/, have become alveolar as in Guaraní and even the intonation patterns have been modified.[9]

Substratum influence is not restricted to phonological features. In the district of Léon in Brittany, the local French has acquired the Bréton rules of stress, quantity and syllabification. In recently anglicized districts in Ireland, the local English dialect has decidedly Irish features in grammar and syntax as well as in phonology. Compare the usual expression of the perfect tense, ' I am after doing it,' or the use of the article in ' I am perished with the cold.'[10]

The most obvious influence of substratum occurs on the lexico-semantic level of language; but even here, to make the entire notion explicit and meaningful requires an explanation based upon semantic gaps in the vocabulary of the target language in relation to items in the environment (names of places, plants and animals etc), or the social and structural reasons why a particular word, already in the target language, was rejected for a substratum word.

Celtic influence on Gallo-Roman and on English reflects substitution of Celtic for Romance words and retention of Celtic names for entities which have no English names. The French numerical system, partially reflecting multiples of twenty seems to have been retained from the Celtic system, *eg, vingt* 'twenty', *quatre-vingts* 'eighty', *quatre-vingt-dix* 'ninety'. In English, place-names occur such as *Thames, Avon, Dover, Stour, Kent, Devonshire, Cumberland* (land of the Cymry), all of Celtic origin. A few other Celtic words are *binn* for basket, *cumb* for valley, *dun* for dark and *crag* for strait or channel.[11] One fairly common type of substratum influence affecting

lexical items occurs when words from both languages come together
to form a new word, as the following examples demonstrate:

> *Latin* rugire   + *Celtic* brag > *French* braire   to bray
> *Latin* tremere + *Celtic* crit   > *French* craindre   to fear

The term 'substratum', then, refers to a certain direction of influence, that is, features in Language A influence Language B, not
vice versa. To make this notion more explicit, the linguistic structures under consideration must be shown to contain perceptual
problems which led to variations in the speech of the substratum
population. A broader perspective of such problems would have to
define (besides the structural/perceptual aspects) the socio-cultural
forces operative in each situation. For example, relevant to each
linguistic modification brought about through learning a new language are certain factors such as the levels of the cultures in contact,
the degree and nature of the contact and the motivations for learning.
Even in present times, these are little-known variables. They can
only be examined in detail within present-day situations. The results
of a number of studies along these lines might lead to answers about
what kinds of structural characteristics are more likely to be preserved under specific conditions and whether or not these characteristics can be ordered in terms of their relative strength *qua* conceptual features innate in human beings.

Superstratum and adstratum

Included in the notion of stratum are superstratum and adstratum.[12]
When conquering, invading or migrating peoples learn the language
of the population they have subdued and leave traces of their linguistic habits in this language, we refer to superstratum influence. An
example of such an influence can be seen in the westerly migrations
of a west Germanic tribe (the Franks) into Gaul in the fifth century
AD where, upon learning the Gallo-Roman language, they superimposed on it characteristics of their own Germanic language. The
strong expiratory Frankish system of accentuation is said to have
influenced diphthongization of the Latin long, free vowels $/\bar{e}/ > /ei/$
and $/\bar{o}/ > /ou/$; the reduction or effacement of the unstressed vowels,
cf Latin *fēmina* > French *femme*; and the closing of secondary
stressed $/\varepsilon/$ and $/\mathfrak{o}/$. The effacement of unstressed vowels brought
into juxtaposition new groups of consonants which previously were
unknown in the language, and the laryngeal $/h/$ which had dis-

appeared from the sound system of Latin was reintroduced.[13] Frankish influence on vocabulary was particularly extensive, further differentiating the Latin language of Gaul from the other Romance languages and giving rise to such words as

danser   <dansōn   'dance'
guerre   <werra   'war'
gagner   <waidanjan   originally 'to gather the crops'[14]
écharpe <skerpa   'scarf'

The influence of Frankish elements in Gallo-Roman is most clearly seen among lexical items. While these words are found in all aspects of the vocabulary, they cluster mainly around the cultural pursuits that interested the Franks the most – war[15] and pastoral occupations. Frankish influence is also evident in word formation. The suffix -ing, for example, gave rise to Old French -enc as in paysan from earlier paisenc. The suffixes -hart and -wald became -ard and -aud as in vieillard and ribaud.

The phonological inventory of Gallo-Roman was somewhat altered by the introduction of /h/ into the system. This sound was carried over to words of Latin origin, usually by lexical contamination as in altus + Germanic hoh which became haut. Heavy Germanic influence in some areas of the Latin-speaking world (as, for example, in northern France where Gallo-Roman and Frankish cultures were intermingled) in part accounts for some of the differences in the Romance languages. In other areas, this influence was slight (in France south of the Loire), or non-existent.

Adstratum influence refers to borrowing that occurs across linguistic boundaries between adjacent languages or dialects. This type of linguistic activity is readily seen at almost all border areas where the political frontier corresponds to a linguistic boundary. For example, in northern Mexico near the border, the term chequear 'to check' is used in place of medir 'to measure' when referring to the oil in an automobile. A great deal of borrowing has occurred between Basque and Peninsular Spanish in the form of adstratum influence, cf Spanish zorra, sapo, vega, arroyo, garra, manteca, from Basque. Many place-names were borrowed from American Indian languages when the English colonists and the Indians lived side by side, cf, Mississippi, Massachusetts, Iowa, just as many place-names in the west were taken from Spanish names, eg, Colorado, San Francisco, Los Angeles.

The extent and effects of these various strata of language change will vary according to the situation. The problems of strata, for remote historical periods, are for lack of data hypothetical in nature. In the realm of vocabulary the situation is somewhat less obscure but even here it is not clear why some lexical forms persist and others do not, except perhaps where the terms coincide with predominant cultural characteristics of the substratum or superstratum. Some aspects of language change, then, appear to be the result of forces outside the linguistic system. Part of the task of historical linguistics is to determine the relationships between these external forces and linguistic structures. Since language is a social instrument, factors in society may sometimes set the conditions for certain changes and not for others. Language is also a highly structured instrument however, which apart from the necessity of meeting the ever-changing needs of society continually makes adjustments to maintain a degree of precision between its parts.

The various external situations outlined above are not necessary for language change. Changes will occur regardless of the presence or absence of external influences. Nevertheless, they cannot be ignored since when they are present, they do act as disruptive forces on language.

Lexical borrowing

When cultures come into contact with one another, borrowing takes place primarily in the realm of lexical items. There have been numerous contacts throughout recorded history in which such borrowings have occurred: the English words *beef*, *veal*, *pork* were borrowed from French along with many other words during the twelfth and thirteenth centuries – a period of strong French influence in England. In earlier times many Latin words found their way into English, *eg*, *street*, and *wine*, but in most cases the borrowing at any given time appears to be primarily in one direction – the culture with the greatest prestige is the primary loaner. Words may be borrowed into the less sophisticated culture for several reasons. Some speakers may adopt loan words to show their superior learning over other members of their culture, or the lexical item in question may fill a definite need in that it is imported along with a new idea or object. In the former, the loan word replaces or partially replaces a native word while in the latter it represents a new concept.

New cultural concepts may also be given labels through the use

of loan translations where native linguistic elements are combined
into new formations to define new notions or objects; for example,
German *Sauerstoff*, *Wasserstoff*, and *Fernsprecher* are loan translations.[16] Instead of utilizing the Greek elements *tele* and *phone*, as did
English, German used native words with similar meanings, *ie : fern*
'far, distant', and *sprechen* 'speak' to convey the idea of the telephone. Similarly, *Wasserstoff* 'hydrogen' and *Sauerstoff* 'oxygen'
are native German compounds.

A given group may borrow words which reflect a more remote
period of its own cultural history, yet these are borrowed with little
or no change in form. These so-called learned words having disappeared at some earlier point in the history of the language are then
reintroduced. This is of course only possible when written records
exist from which the forms are taken. This type of borrowing usually
relates to literary situations but sometimes the words filter down to
the masses and are used throughout the various social levels. Such
words are not uncommon in the Romance languages and have been
taken directly from Latin, for example, Spanish *planta* has not
undergone the normal change of /pl/ to /ʎ/, *cf : pluvia > lluvia*, although there was a medieval variant *llanta*. Similarly, the modern
Spanish word *digno* has not reduced /-gn-/ as in other forms, *eg*,
ligna > leña. Again, however, there was a popular medieval form
dinno.

There is still a further type of intra-cultural borrowing of vocabulary items which move along the ladder of social stratification in
both directions. In unstratified societies there would be some
borrowings back and forth on a regional basis. Some words used in
dialect A would find their way into dialect B and vice versa, but in
stratified societies this would be further compounded by borrowings
between social levels. In Spanish, for example, the Vulgar Latin
cluster /kl/, resulting from the loss of a post-tonic vowel, generally
becomes /x/, *cf : veklus* (earlier *vetulus < vetus*) *> viejo* /biéxo/. The
Spanish word *siglo*, however, comes from Latin *sēculum* in which,
after the loss of the post-tonic vowel, the /kl/ consonant cluster did
not result in /x/ but in /gl/. This has been attributed to the speech
patterns of the upper classes, where, perhaps for purposes of prestige, the unstressed vowel was retained longer than in the uncultiva-
ted speech and the /k/ voiced to /g/ in intervocalic position. The
subsequent loss of the vowel resulted in /gl/. The form containing
this cluster gradually filtered down to the lower classes and became

the accepted form. Vocabulary items which have undergone this kind of influence, *ie*, that have by-passed the regular phonological changes, are known as semi-learned words.

Pidgin and Creole languages

Pidgin languages represent extreme borrowing. The entire language is borrowed but considerably modified in the process: it is sharply reduced in grammatical structure and vocabulary and is not the native language of those who use it. When such a language becomes the native tongue of the users, it undergoes lexical and grammatical enrichment and is then referred to as a creole language. This process of creolization or nativization of a language must have occurred many times during the course of history, as for example when various linguistic groups of Europe gave up their native languages – Iberians, Celts, Visigoths, etc – to learn Latin.

The Romance languages show regular change from Latin. There are no major upheavals, paradigms are regularly retained, etc. There was probably a pidgin Latin period at first in many parts of the empire, but with constant reinforcement from Latin, it left no traces. Pidgins have sprung up in many parts of the world where English, Spanish, French and Portuguese have come into contact with different cultures and where a need has been established for the natives to communicate with the speakers of these languages in order to carry out commercial transactions. Not all pidgins have arisen through these more-or-less voluntary conditions, however; for example the slaves from Africa, brought to the southern United States, South America, and the Caribbean, were forced by necessity to learn the language of their masters (at first in a rudimentary form) in order to communicate with one another since even those who were lucky enough to find a fellow slave from the same region in Africa were separated to prevent any insurrection that might come about through conspiracy.[17]

Morphology and syntax
Pidgin languages show high semantic redundancy and small vocabularies, as well as simplified grammar and syntax. The process of paraphrase is common in which the fundamental vocabulary takes on extended meanings in new syntactic arrangements. 'Plenty breeze live for inside' means 'the tyre was pumped up' or 'has air in it'.[18] Paraphrase may replace one lexical item, *eg*, 'she's pregnant' has

been expressed by 'woman he got family inside'. The expression 'coconut belong him grass no stop' or 'that fellow man coconut belong him no grass' means 'he's bald'. 'Belly belong me walk about too much', stands for 'I was seasick'.[19]

Similar characteristics prevail throughout the various pidgin languages, such as the loss of gender – both *she* and *it* equal *he*. The possessive is often expressed by *belong*.[20] In the above examples the term *stop* means *to be*. 'Rain he stop' means 'it's raining'. Both the verb *to be* and the plural may not be expressed but if the plural is overtly stated it takes the form of *all*, or in pronouns, *eg*, 'me two fella' equals 'we'. Future time is referred to by the term *bymby*, etc.

Phonology

Vowels are generally reduced to /i e a o u/, glides are eliminated and consonant clusters reduced. Somewhat unusual sounds for the pidgin speakers such as English interdental fricatives, may be eliminated.[21]

The dramatic simplification found in pidgins is a universal trait of these languages and operates as much in French and Portuguese pidgins as in English pidgins. The creole languages arising from the earlier pidginized stage reflect these reductions in structure but take on new characteristics of their own or of the language from which they are derived. The amount of influence from the original language will proportionately affect the development of the creole language. Different social strata will reflect this influence to varying degrees. The structural simplicity common to all pidgin languages appears to be little influenced by the native language of the pidgin speakers. It must be emphasized that the term structural simplicity is used to describe pidgins with respect to the language that has given rise to them. It does not suggest that they are devoid of grammar. Pidgin languages offer a field of inquiry in which to explore linguistic reduction on all levels of language structure. The rise of pidgins, entailing concomitant disregard of complex features, especially in phonology, appears to reflect behaviour patterns in which articulations assume the most fundamental or natural properties of language. The motivations underlying this type of behaviour are considerably different from those of other language learning situations. Questions of correctness and style that plague adult learners of a foreign language are simply not relevant in the social atmosphere in which pidgin languages originate.

Lingua franca

There have been a number of lingua francas in recent times which exemplify linguistic interaction among peoples of diverse linguistic backgrounds. The difference between these and pidgin languages is that a lingua franca incorporates features from a variety of languages. Elements from a dozen languages may find their way into a common trade language which is used for commercial transactions in a given area. These types of speech are found in present-day Brazil among non-Portuguese speakers and in Africa where a variety of Arabic is used in this connection among traders of diverse ethnic and linguistic histories, while Ancient Greece had a similar language known as the 'koine'.

In the northwest of the United States, a lingua franca existed among the Indians and was known as Chinook Jargon by the early explorers. As trade developed in the area, elements were incorporated into the Jargon from at least a dozen local Indian languages, from English, and from French through French Canadian trappers,[22] *eg*,

Chinook	etsghot	> itshut	'black bear'
English	fire	> piah	'fire'
French	le mouton	> lemuto	'sheep'

Characteristic of this type of language is the absence of grammatical and phonological complexity.

External factors contribute to language change as in organic evolutionary change for example; however, recourse to external factors tells only part of the story. Internal dynamics are partly responsible for language modification and appear to be somewhat independent of social and cultural contacts that make up external influence on language.

Notes

1 See Jespersen (1922), *p* 70. This theme was taken up later by Paul; many others have at one time or another confronted the problems underlying the psychological and/or physiological motivations of language change, *eg*, Sweet, Jespersen, Martinet, Labov.

2 For the first major comparative study of the Romance languages see Diez.

3 There is a good deal of direct evidence supporting these differences in speech. Numerous inscriptions are available in the *Corpus Inscriptionum Latinarum*, Berlin, 16 *Vol* published between 1863–1943 and in the works of Latin authors, *eg*, the *Appendix Probi* written some time during the first few centuries A D which contains lexical forms in both styles. For reference to class differences and loss of -*s* in Romance, see von Wartburg, *p* 35.

4 A Scotsman and a backwoods Texan could read the same newspaper but they would encounter great difficulty in discussing its contents between them.

5 See Buck, *p* 80.

6 *Ibid*, Attic Greek has /u > ü/; Modern Greek /i/.

7 Martinet (1955), *p* 306, discusses several examples of a similar type, *eg*, the Greeks transcribed Latin *f* as *φ*. Chinook Jargon had /p/ and /h/ but heard English /f/ as /p/, *piah* 'fire', *kauppy* 'coffee'.

8 See Burrow, *p* 95.

9 See Malmberg, *p* 25. Note also the change of *ll > ḍḍ* in certain Calabro-Sicilian dialects.

10 See Sommerfelt (1958), *pp* 213–216.

11 For cases of Celtic influence on Old English in the form of substratum, see Baugh, *pp* 86–129.

12 First used by von Wartburg in 1932 at the Congress of Romance Studies in Rome.

13 For more on Frankish stress and its influence on Gallo-Roman, see Pope.

14 This association is preserved in the word *gagnage* 'pasturage'. For a substantial review of Frankish lexical influence in French, see Elcock, *pp* 232–257. For examples and theoretical notions underlying phonic, grammatical and lexical interference in language contact situations, see Weinreich (1953).

15 Frankish military terminology had all but taken over by the fourth century AD, *cf* Latin *bellum* had given way to *werra*, French *guerre*; *cassis* or *galea* was replaced by *helm* which became French *heaume*; *instruere* was taken over by *warnjan* which became French *garnir*; and *observare* was substituted by *wardân* which became *garder*.

16 See Lehmann (1962), *p* 213.

17 See Hall (1966), *p* xiii.

18 Congolese pidgin English, Jespersen (1922), *p* 224.

19 *Ibid*, Beach-la-mar or Sandalwood English. Beach-la-mar was spoken extensively over the western Pacific. The vocabulary is nearly all English. Two exceptions are the Maori words *taboo* and *kaikai* 'to eat'.

20 For other uses of the term *belong* in South Seas pidgin English, see Hall (1966), *p* 79.

21 *Ibid, p* 51, for an analysis of phonological adjustment in the phonology of Melanesian.

22 For further examples, see Jespersen (1922), *pp* 229–230.

Chapter 6

Structural change (syntagmatic)

It has generally been considered that phonological change entails *unconditioned change* where sounds are modified in all environments unhampered by distributional relationships; *conditioned change* or changes restricted to specific environments; and *sporadic change* in which the modifications are restricted to one or several lexical items.

Many sound changes can be thought of in general terms as involving phonological split and phonological merger, both of which may entail the loss of a sound. For example, given the phonological system

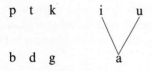

we might find that /t/ > /d/ in all environments, giving us a case of unconditioned merger. On the other hand, if /t/ > /d/ only in intervocalic position, we have conditioned merger. If /t/ displayed an allophone, *eg*, [tʸ] before the vowel /i/ and this allophone became a phoneme /č/, phonological split has occurred. This is sometimes referred to as secondary split to differentiate it from the kind of split that results in merger and produces no new phonemes. The change /-t-/ > /-d-/ would reflect primary split and merger. The loss of /t/ in morpheme final position could be considered a split in which [-t] becomes ø, while [t-] remains.

Phonological coalescence or merger is often the result of a paradigmatic stimulus while phonological split is frequently carried out through syntagmatic processes in which a conditioning factor is responsible for the mechanics of the change,[1] for example,

$$n > \begin{array}{l} n \\ \text{ŋ}/\text{\_\_velar} \end{array}$$

Conditioned change usually results from conditioned allophonic variation in which the formerly non-significant contrast becomes phonemic by loss or change of the original conditioning factor. For example, in a system in which vowels are phonetically long before voiced consonants and short before voiceless consonants, the loss of the consonant may entail a new phonemic opposition between long and short vowels, *cf*

/pæt/ [pæt] > /pæ/ [pæ]
/pæd/ [pæːd] > /pæː/ [pæː]

Conditioned change has been traditionally considered regular or irregular depending on the extent to which it is carried out. If all relevant environments are affected, it is regular. Internal restrictions on change may sometimes be confused with irregularity in that some 'likely' environments are actually inhibited by structural factors. Also, external influence is often a disruptive force which cuts short a regular change before it has had time to affect all relevant environments as the change is diffused throughout the speech community.

Some generalizations concerning regular conditioned change and the syntagmatic conditions most responsible for such changes have been stated.[2]

1 The conditioning factor is more often a phoneme which follows rather than one which precedes, and is usually immediately following or immediately preceding.
2 Vowels are often conditioned by immediate syllables. More remote conditioning is rare.
3 Change is usually assimilative rather than dissimilative; that is, the change results in articulation more like the conditioning phoneme.
4 Final position of syllables, morphemes and utterances are often conditioning factors for change, initial positions only rarely; changes with final position as their conditioning factor are typically those which result in loss or merger.[3] The result is fewer

phonemes in this position. Most languages seem to have more phonemic oppositions in syllable initial position than in syllable final position.

The trend towards a monosyllabic language, implied by the statement that final position is a conditioning environment resulting in fewer phonemes in this position, may be inhibited by stress in the final syllable, or even reversed by drift towards a synthetic-type language from an earlier analytic stage (see Chapter 8). If, on the other hand, forms continue to shorten, or homonyms become more frequent, tones may develop to help identify phonemic oppositions.

Sporadic change

Changes are considered sporadic if under certain conditions they sometimes occur and sometimes do not. They may be consistent in rapid and informal speech as opposed to formal varieties of conversation. They seem to be the result of a change in a distinctive feature and are thus phonemic changes. Sporadic changes have the following characteristics:

1 The most frequently affected sounds are liquids /r/ and /l/, nasals /m/ and /n/, and sibilants /s/ and /š/.
2 The conditioning factor often operates at a distance, *eg*, Latin *peregrinus* > Italian *pellegrino* 'pilgrim.'[4]

Sporadic change implies that the conditioning factor is not known, since it is difficult to conceive of a change that has no stimulus, no motivating factor behind it. The conditioning factors may relate to structural, psychological, and physiological considerations not yet understood. If sporadic change had no motivation apart from phonetic considerations, it would occur in all phonetically identical environments and constitute regular conditioned change. The fact that it is irregular presupposes a disruptive or inhibitive force on one linguistic level or another (see also Chapter I, *Regularity of sound change*).

Changes occurring in the syntagm and in the paradigm are two types of internal change that are evident in any language system. In syntagmatic change only distribution may be affected while the paradigmatic relationships remain the same. This would be the case in phonological split, in which the resultant sounds are already in the language. Given the vocalic system

in which /e/ splits into /i/ and /e/, no new sounds are added to the phonemic inventory. The loss of medial /-h-/ in Old English affected only the distribution of /h/ since initial /h-/ was retained:

teōhan > teōan > teōn   'draw'
heāhes > heāēs > heās   'high' masculine singular genitive
seohan > seōn   'see'

Alternations may be established by syntagmatic changes, as in Old English /a/ to /æ/ where the anticipatory influence of a following back vowel generally inhibited the fronting of /a/:

singular	*plural*	
dæg	dagas	day
mæg	magas/mægas	kinsman
bæd	badu	bath

Vocalic alternations may be inhibited by consonant patterns. In Old English vowels were lengthened before the consonantal sequence *ld*:

čild > čīld > čayld   'child'

No vowel lengthening occurred, however, before the sequence *ldr* as in the plural children:

čildru > čildrən

Phonological processes

There are a number of common processes of change which can be seen in the history of most languages. They are generally motivated by the syntagmatic arrangements of the language in question and in many cases can be considered as the underlying factors responsible for phonological split. It should be kept in mind that phonological processes are best understood in reference to the linguistic systems in which they occur. In one language, a change may occur which has no counterpart in another language although the immediate phonological environments appear to reflect the same conditioning factors. The relative properties of linguistic units in the paradigmatic structure of all languages are different and may inhibit a syntagmatic change in one language while not in another. Most phonological processes on the syntagmatic plane represent a form of anticipation based on the sequential order of sounds influencing each other in the spoken chain. The direction of influence is regulated generally by time and space considerations in that those sounds not far removed from a preceding sound cause the preceding sound to be modified in accordance with the anticipated sound. Consonants and vowels, stress and tone, may be affected in this manner.

Assimilation

Assimilatory phonological changes are frequent and involve the change of a sound which becomes more like a neighbouring sound, *cf* Latin *nocte* > Italian *notte*, *ie*, /kt/ > /tt/.

Assimilatory changes may reflect changes in either manner of articulation, place of articulation, or both. The process is governed by range of allophonic variation; changes take place along a vertical or horizontal axis (see Chapter 7). Thus, given an earlier form *adpretare* and a later form **appretare*, an intermediate stage, either **abpretare* or **atpretare* could be posited with assurance. Assimilation is essentially an anticipatory change and can operate in either direction, *eg*, *kt* > *tt*, or *kt* > *kk*.[5] Both directions are demonstrated in the following examples:

Latin octō   *Italian* otto 'eight'
Latin fēminam   *Old French* femme 'woman' (via Gallo-Roman
                          mm)

Assimilation may be influenced by non-juxtaposed conditioning sounds such as in certain types of vowel harmony, *eg*, in Turkish, where restrictions are placed on the types of vowels in the successive syllables of a word, *cf* Turkish [sevildirememek] 'not to be able to cause to be loved' (all front vowels) and [jazïldïramamak] 'not be able to cause to be written' (all back vowels). Assimilatory influences can take place over morpheme boundaries, *cf* 'How did you do that?' [hawdž + duwðæt] or [hawdidž + duwðæt] where *d* + *y* > *dž*.

Assimilation is regular inasmuch as the phonological units modified by this influence are modified in all identical environments. All instances of /-kt-/ have become /-tt-/ in Italian, all velar sounds /k/

in English show assimilated front allophones before front vowels, all
nasals in Spanish have assimilated to the point of articulation of
following occlusives, *eg*, /mp/, /nt/, /ñč/ and /ŋk/, etc. Assimilation
is found in English where nasals assimilate to the point of articulation in some words (*eg, impossible*), but other words (*eg, inflammable*)
suggest the process is incomplete but not necessarily static. The
variant *im + f* is also found in some styles of speech.

Dissimilation

This process, the opposite of assimilation in that one sound is
modified to become less like another, appears to be less frequent in
the known histories of languages than assimilation. The conditioning factor may be juxtaposed to the sound which undergoes change,
or may operate at a distance. The first case is illustrated by Vulgar
Latin *luminosu* > Spanish *lumbroso* in which, after the loss of unstressed /i/, the resultant cluster *mn* dissimilated to *mr* and subsequently became *mbr*.[6] The nasal /n/, by losing its nasal quality and
changing to /r/, became less like /m/. The second case is illustrated
by Latin *arbor* which became Spanish *arbol*, presumably by changing /-r-/ to /-l/ under the influence of the preceding /r/. An interesting form of dissimilation occurred in early Greek. If two successive
syllables contained aspirate occlusives, the first occlusive lost the
aspiration:

Proto-Indo-European	>	*Pre-Greek*	>	*Greek*
*drighm		*thrikha		trikha
*bhewdhomaj		*phewthomaj		pewthomaj[7]

Dissimilation may be regular in its modification as in the de-
aspiration of Greek aspirates, or limited to one or several lexical
forms as in Spanish *arbol*.

Palatalization

Palatalization is a common feature of Indo-European languages and
has been discussed earlier (see Chapter 3). This process is also the
result of anticipation leading to allophonic variation. A situation of
this kind may lead to phonemicization of the allophonic variants in
several ways. In Latin, for example, the reduction of labial velars
resulted in new palatal phonemes.[8] In Sanskrit, palatal phonemes
occurred through the merger of the conditioning vowels resulting in
new phonemic oppositions through secondary split.[9]

The results of syntagmatic changes may affect the paradigm in that new phonemes occur which cause a readjustment in the relationships of the sounds to each other. In Early Old English, the frontal allophones of /k/ occurring before high front vowels became /č/, establishing such alternations as *cock, chicken*.[10] Palatalization also affected certain combinations of sounds, *eg, sc* /sk/ became /š/ in Old English.[11] Anticipation of /k/ caused a more palatal articulation of the /s/ resulting in the appearance of the new sound. The phonetic facts underlying these changes are discernible from the changes themselves; that is, there are a limited number of plausible articulatory events that may lead to specific changes. Nevertheless, the phonetic facts are not enough to account for change, since even within the framework of specific environmental influences leading to certain modifications such as /sk/ to /š/, the phonological paradigm must be taken into consideration. The change of /sk/ to /š/ would in fact create a more symmetrical pattern with /š/ as the fricative counterpart of /č/. The function in the paradigm of the sounds that undergo modification may also influence the modification itself. In this case no ambiguity in the form of homonyms would result from the change since palatals were not previously part of the phonological system.[12]

Whether the frontal [ḳ] in Modern English *keep* as phonetically different from the [k] in *cool* eventually results in a new phoneme of a palatal variety will presumably depend somewhat on the nature of the linguistic system of English and not just on the phonetic environment. It is interesting to note that the frequent occurrence of /č/ in English might act as an inhibiting condition preventing further modification of [ḳ] in the direction of /č/ even if a stimulus for such a change were provided. It would be expected that a merger with /č/ might more readily arise if [ḳ] occurred only before high front vowels such as /iy/ and /i/ than under more general conditions such as exist in English where [ḳ] occurs before all front vowels:

	/iy/		/uw/
	/i/		/u/
[ḳ]	/ey/	[k]	/ow/
	/e/		/o/
	/æ/		/a/

The fact that a few homonyms arise from phonological merger seems not to greatly hinder some modifications. Where a distributional rule is very extensive, however, such hindrance may be a factor. Compare just a few examples of potential homophony:

keep	cheap
kin	chin
cane	chain
cat	chat

The function of a phoneme depends on its relations with other phonemes in a system and its frequency in distinguishing lexical forms. To determine semantic constraints on phonological change, at least with regard to the restrictions placed on change by the influence of homonyms, is difficult since the investigation must proceed with 'what might have happened if . . .'. Like the development of the palatals in English, the emergence of the velar nasal /ŋ/ reflects a phonetic process, first of assimilation in which the nasal became more like the following sound by becoming velar in articulation before /k/ and /g/. The loss of /-g/ exposed /ŋ/ in final position, *cf* : *sing* (Middle English *singen*), widening its distribution and allowing it to oppose other phonemes in this position, *cf* : *sin*. The phonetic facts again, however, only tell part of the story in that the emergence of this sound was not inhibited by structural or functional factors and was allowed to proceed.

Paradigmatic factors appear to be responsible for the direction of syntagmatic change in Latin /-kt-/ > Spanish /-yt-/ > /č/, *cf* /nokte/ > /nóče/. Paradigmatic restraints would have prevented /-kt-/ > /-tt-/, since the phonological opposition between geminated and single consonants had earlier disappeared. In Italian, on the other hand, geminates persisted and the change /-kt-/ > /-tt-/ readily occurred, *cf* Italian /nɔtte/.

In some of the Romance languages, palatalization has occurred in a number of diverse environments, *eg* Spanish:

/pl-/ > /λ-/	plēnu > lleno	/λéno/
/-kt-/ > /-č-/	nocte > noche	/nóče/
/-kl-/ > /-x-/ (via ž)	apicula > abeja	/abéxa/

As these Spanish examples indicate, palatalization does not necessarily depend on the quality of a following vowel, but may be conditioned by consonantal relationships which give rise to a change in articulatory movements through anticipation. Phonetic environments *per se* appear to be subservient to non-phonetic considerations. In French, for example, /pl/ *plein*, remains unmodified while in Italian /pl/ > /py/, *eg, pieno*. Environment provides the conditions in which the change can occur and not radically disrupt the system of communication.

Nasalization

Processes of this type are essentially anticipatory and assimilatory and, if carried through, the conditioning factor may become redundant and disappear. Latin *vīnu* developed in Old French (along with the loss of the final vowel) a nasalized vowel /ĩ/ as in /vĩn/ conditioned by the following nasal. The loss of the nasal resulted in Modern French *vin*, /vɛ̃/, in which the nasal vowel has been lowered.[13] Both French and Portuguese have undergone extensive nasalization while Spanish and Italian have not. The geographical location of French and Portuguese, disrupted by Spanish, indicates that they did not share a common substratum responsible for nasalization, nor other common external influences. In French at least the loss of final consonants may have been a factor in the process of nasalization. Nasal vowels could then carry some of the functional load formerly carried by consonants and continue to distinguish such forms as *bellus > beaux* /bo/ and *bonum > bon* /bõ/, *cf* also *eau* /o/, *on* /õ/.[14]

In some dialects of English, nasalized vowels are prominent but consist of allophonic variants of non-nasal vowels before a nasal consonant. The loss of final consonants at some future period in these dialects might result in a distinctive opposition between nasal and non-nasal vowels as follows:

[pæt]   /pæt/ > [pæ]   /pæ/
[pæ̃n]   /pæn/ > [pæ̃]   /pæ̃/

Mutation (umlaut)

This phonological process modifies vowels through anticipation of a vowel often (but not always) a high front vowel (yod) in a following syllable. The effects may be varied but the vowel sound affected becomes more like the high front vowel resulting for example in

vocalic fronting ū > ū̄

Proto-Germanic */mūsiz/ > Old English /mūs/ (Modern English

mice through the Middle English stage /mīs/), or

> Vocalic raising e > i
> *Latin* fēcī > *Spanish* hice /iθe/   *French* fis /fi/
> *Latin* vēnī > *Spanish* vine /bíne/

In the Spanish example the conditioning vowel remains but has lowered from /i/ to /e/. In the other example the conditioning factor is lost and is reconstructed for the Proto-Germanic form. Old Norse shows the assimilation of /a/ toward a back vowel /u/, as in */saku/ 'accusation', *cf* Old English *sacu* 'dispute', which appears in Old Norse as /sɔk/.[15] This and other processes are repetitive in the history of languages. After a modification has occurred new conditions may arise from various sources that again set changes in motion.

Influence of yod

The phoneme /i/ in Classical Latin acted as a yod in consonantal position, *ie*, /y/, *cf iam, iungere, maior*. This gave rise to a palatal phoneme in Romance, *cf* Spanish *mayor*. At a later stage of Latin the vowels /i/ and /e/ in hiatus with a following vowel gave rise to a palatalizing influence, *cf : vinea > vinia > vinya*. The yod developed independently through phonological change in the various Romance languages. For example, a new high, front vowel developed in *factu > fait* /fɛ/.

The effects of this palatal sound appear to be more diverse than those of its counterpart the vau, that is, the phoneme /u/ in consonantal position. Unlike the yod, which frequently was the cause of palatalization in the Romance languages, the vau (often resulting from vocalization of the /l/) affected the preceding vowel. Compare Latin *alteru* which gave rise to *autro > otro* in Spanish and *autre* /otrə/ in French.

Metathesis

The transposition of sounds is very common and can be attested in the history of most languages with documented histories. It is often heard in present-day speech but, like many so-called sporadic events, it occurs and is lost without imitation by others. Metathesis is not simply an articulatory phenomenon, however, as witnessed by the many times it takes place in typing (once a little speed has been worked up). This suggests that neurological structures underlying certain types of muscular activity pertaining to language are affected.

There are basically two related types of metathesis: metathesis in which two sounds are transposed over some distance, *eg, mirāculu >* Spanish *milagro* 'miracle', and metathesis in which juxtaposed sounds change places. This latter type of linguistic change was remarkably frequent in late West Saxon resulting in *axian > ask*, *dox > dusk, waxan > wash*, and a number of others. In Spanish the form *espalda* from Latin *spatula* displays voicing of /t/ > /d/, loss of /u/ and metathesis of /dl/ > /ld/. Motivation for metathesis in this case may stem from the fact that an occlusive plus /l/ was not a compatible combination within the phonosyntactic rules of Spanish. Metathesis of consonant and vowel also occur, *cf : hros > hors* in Old English.[16]

Prothesis

The modification of the initial consonantal sequence /sp/ in *spatula* to /esp-/ *espalda* by the addition of /e-/ appears as a regular occurrence in Western Romance languages such as Spanish and French, *cf : schola >* Spanish *escuela*, French *école* (Old French *escole*).

When first learning English Spanish speakers find initial clusters of the type /sp/, /st/ and /sk/ somewhat strange and substitute their own sequence /esp-/, /est-/ and /esk-/. Similar external influences may have been responsible for the prothetic sound during the formative period of the Romance languages in the form of substratum or adstratum contacts. However, internal factors based upon distributional readjustments cannot be disregarded as a possible motivation for the change, or at least as a system which offered enough leeway for the change to proceed in the direction that it did. These initial clusters may have responded to syllabic pressure to organize clusters in conformity with prevalent patterns. The addition of /e-/ to these clusters appears to have caused a new syllable division, *cf : stāre* (*sta-re*), to *estar* (*es-tar*). A similar situation existed in French but the preconsonantal /s/ was later lost as in *être, école*. In Spanish, syllable final and morpheme final consonants correspond to a distributional relationship in that certain consonants occur in both positions while certain others occur in neither position. This relationship may have exerted some pressure on /s/ in the clusters /sp/, /st/ and /sk/ to align with the same syntagmatic situation by becoming syllable final in the form of /es/ corresponding to morpheme final /s/. In French the loss of syllable final and morpheme final /s/ appear to have been related events.[17] The seemingly sporadic development of a prothetic vowel in Italian, *eg : iscuola/scuola*, on the other hand, may be related to the fact that the early loss of /-s/ disrupted the process of prothesis by alleviating distributional pressure to force /s/ to conform to syllable final position, *ie*, /is-kóla/, *cf* Italian *stare*,[18] and Spanish *estar*.

Syncope

The loss of medial vowels, known as syncope, is a common occurrence in many languages. Old English *stānas* became *stones* /stównz/ through the reduction and loss of the unstressed vowel, *ie*, /a/ > /ə/ > /ø/. In present-day English, an unstressed vowel is often lost in the environment of a voiced palatal /ǧ/ and a voiceless occlusive /t/, *cf : vegetable* /véǧtibl̞/. Syncope does not always occur in this environment, however, as evidenced by the word *vegetate* /véǧiteyt/ and *fidgety* /fíǧitiy/. As articulatory energy is expended on a certain syllable, neighbouring unstressed vowels may weaken and disappear. In the environmental framework *nt-r* in the word *interesting*, the vowel may be lost when stress is placed on the first syllable, *cf* /íntrestiŋ/ and /intəréstiŋ/. Retention or loss of the vowel, however, may depend on the dialect, on matters of style, or on syntagmatic constraints inherent in the distributional system of the language.

Phonological processes such as syncope can be stated in terms of the environments in which they occur. Often, however, the environments cannot be stated in terms of the process. Proparoxytonic forms in Vulgar Latin, for example, do not give identical results in the various Romance languages, *cf : tábula* > French *table* but Italian *tavola*, and even specific environments in a given language may not yield similar results. Syncope occurs between a liquid and an occlusive in early Spanish, *eg*, *cálidus* > *caldo*, but Spanish also has *álaga* from Vulgar Latin /álika/. Syncope may be more regular, however, in its operation than the apparent exceptions suggest. This regularity must be sought in the overall structure or design of the language since only in this way can the inhibiting factors be determined which for one reason or another limit the changes to certain environments. Since syntagmatic change involves changes in distribution, an investigation of the distributional arrangements of the language under consideration is the first step in linking this type of change to inhibiting factors.

In many languages there is a relationship between consonant distribution and intervocalic clusters which can be measured by the degree of compatibility of intervocalic consonant clusters (-cc-) to morpheme initial (c-) and morpheme final (-c) consonants. Inter-vocalic clusters may be termed compatible if they are dissolvable. They are dissolvable if the second member occurs in morpheme initial position and the first member occurs in morpheme final position. If all the morphemes in a language correspond to the shape $C_1VC_3C_4VC_2$ where $C_1 = C_4$ and $C_2 = C_3$, clusters are dissolvable. If a language has medial consonant clusters and only morpheme initial and morpheme final vowels, no clusters are dissolvable. In Spanish, for example, /-nt-/ is dissolvable since it is composed of /t-/ as in *tu* and /-n/ as in *ven*. The cluster /-bd-/ on the other hand is not since there is no final /-b/ in the system.[19]

A schematic arrangement of possible cluster combinations yields four classes of cluster concatenations which correspond to degrees of compatibility in the following hypothetical system:

Consonant clusters

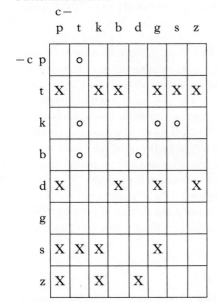

		p	t	k	b	d	g	s	z
−c	p		o						
	t	X		X	X		X	X	X
	k		o				o	o	
	b		o			o			
	d	X		X		X			X
	g								
	s	X	X	X			X		
	z	X		X		X			

The language represented in the above chart has the following distributional arrangements:

initial position: all consonants
final position: /t, d, s, z/

The medial consonant cluster arrangements can thus be classified into four major groups:

Occurring clusters
 Class 1A, compatible, *eg*, /tp/, /tk/, /tb/, etc represented by X
 Class 2A, marginal, *eg*, /pt/, represented by o

Non-occurrent clusters
 Class 1B, potential, *eg*, /dk/, /zb/
 Class 2B, incompatible, *eg*, /gt/

Among the non-occurrent clusters, Class 1B would be compatible to the distributional system if they were to occur. Class 2B, if they were to occur, would not be compatible. From a diachronic point of view, the creation of a new cluster in a 1B slot would entail its re-classification to 1A. The loss of a 1A cluster would present a new 1B hole in the system of distribution. Similar reclassifications would occur between Classes 2A and 2B. The occurrence of syncope in the phonological sequence CV́CVCVC resulting in CV́CCVC, where the resultant -CC- = Class 1A, would have the highest expectation of realization. Class 1B would also have a high expectation of occurrence since they do not run counter to the distribution of initial and final consonants. Class 2A would be expected to have a relatively low frequency of occurrence since the resultant clusters would not be compatible, *ie*, dissolvable. This class nevertheless would yield more clusters from syncope than Class 2B, since marginal clusters already exist in the system. Class 2B would be the most inhibited and would be expected to result in the majority of the exceptions to syncope under identical syllabic and prosodic conditions. The so-called exceptions, however, are governed by phonological rules of con-catenation. The inhibiting factor is the degree of incompatibility of the system of distribution to the potentially new clusters.

Phonetic patterning

Within the framework of Class 1B, some potentially new consonant clusters have a higher possibility of occurrence than others. If the distribution of phonemes is such that some general statement can be made, *eg*, that dentals /t, d/ do not occur with dentals, then the possi-bility of their emergence from phonological processes appears less than that of other potential clusters whose distribution does not correspond to such a structural hole,[20] *eg :*

```
tp  [ ]  tk
tb  [ ]  tg
```

Non-occurrent clusters of the type 1B that do not relate to structural holes correspond instead to accidental holes, for example, dentals concatenate with velars, /tk/, /dg/, but /dk/ does not occur, (where ( ) = accidental hole).

```
( )  tk
dg   tg
```

Similarly, among Class 2B, some clusters will be more likely than others since some will correspond to structural holes and others to accidental holes in the paradigm. Labials, for example, do not pattern with velars, making this combination even less likely to arise than the already unlikely 2B type in general.

There is, then, not only a syntagmatic relationship between the various classes that governs phonological change, but syntagmatic-paradigmatic factors within several of the subclasses that also inhibit or direct phonological modifications.

Changes in both the distributional arrangements of the sound system and the paradigmatic arrangements constantly modify the relationships of the classes to each other. Given CVC where − C = /t/ and CVCCV where -CC- = /ts/ or Class 1A, and a change in distribution in which CVC becomes CV by loss of /-t/, then /-ts-/ becomes Class 2A or marginal. Conversely, the addition of a new consonant in morpheme final position may change marginal clusters into integrated clusters. The addition of a /-t/ (CV > CVC or CVCV > CVC where − C = /t/) would change /-ts-/ from 2A to 1A. A new final consonant might be added either through normal linguistic evolution or by the incorporation of a borrowed word in the language. Just as a marginal cluster would be less likely to arise through syncope, it would be theoretically more prone to disappear than other well integrated clusters of the type 1A.

Theoretically, words would more readily be accepted into the language if they conformed to the distributional arrangements of the compatible Classes 1A or 1B. Those borrowed words containing distributionally non-compatible clusters would be either not borrowed or substantially modified in the process. Borrowed words introducing new final consonants would be readily accepted if the -C rendered a marginal cluster compatible, *ie*, a new /-k/ would render the cluster /-kt-/ Class 1A. The cluster /zt/, if borrowed, would fill an accidental hole in 1B and would enter the language unmodified.

The relationship of -CC- to -C and C-, *ie*, of syllable onset and coda to morpheme onset and coda, is not restricted to clusters of two members. Larger clusters such as -CCC- would relate to CC- and -C or to C- and -CC. Vague notions concerning tendencies and pressures in language change are made more explicit by an examination of inhibiting forces based upon structural relationships. Sociological factors, however, interfere with structural changes insofar as the latter are consciously rejected by one or another social group for prestige or other reasons. An investigation of syntagmatic inhibiting factors and their relationships to various phonological processes such as assimilation, dissimilation, epenthesis, cluster reduction, umlaut, etc can only lead to a better understanding of structural principles underlying these processes.

Apocope

Apocope pertains to the loss of a vowel in final position of lexical items. Old English *ic singe* became *I sing* whereby /-e/ > /-ə/ > /ø/. French has undergone a great deal of apocope resulting in effacement of final vowels throughout the lexicon regardless of vowel type or grammatical categories:

```
heure    < hōra
chef     < caput
cher     < cāru
chien    < cane
couleur < colōre
prouver < probāre
```

The loss of unstressed vowels in French is generally associated with the Frankish invasions of Gaul which introduced into Gallo-Roman a more pronounced stress accent on the relatively weak accentual system inherited from Latin. This led to the reduction and loss of many unstressed vowels that were not lost in other Romance languages. Spanish, for example, underwent a more limited type of apocope:

no apocope	apocope
hora < hōra	probar < probāre
caro < cāru	ciudad < cīvitāte
cabo < caput	color < colōre

Apocope in Spanish was restricted to a position after certain consonants (*l, r, s, n, d, θ, ć* and *y*) and to certain vowels (primarily *e*
and *o*), and to some syntactic positions, *eg, bueno* but *buen hombre*.

Epenthesis

The phonological process of epenthesis refers to the insertion of a
sound within a morpheme. The phonological environment generally
determines the nature of the inserted sound. The modification of
consonant clusters by the addition of an epenthetic consonant occurs
often in the history of English as well as other languages. It appears
to relate to a phonetic process inasmuch as it is motivated by the
environment but, as the following examples suggest, it may well be
inhibited by other factors associated with phonosyntactic or
morphological characteristics of the language in question. Epenthesis may occur in specific environments in one language but not
under similar conditions in another language. In English epenthesis
occurred in *timber < *timron* but not in German *Zimmer* or Swedish
timmer. Middle English *θuner* became Modern English *thunder* but
in German *Donner* epenthesis did not take place.

The phonetic basis for epenthesis is reasonably clear. Through
anticipation of a non-nasal sound such as /r/, air is diverted through
the buccal passage while articulating the nasal, *ie,* /m/ or /n/. The
result is a change in one phonetic feature. The phoneme /m/, for
example, is labial, voiced and nasal but if nasality is disrupted before
the articulation of /m/ is complete the ensuing sound is labial, voiced
and non-nasal or /b/. Epenthesis, for example, occurs in several types
of environments such as between nasals and /s/, /r/ and /l/; *cf* Old
English *glimsen > glimpse, ganra > gander* and *bremel > bramble*. A
transitional consonant does not always arise in these environments,
however, and we find words such as *slimmer, summer* and *dinner* with
no epenthetic consonant. While there was some alternation in
Middle English between epenthetic consonants and geminated consonants, *eg, stamber/stammer,* in general epenthesis did not occur

after geminates. The lack of an epenthetic consonant in environments such as *mm-r* and *nn-r* points to a phonological restriction on its occurrence.

On the other hand epenthesis occurs or fails to occur in other potential environments for reasons which do not seem to be phonological. In the environmental frames *m-z*, *n-z*, and *ŋ-z*, eg, *hams*, *fans*, and *sings*, no intrusive /b/, /d/ or /g/ arises. A morpheme final nasal plus /z/ generally signals a morpheme boundary in English and does not readily occur in morpheme final position, except over morpheme boundaries (though some counter examples do exist, *cf: lens*).[21] Epenthesis in the environments *m-s*, *n-s*, and *ŋ-s* as in *glimpse*, *fence* /fents/ (Old English *fens*) and *lynx* occurs at non-morpheme boundaries and appears to have inhibited the normal assimilation processes characteristic of English by maintaining the voiceless sibilant, or preventing *ms* > *mz*, *ns* > *nz*, *ŋs* > *ŋz*. Epenthesis may act here as a functional device to check a phonological change that would otherwise result in more overlap between phonological sequences at morpheme boundaries and non-boundaries.[22]

Sonorization

The voicing of intervocalic voiceless consonants appears to be motivated by the phonetic environment inasmuch as it occurs between voiced sounds. The frequency of this process is attested by many languages that have voiced allophonic variants of voiceless occlusives and fricatives in intervocalic position.

That all medial consonants under vocalic influence are not solely conditioned by the syntagmatic environment is evident from the change of intervocalic /z/ to /s/ in Medieval Spanish.[23]

In some of the Romance languages sonorization appears to have been prompted by the reduction of geminate consonants, *cf:* -*pp*- > -*p*- > -*b*- (and -*v*):

Latin	Italian	Spanish	Portuguese	French
cuppa	coppa	copa	copa	coupe
cūpa	copa	cuba	cuba	cuve

Vocalization

As the name suggests, this process involves the modification of a consonant – usually /l/ or /r/ – to a vowel. Latin *alteru* became French *autre*, Spanish *otro*. The latter change passed through the stage

/alt-/ > /aut-/ > /ot-/. Vocalization can be seen in present-day English in the alternate pronunciation of lexical items containing /l/ plus a consonant, *cf*: *milk* /məlk/ and /məuk/ and *film* /fəlm/ and /fəum/. In some dialects of Portuguese the vocabulary items *mau* 'bad' and *mal* 'badly' are both pronounced /mau/.

Rhotacization

Intervocalic /s/ in Latin became /r/, *cf* */genesis/ > /generis/ and */asēna/ > /arena/. Elsewhere /s/ remained as in *est*, *senex* and *equus*.[24] /s/ would not be expected to become /r/ directly, however, and the intermediate stage */z/ can be posited. The voiced environment of the surrounding vowels was responsible for the first part of the change, but */z/ > /r/ cannot be equated with any such combinatory influence.[25] Paradigmatic motivations appear to influence */z/ > /r/ without recourse to specific phonological environments.

Haplology

For the form *nūtriō* 'I nourish' in Latin, the regular feminine agent noun should be *nūtri-trix 'nurse' but the form is *nūtrix*. Similarly, *stipipendium 'wage payment' appears as *stipendium*. In both cases syllables were lost which were phonologically similar to an adjacent syllable.[26]

A catalogue of phonological processes would include many more than those mentioned in the foregoing pages. It would appear that many of the phonological features found in language are derived through structural processes. Some consonants, for example, besides undergoing the process mentioned above, may become aspirated, pre-aspirated, glottalized, prenasalized, affricated, imploded or produced with simultaneous closure at two points of articulation, *eg*, /gb/ (found in some African languages). Vowels may be raised and lowered, fronted and backed, rounded and unrounded, lengthened and shortened, nasalized and even pharyngealized. To think of some of these phonological characteristics such as aspiration and glottalization as an extension of a basic or underlying sound presupposes a given set of natural speech sounds from which other sounds are derived by the addition of phonological features. The various phonological processes or their results are not evenly distributed throughout the world's languages. Different languages or groups of related languages often demonstrate a decided preference for some features rather than others. One further example of possible syntagmatic constraints on phonological processes related to a higher linguistic level of organization is considered in this chapter.

Consonant cluster reduction in English

The tendency to reduce clusters is not only clear from the actual loss of consonants, but also from the alternate pronunciations of clusters such as /-lp/ *help*, /-lt/ *belt*, /-lk/ *milk* which display a continuing trend toward vocalization.[27] Some combinations are more prone to reduction than others. Whether or not a cluster will be modified by loss of one or more of its members seems to depend somewhat on the function of the lexical item, and theoretically upon its resultant shape. The reduction of /fifθs/ *fifths* to /fiθs/ or even /fifs/ presents no difficulties. Both are compatible to English phonotactics and neither results in lexical ambiguity. On the other hand, the loss of /θ/ in /warmθ/ or /warmpθ/ *warmth* would result in /warm/. The fact that these words have different functional roles in English, yet occur in syntactically similar positions is probably a strong inducement to inhibit modification.

/-nd/ is often reduced to /-n/ in utterance final position and before consonants across lexemic boundaries.[28] The allomorph /læn/ replaces /lænd/. Pattern formation suggests that the replacement processes will continue until /læn/ becomes the only form. The reduction appears to be part of a larger framework in which /-mb/ and /-ŋg/ have been reduced to /-m/ *eg : comb* and /-ŋ/, *eg : sing*. There seems to be little structural interference with this modification, indeed, the minimal phonetic difference between [n] and [d], the pattern arrangement, the reduction of identical sequences at morpheme boundaries (M B) and at non-morpheme boundaries (N M B) (*cf : land* /lænd/ and *fanned* /fænd/), and the scarcity of homonyms resulting from such a change are all compelling factors exerting pressure towards modification. The replacement of the allomorph in /-nd/ by /-n/ *eg :* /læn/, /hæn/, /sæn/, etc presents few difficulties with homonymy. Although this notion is theoretically difficult to sustain, there is undoubtedly a threshold of tolerance in every language related to the number and types of possible homonyms the system will support. The sequence nasal plus voiced occlusive carries little information at N M B, *ie*, possible equivalent messages without /-d/ are few. This was also true for /-mb/ and /-ŋg/, although examples to the contrary do exist, *eg : tend* and *ten.* In this case, however, the two forms would rarely be opposed in a syntactic environment. The retention of /-mp/, /-nt/ and /-ŋk/ may in part be due to multiple phonetic differences between the sequential components (although this by itself does not appear to be a strong factor in language change) and homonymous considerations. Lexemic shapes of the type *hump, slump, tent, dent, sink, think* would result in homonyms if reduced; perhaps for this reason they do not display positional allomorphs. The maintenance of /-nǧ/, *hinge* without allomorphs in /-n/ seems to reflect similar considerations. The fact that some similar forms would not culminate in homonyms if reduced (*eg, link*) does not invalidate the general proposal. Theoretically, high frequency of occurrence of lexical items coupled with formal and syntactic similarities would inhibit changes leading to homonyms.

English consonant clusters in morpheme final position display specific patterns of concatenation which appear to exert syntagmatic direction on phonological change. The underlying distributional patterns are readily discernible by arranging the clusters into two major groups: those whose initial cluster belongs to the phono- logical core system of English, *eg*, occlusive and fricatives; and those whose initial consonant belongs to the non-core system, *eg*, /l, r, m, n, ŋ, h/.

Voiceless consonants pattern with voiceless consonants at N M B, for example, /-pt/ *apt*, /-sk/ *ask*, while non-core consonants can be followed by voiceless or voiced, or non-core consonants, *eg*, /-lp/ *help*, /-lb/ *bulb*, /-lm/ *film*.

The absence of clusters revolves around the following patterns representing structural holes (S H): voiceless plus voiced, voiced plus voiced, voiced plus voiceless, core plus non-core.[29]

	vls	vd	non-core
core vls	+	−	−
vd	−	−	−
non-core	+	+	+

+ = occurrent clusters
− = structural holes

Within the framework of the occurrent patterns certain combina- tions do not occur, for example, palatal /č/ or /š/ with any core consonant and geminated clusters, etc. These point to more restricted structural and accidental holes (AH) based upon hierarchically lower features in the phonological matrix, such as place of articulation. Compare, for example, core plus core clusters:

	p	t	č	k	s	š	f
p		pt			ps		
t					ts		
č							
k		kt			ks		
s	sp	st		sk			
š							
f		ft					

wasp script   mask lapse
     fact   blitz
     fast   axe
     raft

The effect on processes of phonological change, by restrictions on consonantal sequences manifest in structural and accidental holes, is not obvious and needs more attention from linguistic historians. For example, some overlap arises with respect to MB and NMB among voiceless plus voiceless sequences since /-t/ and /-s/ in postconsonantal position sometimes function as morphemes, and sometimes not, *eg*: *hacked* /-k·t/, *fact* /-kt/, and *boxed* /-ks·t/, *text* /-kst/, *tacks* /-k·s/, *tax* /-ks/. Morpheme boundary perception may be relevant in maintaining the major structural holes (*eg*, voiced plus voiced) by inhibiting changes in cluster composition among -CC that would lead to more overlap between -CC or NMB and those at MB.

English consonant clusters, both core and non-core, in morpheme final position can be derived in a general way according to the following schematic representation:

(1)	(2)	(3)	(4)
-C	-CC	-CCC	-CCCC
(-k)	(-ks)	(-kst)	(AH)
(-s)	(-sp)	(AH)	(SH)
(-č)	(AH)	(SH)	–
(-l)	(-lb)	(SH)	–

All final clusters of three members, for example, are composed of -CC plus /s/ or /t/: cf /l/, /lt/, /lts/, *bell, fault, waltz*.[30] The dependence of a cluster of three members on the components of clusters of two members, causes an accidental hole at the -CC level to become a structural hole at the -CCC level of composition. For example, the accidental hole */-lg/ (we find /-lk/ *milk* and /-ld/ *cold*) among -CC becomes a structural hole among -CCC. If a certain -CC occurs but is not represented on the -CCC level, it becomes an accidental hole among -CCC: *eg*, /-lp/ *help* does not expand as */-lpt/, */-lps/ (except over morpheme boundaries /help·t/).

One type of -CC (non-core plus voiced) automatically becomes a structural hole among -CCC without passing through the accidental hole stage. It conforms to the rule that only voiceless plus voiceless core consonants can occur, *eg*, /-lb/ *bulb* becomes a structural hole */-lbs/, */-lbt/.

Structural and accidental holes in the consonant cluster paradigm and the nature of cluster concatenation present a framework in which to investigate modifying factors. The most obvious effect of the interlocking network of relationships among morpheme final clusters revolves around external influences on the language. Theoretically, lexical items would not be readily incorporated into English from external sources if they contained consonantal sequences corresponding to structural holes. Sequences filling accidental holes, however, would be compatible, as would those identical to existing -CC. Morphemes ending in /-ts/ or /-lts/ may have been readily borrowed precisely because they filled an accidental hole. *Cf*: *blitz* /-ts/ voiceless followed by voiceless patterns with /-ps/ and /-ks/. *Waltz* /-lts/[31] fills an accidental hole when /-lt/ > /-lts/. This would change the structural hole for */-ltst/ into an accidental hole. Lexical borrowings appear not only to be influenced by linguistic structure but to influence that structure themselves.

Physiological aspects of the human organism and their relationship to language change are not well understood. It is entirely feasible for example that the average frequency of a consonant cluster is a function of the difference between the sounds of the cluster. Low frequencies of occurrence could mean extremes which are too close or too distant phonologically, high frequencies non-extremes. Maximum effort for both encoder and decoder would be avoided if the distribution of average frequencies followed a normal curve. This would avoid the problem of minimum effort by the speaker entailing maximum effort for the listener, and vice versa.[32] The historical implications of this hypothesis would suggest that language change is, in part, governed by subconscious efforts to modify the system in accordance with an economy of communication. The processes discussed in this section are often simply the means by which the underlying motivations are temporarily satisfied.

There are as many historical processes as there are synchronic conditions in language. In some cases syntagmatic influence may be the dominant force in initiating or inhibiting the change; at other periods and under different conditions, paradigmatic forces may be stronger. An analysis of the relative strength of these internal factors and the relationship of the relativity to a particular structural design is a matter of some importance in historical studies. To view these things in their proper perspective, external influences must be delimited and their effect on internal forces assessed.

Investigations of causes and determinants of language change are still in the embryonic stage. Phonological processes are generally considered simply as syntagmatic events. Examined in isolation, they tell us little about language change except perhaps for the fact that they occur in all languages. Investigated in a broader framework of syntagmatic and paradigmatic structure and ultimately in an even wider context of selective morphological, syntactic and semantic factors, they may lead to a better understanding of the dynamic forces embedded in man's capacity for language.

Notes

1 For details of these and their variations, see Hoenigswald (1960), *pp* 86–98. For a discussion of phonetic versus phonemic change, see Bloomfield, *p* 369.
2 See Osgood and Sebeok, *p* 148.
3 See Bloomfield, *p* 371.
4 See Posner for many such examples.
5 Sturtevant, *An Introduction to Linguistic Science*, *p* 86 refers to the latter process as *lag* which appears to be less frequent than *anticipation*.

6 See Entwistle, *p* 150.

7 See Bloomfield, *p* 350.

8 For a discussion of this see Chapter 7.

9 See Chapter 3.

10 *Cf* Old English *cicen* < **ciucin* and Low German *küken*. For further details and intermediate stages, see Stevick (1968), *pp* 59–61.

11 *Cf* Old English *sceāp* > *sheep*.

12 The change of /sk/ > /š/ was regular since it affected all such consonant combinations in the language. Modern English words that contain /sk/ clusters are from foreign sources reflecting a multitude of different origins, *cf* : *skin, sky* < Scandinavian; *scribe* < Latin; *scholar, risk* < French; *skate* < Dutch, and the native word *ask* < Old English *axian* which underwent the process of metathesis, *ie*, /ks/ became /sk/.

13 For further examples of this process in Old French, see Ewert, *p* 63. Also discussed is the process of denasalization in the Middle French period which results in such words as *femme* /fam/.

14 For phonological constraints on nasalization in French and paradigmatic readjustment in a transformational framework, see Schane, *French Phonology and Morphology*, *pp* 45–50.

15 See Bloomfield, *p* 381.

16 See Lehmann (1962), *p* 169.

17 A similar process has occurred in Andalusian Spanish where morpheme final and syllable final /s/ has been lost.

18 The loss of /-s/ and the rise of prothetic vowels /i/ and /e/ occurred during the same general period. For reference to inscriptions and comments on these events, see Grandgent, *pp* 98 and 126. Italian does employ prothetic /i/ after a word ending in a consonant, *cf* : *in iscuola*.

19 For a descriptive analysis of this relationship in Spanish, see Saporta and Olson.

20 See Vogt, *pp* 28–34 for a more precise statement on structural and accidental holes. Pure distributional statements are not entirely satisfactory in this respect.

21 Many cluster combinations in English are found only at morpheme boundaries, *eg*, /čl/ *searchlight*, /šs/ *washstand*, /čs/ *matchstick*, etc. The lower limit of morphological structures can often be determined by an examination of the distribution of phonemes, allophones, stress, and juncture. See Nida, *pp* 102–103. To the extent that phonological border phenomena are relevant, one can determine the interdependence of phonology and morphology. The degree of dependence of the two systems would be reflected in linguistic change.

22 The word *lynx* may have entered the language with the [-k-] intact, *cf* Latin *lynx* but German *luchs*. Similarly, *tempt* is from Old French *temptare* > *tenter*. *Tinct* is from Latin *tinctus*. The Middle English forms *glimsen, fens*, etc have been orthographically altered for the epenthetic consonant.

23 The sound /z/ occurs in Ladino where Spanish now has /θ/, *cf* /káza/, /káθa/ *caza*.

24 de Saussure, *p* 144.

25 *Ibid, p* 146. de Saussure refers to the second part of this change as spontaneous modification.

26 Bloomfield, *p* 385. For a treatment of haplology in Indo-European, see Cardona.

27 For examples of the early loss of /l/, see Wyld, *p* 213.

28 Consider the utterances: The /lænd/ is . . ., The /læn/ she bought . . . .

29 There are a few infrequent exceptions, *eg : adze* and nicknames such as *Bugs*.

30 For a discussion of the general patterning process in the distribution of consonants in clusters, see Jones; clusters containing syllabic /r/ as in *world, corpse* and *quartz* are not included here. For the syllabic nature of /r/, see Hultzen.

31 The variant /wɔls/ is also common.

32 See Saporta. For further endeavours along these lines for French, see Bursill-Hall. Also see Carroll for a statistically more conclusive approach to Saporta's hypothesis.

Chapter 7

Structural change (paradigmatic)

Internal considerations of language change involve both the syntagm and the paradigm. Syntagmatic changes are in part motivated or inhibited by the influence sounds have on each other in their spatial and temporal linear arrangements. Structural considerations have in the past been primarily concerned with the relationship between sounds in distributional or syntagmatic patterns, and the modifications affecting these patterns. An inventory of sound changes would be drawn up between two stages of a language and, where possible, accounted for by syntagmatic events and their relationship to the environment, for example, Latin voiceless /-t-/ in *vita* became Spanish voiced /-d-/ *vida* under the influence of surrounding voiced vowels. The change in French, however, of /u/ to /ü/ could not be accounted for by syntagmatic environments. Recourse to external influences such as substratum influence became important as an explanation of the motivating forces behind such changes. However, by taking into account the functional aspect of sounds in the paradigm of a particular language some changes once attributed to external forces have been seen as internally motivated. Attempts to establish paradigmatic factors in language change, at least with regard to unconditioned phonological merger, have been made. They should not be taken at face value, however, and some critical comments are in order.

1 *The more uncommon a phoneme is in human speech in general, the more likely it is to be merged with another phoneme.*[1] As Hoenigswald points out with regard to this generalization:

Aside from the question of factual support, one would like to know whether it is implied that there are only processes which eliminate 'uncommon phonemes', or also others, not named, which give rise to new uncommon phonemes . . . If the former is meant, this would attribute to the human race a consistent history of uniformization, at least in point of sound structure. Would we not then have to extrapolate back to a phylogenetic babbling stage, and extrapolate forward to a radical reduction in the number of existing areal types? P. Friedrich reminds me that such strikingly aberrant traits as are revealed to the present-day typologist (say, the southern African clicks?) could then *ipso facto* be recognized as survivals – not in terms of ordinary microhistory with its mutually compensatory *plus-ça-change-plus-c'est-la-même-chose* reshuffling, but as true fossils against a background of serious mutation.[2]

2 *The closer the points of articulation shared by two phonemes the more likely they are to merge.* This generalization and the following are stated with the condition: other things being equal. The concept 'other things being equal' is a theoretical nicety but it must be kept in mind that the whole notion of diachronic structural studies revolves around an attempt to unravel and delimit the unequal factors involved in language modification.

3 *The more distinctive features shared by two phonemes the more likely the phonemes are to merge.* Phonemes with one, two, or more shared features but with several distinct features are only likely to merge over a period of time in which each feature is replaced in the direction of a possible merger. Phonemes with two shared features are no more likely to merge than those with one. Only phonemes with all but one common feature are likely to merge at any given time.

4 *The fewer the pairs of different linguistic forms which are distinguished by the phonemes, the more likely they are to merge.* This would appear to be particularly true for phonemes participating in isolated or non-integrated oppositions, but phonemes participating in the major phonemic correlations, *eg*, English /š/ and /ž/, even though distinguishing few linguistic forms, would find a strong inducement to retain their identity based upon the correlation of voiceless/voiced which permeates the system.

5 *The lower the frequency of a phoneme in a given language the more likely it is to merge with another phoneme, providing this second*

phoneme is not itself of excessively high frequency. Frequency would only be a factor if other conditions prevailed such as (2) and (3) above. Since phonological change proceeds through allophonic steps, the phonemes /t/ and /g/ would not be expected to merge even if they met the requirements of the statement.

The theoretical importance of these factors as general or universally valid statements about language has yet to be completely demonstrated within a coherent model of language change. Relating to both the function and the structure of phonemes, however, the notions contained in these statements appear to account for some aspects of language change within the framework of paradigmatic relationships.[3]

Paradigmatic relationship is concerned essentially with the opposition of phonological features in the sound system of a language. The phoneme /p/ in English in the environment /-in/ stands in paradigmatic relation with /b/, /f/, /t/, /d/, /θ/, etc by virtue of the minimum difference between lexical items such as *pin, bin, fin, tin, din, thin*, etc. The vowel /i/ stands in paradigmatic relation to other vowels in English, *eg, pin,* /e/ *pen,* /æ/ *pan*. Paradigmatic relations can be thought of as operating on a vertical axis entailing substitution of phonemes while syntagmatic relations operate along a horizontal axis such as the relationship between /p/ and /i/ and /n/, *eg :*

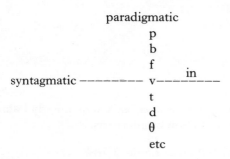

The following discussion examines the basic principles underlying phonological change in which the motivation for change appears to stem from paradigmatic considerations.[4] The application of paradigmatic criteria takes into account both the function and the structure of the phonemes in the particular language during the period of time under investigation. This method attempts to go beyond the data in order to explain language change by recourse to hypotheses about the data. Such considerations must be based upon ample documentation of the facts. The two thousand years and more of Latin and its descendant languages offer, if not ideal documentation, at least sufficient written records to adequately examine the principles of this approach.

Proto-Indo-European is thought to have contained six diphthongs:[5]

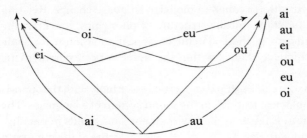

ai
au
ei
ou
eu
oi

These glides generally merged with long vowels until Classical Latin contained only three,

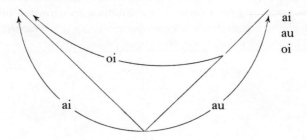

ai
au
oi

Compare, for example, the presence of *ei, ou*, and *eu* in Early Latin and Greek and their Classical Latin counterparts.

PIE >	Early Latin	Classical Latin	Greek
*ei	deicō	dīcō	–
	–	fīdō	peithō
*ou	doucō	dūcō	–
	–	ūrīna	oureī
*eu	–	lūx	leukós

Of the three Classical Latin diphthongs the least integrated, /oi/, disappeared during the period of written Latin merging with /ē/, *cf*: *póena > pēna*. The reduction of the diphthongs appears to be involved with the more general processes of reduction affecting long vowels and long (geminated) consonants.[6] By the time of the Empire, only the equipollent diphthongs /ai/ and /au/ remained. Likewise, /ai > ɛ/ and au > ɔ/ were tending to be reduced. This tendency towards reduction of long components coupled with the nature of the non-distinctive features among vowels and the increasing articulatory force placed on stressed vowels are all intimately integrated forces which paved the way for profound changes leading to a new phonological structure.

Latin vowels

The Classical Latin vocalic system of oppositions consisted of five long and five short vowels, *eg*:

| dĭcō 'I dedicate' | pŏpŭlus 'a people' |
| dīcō 'I say' | pōpŭlus 'a poplar' |

arranged in three degrees of aperture, *eg*:

rĭgō 'I irrigate'
rĕgō 'I rule'
cădō 'I fall'

They can be shown schematically as

phonemic

The long vowels were phonetically close or tense, and the short vowels were phonetically open or lax.

phonetic

The reduction of /ai/ to open /ɛ̄/ established a new opposition among the mid vowels ē/ɛ̄ based upon quality or aperture.

$$[ɛ̆] = /ɛ̆/$$
$$[ɛ̄] = /ē/ \quad \left\{ \begin{array}{l} \text{opposition of vocalic quantity} \\ \text{new opposition of vocalic quantity} \end{array} \right.$$
$$/ai/ > /ɛ̄/$$

The increasing articulatory energy expended on stressed syllables tended to shorten unstressed long vowels and to lengthen short stressed vowels. This loss of quantity allowed /ɛ̆/ and /ɛ̄/ to merge as /ɛ/, neither long nor short, *ie*

$$/ai/ > /ɛ̄/ \left\{ \begin{array}{ll} /ɛ̄/ & [ɛ̄] \\ /ɛ̆/ & [ɛ̆] \end{array} \right\} > /ɛ/$$

Long and short vowels did not then simply coalesce with the increasing stress and subsequent loss of quantity accompanied by the reduction of /ai/. Rather, the phonetic difference in aperture acquired phonemic or distinctive characteristics, beginning first with the mid vowels and later spreading to the entire system. Short /ĭ/, for example, was more open than /ī/, and /ē/ was more close than /ĕ/ phonetically. This set the stage for the merger of /ĭ/ and /ē/ instead of /ī/ and /ĭ/. Similarly, /ŭ/ fell together with /ō/ as a result of their phonetic proximity in aperture. The resulting vocalic system formed the basis for peninsular and general European Vulgar Latin.

Characteristic of the vowels that underwent the modification outlined in the following analysis is the fact that they were both stressed and in free position vis-à-vis the syllable; for example, the vowel /o/ in *po-tes* is considered free since it ends the syllable. The vowel /o/ in *por-ta* is considered checked since it is blocked by a consonant. Unstressed and checked vowels behave somewhat differently from the stressed and free vowels and would be taken into account as vocalic subsystems in a comprehensive treatment of the Romance languages. Compare, for example, the following modifications in Spanish (where ( ) = analogical formations):

Latin	>	*Spanish*
póssum		(puedo)
pótes		puedes
pótest		puede
possúmus		(podemus)
potéstis		podéis
póssunt		(pueden)

Free stressed /o/ > /ue/ while unstressed /o/ remained.[7]

The free stressed vowels of Latin were modified in the following manner:

$$\bar{\imath} > i \qquad\qquad\qquad \bar{u} > u$$

$$\left.\begin{matrix}\breve{\imath}\\ \bar{e}\end{matrix}\right\} > e \qquad\qquad \left.\begin{matrix}\breve{u}\\ \bar{o}\end{matrix}\right\} > o$$

$$\left.\begin{matrix}\breve{e}\\ ai > \bar{\varepsilon}\end{matrix}\right\} > \varepsilon \qquad\qquad \breve{o} > \mathit{ɔ}$$

$$\breve{\bar{a}} > a$$

The result of the modifications outlined above was a new system for the free stressed vowels based on seven vowels and four degrees of aperture.

Differences in quality now underlie the vocalic organization, but the non-integrated long component /au/ remains as an unstable unit in the system around which further modifications were to occur. The continuing tendency towards reduction of /au/ to a low back vowel maintained a labile condition in the vocalic paradigm.[8]

Margin of tolerance

Diphthongization of the lower mid vowels /ɛ/ > /iɛ/ and /ɔ/ > /uɔ/ occurred in early Romance. This change is attributed to the small margin of tolerance between the mid vowels, and the tendency to reduce the diphthong /au/. The assumption underlying the notion of margin of tolerance is that the change from a system of three degrees of aperture to one of four degrees compresses the phonological space in which each vowel operates. Any vowel may fluctuate within a certain limited area, the limits being defined by the neighbouring vowels. If two vowels overlapped in any of their allophonic variations their distinctiveness would be lost in the environment in which this occurred. The back vowels would have been the first to undergo modification since they are closer together from an articulatory viewpoint. There is less distance between /a/ and /u/ than between /a/ and /i/.

The movement, inherent in Latin and early Romance, to reduce long phonological components continued to eliminate the last of the diphthongs, *ie*, /au/ moved towards /ɔ/.

To make room for this development, the vowels /ɔ/ and /o/ theoretically could have merged, or /ɔ/ and /au/ could have fallen together. Instead, merger was avoided and the vowels were kept distinct through vocalic differentiation in which the low mid vowel /ɔ/ > /uɔ/, effectively differentiating it from both /o/ and the developing /ɔ/ from /au/. This was followed by diphthongization of /ɛ/ > /iɛ/, possibly for reasons of vocalic symmetry in the form of an equipollent partner to /uɔ/, *ie* i:u = e:o = iɛ:uɔ, where /iɛ/ and /uɔ/ are correlative partners of the type

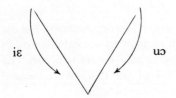

The system common to early general Romance was thus

Italian has remained at this stage of modification, while Spanish has continued a step further by changing /uɔ/ to /ue/. The latter change may be considered a kind of paradigmatic analogy motivated by subconscious aspects of linguistic economy towards less differentiation inasmuch as one feature is now utilized to distinguish the reflexes of the mid-open vowels, namely high front versus high back on-glides. The inhibition of this change in Italian must be sought in the interaction of dialectal structural and psycho-sociological factors. The present vocalic systems for Spanish and Italian reflect these developments:

Note that Spanish /iɛ/ and /uɛ/ and Italian /iɛ/ and /uɔ/ are often treated as combinations of vowel phonemes but historically they are different from juxtaposed vowels forming glides or diphthongs which stem from syntagmatic conditions in Latin, *eg : dies* > Spanish *día*, or from syntagmatic processes such as loss of a consonant which brought into contact formerly non-contiguous vowels, *eg*, Latin *bŏve* > Italian *bue*, Spanish *buey*; Latin *lēgāle* > Spanish *leal*, etc.

The diphthong /au/ reduced to /ɔ/ remained in Italian, *eg : causa* > Italian *cosa* /kɔza/ but merged with /o/ in Spanish *cosa* /kosa/. Note also that free stressed /ɛ/ did not always diphthongize in Italian, *eg : pĕde* > *piede* /piɛde/ but *bĕne* > *bene* /bɛne/. Another state of affairs existed in Gaul where the vocalic pattern of Vulgar Latin was radically modified, so that in its present form French shows little resemblance to Spanish or Italian.

Gallo-Roman vowels

External influence on the development of the French vocalic system cannot be discounted. The situation can be made more explicit, however, by an examination of how the system was affected in terms of the repercussions on the entire pattern caused by these influences and which led to a new system of structural arrangements.

Without going into detail of the history of vocalic development in French – a study more appropriate to a history of the French language – let us examine some of the structural highlights of free stressed vowels in the evolving Gallo-Roman system: Vulgar Latin /a/ was spoken with a frontal articulation in Gaul, often accredited to substratum (Celtic) influence, and underwent diphthongization forming a partnership with /au/, hence /ai/, /au/:

For example, Vulgar Latin /măre/ > (*/maire/?) Modern French *mer* /mɛɹ/, and /mănu/ > *main* /mɛ̃/. In Northern Gaul, the palatalization of /k/ > /č/ before /a/, eventually reducing to /š/, suggests a more frontal articulation of /a/ since /k/, while palatalizing before front vowels, did not palatalize before /a/ in other regions, *cf* Latin *cantāre* > Spanish *cantar*, Italian *cantare*, French *chanter* /šãte/.

The higher mid vocalic series also diphthongized in Gallo-Roman and became /ei/ and /ou/. The greater extent of diphthongization in Gaul compared to other Romance languages has been attributed generally to strong Frankish influence with its accompanying heavy stress accent. This diphthongization, however, can also be attributed to internal developments affecting the high mid vowels. Monophthongization of /ai/ (from /a/) > /æ/ > /ɛ/ and of /au/ > /ao/ > /ɔ/ tended to reduce the margin of tolerance between /o/, /uɔ/ and /ɔ/ in the back vocalic series and /e/, /iɛ/ and /ɛ/ in the front series. To become more distinct from each other /e/ > /ei/ and /o/ > /ou/, giving rise to the following system:[9]

The crowded situation in the back order was not sufficiently relieved and as /au/ became /ɔ/, the vowels were pushed upwards, forcing the high back vowel /u/ to palatalize to /ü/ in Old French, for example, /dūru/ > *dur* /dür/; /ūna/ > *une* /ünə/. This set up a pattern in French that would drag other vowels along into it. Back vowels, *eg*, /ou/ and /uɛ/ (< /uɔ/), moved towards the front rounded position proceeding along the lines established by /ü/ concentrating most of the vowels in the frontal region and leaving phonological holes in the back series, *cf* /fõcu/ > *feu* /fö/.

The overcrowded front positions and the absence of vowels in the back series led to a movement of front vowels towards the back, *viz* /mẽ/ > /moi/.

i   ü

┌──────────→ oi

ei   ö

   iɛ   ɔ̃

      ɛ

Compare the vocalic modifications among the following stages of French:

Vulgar Latin		*Gallo-Roman*		*Old French*		*Modern French*	
mē	/ē/	mei	/ei/	moi	/ei/ > /oi/ > /uɛ/	moi	/u̯ɛ/ > /wa/
pĕde	/ĕ/	piet	/iɛ/ > /ye/	pieθ	/ye/	pie	/ye/
nōdu	/ō/	nou	/o/ > /ou/	neu	/ou/ > /eu/ > /ö/	nœud	/ö/
bŏve	/ŏ/	buɔf	/uɔ/ > /ue/	buef	/ue/ > /ö/	bœuf	/ȫ/
māre	/ā/	*maire	/ai/ > /ɛ/	mer	/ɛ/	mer	/ɛ/
auru	/au/	ɔru	/ɔ/	or	/ɔ/	or	/ɔ/

Note that Latin ī > i and ū > u while i/ē, ŭ/ō and ă/a merge.

Besides the paradigmatic pressures that shape the changes in the system revolving around such factors as margin of tolerance between mid vowels, *eg*, e/ɛ and o/ɔ, symmetry in the system which appears to be responsible for the modification of the front vowel /ei/ > /oi/ and equipollence, a kind of pairing of phonological units, *eg*, ai/au, there are also a number of distributional (syntagmatic) limiting factors. Certain environmental situations inhibit modification: the change *sŏnu* /sonu/ to *son* /sõ/, for example, prevents /o/ before a nasal from becoming front rounded.[10] French vocalic changes reflect the high degree of modification a system may undergo in a relatively short period of history.[11]

Modern French vowels

Modifications in French, revolving around nasalization of prenasal vowels and the integration of unstressed vowels into a general vocalic system in which word stress is no longer relevant, leads to the vocalic design of Modern French. The various forces, both internal and external, that shaped the French language through two thousand years have radically altered the vocalic paradigm so that it bears little resemblance to Latin. Modifications are still occurring which are an extension of the structural processes that shaped the present system. (Vocalic arrangement I (Modern French) is tending towards system II.)

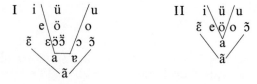

In some dialects, *eg*, Parisian French, /œ̃/ has merged with /ɛ̃/, *cf*:
un, while /ɔ̃/ and /ö/ have merged. This appears to reflect the small
functional load between these vowels as well as the crowded situation
or severe limitations on phonological space. There is, for example,
only one pair of lexical items distinguished by /ö/ and /ɔ̃/: *jeûne*
'fast', and *jeune* 'young'. Elsewhere they are simply relegated to
open and closed syllables. The functional difference between /e/ and
/ɛ/, as in the first person of the future and conditional tenses *je serai*,
je serais has not deterred their coalescence, at least in the areas where
the change has occurred. Similarly, in some words /o/ and /ɔ/ have
merged suggesting a general tendency to eliminate mid open vowels.
Similar forces are operative with regard to front and back articulation of /a/ which are again supported by few minimal pairs such as
patte /pat/ 'paw', and *pâte* /pɐt/ 'dough'. These changes are by no
means completely uniform. Some speakers may have merged some
vowels while maintaining a distinction among others. The distinctions in system I are often taught in schools and vary among dialects.
Nevertheless, the general pattern seems to indicate that system I is
being transformed into system II. The exact degree to which the
theoretical considerations outlined above operate as viable factors in
vocalic change is difficult to pin down. Similar motivating forces
appear to operate, however, among other vocalic systems in which
written documentation is available.

English vowel shift

Long vowels in Late Middle English may serve as another illustration of paradigmatic or functional-structural principles of language
change. The short vowel subsystem remained relatively stable affected primarily by syntagmatic events. The Middle English long
vowels, however, underwent a shift. They are commonly assumed to
have been

During the fifteenth century, the vowel shift in English raised all
long vowels with the exception of /ī/ and /ū/ which could not be

raised further and still remain vowels. They were diphthongized
into /ei/ and /ou/ to become /ai/ and /au/ subsequently. In most
cases, English spelling had been fixed before the shift, constituting
one of the main reasons for the divergence between orthography and
sound in Modern English. The shift may be represented as

Examples:

| | | | | Modern |
Middle English	Chaucer	Shakespeare	Present	Spelling
bite	/bītə/	/beit/	/bayt/	bite
bete	/bētə/	/bīt/	/biyt/	beet
bete	/bǣtə/ (or ɛ̄)	/bēt/	/biyt/	beat
abate	/a'bātə/	/ə'bǣt/	/ə'beyt/	abate
foul	/fūl/	/foul/	/fawl/	foul
fol	/fōl/	/fūl/	/fuwl/	fool
fole	/fɔ̄lə/	/fōl/	/fowl/	foal

The changes of a single vowel cannot be considered in isolation:
they are all part of a general movement which affects long vowels in
all environments, apart from a few syntagmatic restraints.[12]

The question confronting a structural approach to this shift must
deal with the problem of origin, or of the impetus which gave rise to
the movement. It can be considered primarily from two approaches:
(1) a *push* effect in which the lower vowels moving upwards dis-
lodged the high vowels, or (2) a *pull* effect where the high vowels,
having diphthongized, left vacancies in the system into which the
lower vowels were free to move.[13] One structural-functional account
relates the vocalic shift to the loss of /ī/ and /ū/ giving rise to a *pull*
chain effect. The loss of these high long front vowels is related to the
levelling of vocalic quantity (isochrony) and to the simplification of
geminates.[14]

Prior to the shift vocalic length began to disappear as a functional
opposition among vowels. Through syntagmatic processes long
vowels were relegated to open syllables and short vowels to closed

syllables.[15] All vowels except ī/ĭ and ū/ŭ were affected, resulting in a vocalic system as follows:

During this period the high vowels participated in an isolated opposition of quantity and as such were under pressure to eliminate length which was no longer functional except in these limited oppositions. /ī/ and /ĭ/, /ū/ and /ŭ/ did not fall together, perhaps inhibited in this direction by homonymic factors, nor were they regulated to predictable environments: instead /ī/ > /ei/ and /ū/ > /ou/, which eliminated vocalic length among pure vowels but maintained a distinction between them. The simplification of consonantal geminates reinstated functional vocalic length. Long vowels occurred in open syllables, *eg*, *āta*, and short vowels were found in closed or checked syllables, *eg*, *ătta*. The reduction of geminates passed to the vowels the burden of opposition, and length again became phonemic:

$$\frac{\text{āta}}{\text{ătta}} > \frac{\text{āta}}{\text{ăta}}$$

The mid long vowels were free to move into the holes left in the system which were vacated by /ī/ and /ū/ through the process of diphthongization,[16] for example:

$$[\ ] \diagdown \diagup [\ ]$$
$$\bar{e} \diagdown \diagup \bar{o}$$
$$\overline{æ} \diagdown / \bar{ɔ}$$
$$\bar{a}$$

The modern English vocalic system which no longer makes use of quantity as a functional characteristic reflects the earlier oppositions of long and short vowels. The short vowels were phonetically more open or more lax than long closed or tense vowels. They have remained as open /i/, /e/, /o/, /u/ and /a/ while the long vowels developed glides which helps to distinguish them from the open vowels, *ie*, /iy/, /uw/, /ey/, /ow/. The modern English vocalic system (for many but not all dialects) can be represented as follows:

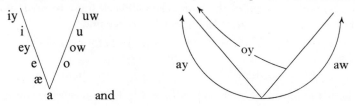

iy uw
i u
ey ow
e o
æ
a   and

ay   oy   aw

Latin consonants

As the preceding examples demonstrate, functional-structuralists are concerned with the relationship of language modification to the overall linguistic framework in which the modifications occur. The modification of consonants from Latin to Modern Spanish will further illustrate the notions underlying the relationships involved in internal paradigmatic change. Like the French vocalic system, Spanish consonants display a wide latitude of modification in one system over a relatively short time span. Only the core consonants are taken into consideration here except when they are directly influenced by non-core modifications.

The Latin consonantal system consisted of four orders: labial, dental, velar and labiovelar; and three series: voiceless occlusive, voiced occlusive and fricative (among core consonants):

core	p	t	k	kʷ
	b	d	g	(gʷ)
	f	s		(h)
non-core	m	n		
	l			
	r			

All the consonants, except labiovelars and /h/ could be geminated intervocalically; /h/ disappeared from the system early and /gʷ/ from P I E remained only after a velar nasal, *eg, inguen.*[17] Two major factors should be kept in mind with regard to the Latin consonantal system: long phonological components were in general in the process of reduction, *ie*, geminates and labiovelars; the consonantal pattern did not make economical use of the available distinctive features. The Latin fricatives were phonetically voiceless. Failure to extend fricativity and voice – features already in the system – to voiced fricatives resulted in an uneconomical arrangement. Latin also had fronted velar allophones conditioned by front vowels, *eg*, /y i e/; the reduction of the labiovelars allowed these fronted allophones to phonemicize.[18] In Vulgar Latin, we find

	[ts] before y, i, e		[dz] before y, i, e
/k/		/g/	
	[k] elsewhere		[g] elsewhere

The reduction of /kʷ/ > /k/ before /i/ and /e/ (as well as other vowels) opposed the frontal allophone [ts] to /k/ in these environments, and [ts] became /ć/. (/ć/ is used here as the phonemic symbol equivalent to phonetic [ts].) Compare:

(1) kʷi   >ki
(2) ki [tsi] > ći

Concurrent with these palatalizing events a new voiced fricative series of consonants began to form.[19] The allophone of /u/ (*ie* [w] in consonantal position), became a voiced labial fricative, *eg* :

	[u] vocalic position
/u/	
	[w] elsewhere > /v/ /wentum/ > /véntu/[20]

The new labial phoneme now formed a paradigmatic opposition among the labial order resulting in a new consonantal paradigm based on a quadratic system instead of the previous triadic pattern:

Classical Latin

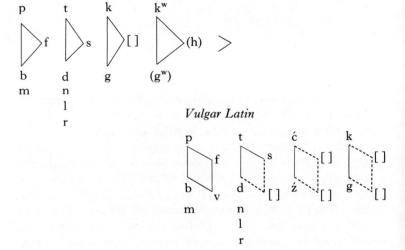

Vulgar Latin

The introduction of the voiced fricative series made more economical use of the distinctive features by extending fricativity and voice to include more phonemes, *eg*

p	labial	voiceless	occlusive	p	labial	voiceless	occlusive
b	labial	voiced	occlusive	b	labial	voiced	occlusive
f	labial		fricative	f	labial	voiceless	fricative
				v	labial	voiced	fricative

Further symmetry and efficiency would be achieved by extending the voiced fricative series throughout the remaining three orders, *ie*, dental, palatal and velar. The net result of such activity would be four orders and four series in the core system containing the maximum number of phonemes in relation to the phonemic correlations.[21] The holes in the phonological paradigm are characterized by a general condition of lability. Phonological modification revolved around these unstable holes since they were instrumental factors in the equilibrium of the system.

The general loss of quantity in Vulgar Latin affecting particularly Western Romance resulted in the reduction of long consonants or geminates. The geminates did not simply shorten and merge with their short counterparts, however, but maintained their functional capacity while changing their structure. Thus

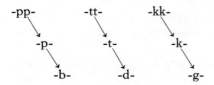

These changes involving geminate reduction and sonorization (*-p-* > *-b-* etc) are related processes, *eg*

Vulgar Latin		*Spanish*	
cŭppa	/pp/	copa	/p/
rīpa	/p/	riba	/b/
gŭtta	/tt/	gota	/t/
vīta	/t/	vida	/d/
văcca	/kk/	vaca	/k/
lăcu	/k/	lago	/g/

This chain of events continued in Spanish. The phoneme /d/ was

realized in intervocalic position as [ð], [kantáðo], but in some social dialects of Castilian the [ð] is lost, [kantáo], hence in these dialects -tt- > -t- > -d- > ø. The simplification of /-ss-/ to /-s-/, followed by the sonorization of /-s-/ to /-z-/, created a new phonemic partner for /s/; consequently the voiced fricative series was extended by filling the hole in the dental order. The equation $p : b : f : v = t : d : s : z$ is now balanced:

pāssu /ss/ > paso (Old Spanish /páso/) /s/
mēse /s/ > mes (Old Spanish /méze/) /z/

Further events of a paradigmatic and syntagmatic nature extended the palatal oppositions and forced a realignment of phonemes and orders. Syntagmatic changes gave rise to new phonemes: /-kt-/ > /-č-/ *nŏcte* /nókte/ > *noche* /nóče/; /-ks-/ > /-š-/ *lūxu* /luksu/ > *lujo* /lúšo/ (Modern Spanish /luxo/); but /-ll-/ > /-λ-/ while earlier /-λ-/ from /-lʸ-/ and /-kl-/ became /-ž-/, *cf* : *fŏlia* /folya/ > /fóλa/ > /foža/ (Modern Spanish *hoja* /óxa/). This change is part of the larger framework involving the reduction of long phonological elements in which the change from /-λ-/ to /-ž-/ appears to be prompted by the reduction of /-ll-/ to /-λ-/,[22] *ie*

/-ll-/ > /-λ-/
/-λ-/ (< -kl-, -lʸ-) > /-ž-/

The modification of /λ/ > /ž/, avoiding a merger with /λ/ from /ll/, appears to reflect a tendency to maintain a distinctive opposition between the sounds.

The medieval Castilian consonantal system appears as follows:

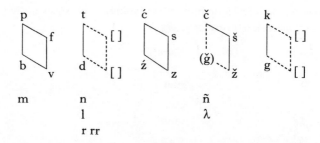

Not all internal and external factors are clear with regard to these developments and subsequent events, but the system under discussion from a structural view appears to have had little margin of tolerance in the overcrowded palatal area, to be asymmetrical in overall design (five orders and four series), and to display holes in the dental and velar regions marking areas of phonological imbalance. Further conditions for change may have also revolved around a low functional yield for some of the new palatal sounds. A number of phonological mergers occurred which ultimately reduced the number of palatal sounds and created new dental and velar oppositions.

These mergers revolved around the devoicing of the sibilants – a consonantal shift on a par with any major phonological change known so far. The phoneme /v/ merged with /b/ (orthographic inscriptions indicate confusion between these sounds from the earliest period of peninsular Romance), and the remaining voiced fricatives also disappeared, merging with their voiceless counterparts, ie, /z/ > /s/, /ž/ > /š/, effectively eliminating the voiced fricative series. Similarly /ź/ [dz] > /ć/ [ts] along with the loss of [ǧ],[23] thus reducing the overcrowded sibilants and affricates to /s/, /ć/, /č/ and /š/ through the loss of /z/, /ź/, /ǧ/ and /ž/. The elimination of the voiced/voiceless opposition among fricatives appears motivated by paradigmatic factors reflecting a small margin of tolerance between the numerous apicoalveolar and palatal sounds among which, at least according to medieval orthography, vacillation was fairly common.[24]

Perhaps more important from a theoretical point of view was the distribution of the voiced fricative phonemes which were relegated to intervocalic position. They were then not widely represented throughout the language and merger with their voiceless counterparts presented no major difficulties with homonymy. The very nature of the change is in itself a striking example of phonological modification that runs counter to expectations if only phonological environmental forces were at work. The development of the voiced fricatives generally via sonorization would not have been unusual, in that intervocalic position often has this effect, ie, voiceless sounds become voiced between voiced sounds. Devoicing in a voiced environment, however, was clearly not a matter of environmental influence. Several subsequent modifications in the core consonantal system leading to Modern Castilian also appear to represent unconditioned changes, ie, /ć/ > /θ/ and /š/ > /x/, the former a voiceless interdental fricative and the latter a voiceless velar fricative.

The modern Spanish consonantal system has changed considerably from its medieval form and can be presented schematically as follows:

```
p   t   č   k
b   d   y   g
f   θ   s   x

m   n   ñ
    l   λ
    r
    rr
```

Only the geminate /rr/ remains as a relic from Latin and represents in modern Spanish an isolated opposition of quantity which in some dialects is being lost by the modification of /rr/ to /ž/, *eg*, [pérro] > [péžo] 'dog'. /y/ came from various sources such as /d/ plus yod, *eg*, *rădiu > rayo*, and is in some areas becoming /ž/ or /ǧ/, *eg*, [yo] > [žo]~[džo]. The latter sound would form an equipollent partner to /č/ and act as a more integrated member of the paradigm than does /y/.

The development of /θ/ and /x/ in Spanish reflects related events and points to what appears to be another structural principle of modification. Allophones of any phoneme are unidimensional, *ie*, viewed from the point of reference of a chart of articulation, they occur on the vertical or horizontal axis but not diagonally. They may be contiguous or non-contiguous but they seldom differ from the phoneme to which they are associated by both place and manner of articulation at the same time. Since sound change involves changes in allophonic status, then sound modifications occur along one axis at a time. This being the case, /ć/ could not have become /θ/ directly.[25] The direction a sound shift takes, however, is not always clear from the result. Latin *cantāre* became French *chanter* /šãte/, but the actual process could have occurred in two ways:

```
k        tš←k
↓         ↓
š←x       š
```

The sound [x] could be an allophone of /k/ as could [tš]. The fact that the change passed through the stage [tš] is clear from the written records of Middle English which borrowed words such as *chaunt* from Old French.[26] The change of /ć/ to /θ/ occurring late in Spanish did not pass through the stage /t/ or it would have merged with /t/

which was already in the system. Instead, the modification must have proceeded as follows:

```
p   t   ć          č   k
b   d   ↓              g
f   [ ]←[ṣ]   →s→š→[ ]
```

/ć/ developed an allophone in the vicinity of /s/. The close proximity of these sounds, including /š/, forced a separation, with /s/ moving into the back palatal region and aligning with /č/. This in turn pushed /š/ into the velar region to become /x/. The phoneme /ć/ (phonetically [ts]), became /ṣ/ when the occlusive element was lost in all environments. Being the only representative of its order and under pressure to move away from /s/, it aligned with the dental order to become /θ/.[27] Other Romance languages followed a different course of consonantal change.

French consonants

In the French core consonantal system, the voiced fricatives (the result of palatalization and sonorization) remained. The palatalization of /k/ and /g/ before /a/ gave rise to /č/ and /ǧ/ which subsequently lost the occlusive element, *cf* Latin *cārum* > French *chier* /čiɛr/ > Modern French *chère* /šɛɾ/ and *gamba* > /ǧambə/ > *jambe* /žãb/. The affricates /ć/ and /ź/ merged with /s/ and /z/ respectively (*eg, centum* > /ćentu/ > *cent* /sã/) culminating in Modern French.

Old French				>	Modern French			
p	t	ć	č	k	p	t	[ ]	k
b	d	ź	ǧ	g	b	d	[ ]	g
f	[ ]	s	š	[ ]	f	s	š	[ ]
v	[ ]	z	ž	[ ]	v	z	ž	[ ]

In French, as in Spanish, the main developments in the consonantal system occurred in relation to the palatals. During the growth of the standard Romance languages these sounds were more subject to modification than the other core sounds. Distributionally they were not as widespread and statistically they were not as well represented in the language since, among other things, they were not reinforced by the simplification of geminates.

Italian consonants

Standard Italian has remained more conservative than French or

Spanish with regard to phonological change:

Modern Italian

```
p  t  ć  č  k
b  d  ź  ğ  g
f  []  s  š  []
v  []  z  []  []
```

While it has appeared to some scholars that the language more closely associated with the geographical area of the proto-language of a given group of languages reflects the proto-form more than the other offshoots (Lithuanian appears to resemble Proto-Indo-European more than most of its descendants), such a position is not always tenable, especially on all levels of language. French, for example, could be said to be morphologically more conservative than Spanish or Italian in the Middle Ages by retaining a two-case system. Modern Romanian still retains a case system which has not existed in Italian since the period of the break-up of the languages.

The core consonants of Modern Standard Italian have undergone a good deal of modification in specific environments, *eg*, /sk/ > /š/, /kt/ > /tt/, but the overall system remains closer to Vulgar Latin than French or Spanish. Marked phonological differences do, however, characterize Italian. The loss of final /-s/ (which occurred also in French) had a profound effect on the morphological system of Italian and is taken up in the chapter on morphology. Some geminates were retained while others were created through assimilation of consonant clusters, *eg* /nókte/ > /nótte/. The somewhat sporadic nature of sonorization in Italian, compared to its regularity in Spanish and French, left a functional difference between geminate and nongeminate consonants.

English consonants

Changes in the English consonantal design since the period of Old English have led to a more economical use of distinctive features through the creation of a voiced fricative series among the core consonants.

Early Old English			>	*Middle English*				>	*Modern English*			
p	t	k		p	t	č	k		p	t	č	k
b	d	g		b	d	ğ	g		b	d	ğ	g
f	θ	s	x	f	θ	s	š	x	f	θ	s	š
				v	ð	z			v	ð	z	ž

The appearance of a voiced fricative series was structurally favoured. No new distinctive features were needed to distinguish the new phonemes. Similarly, a palatal order arose unhindered by the Old English system. While paradigmatic factors may govern the direction of modification, many of the actual changes were carried out through phonological processes under specific syntagmatic conditions. The phonemes /č/ and /ǧ/ were the result of palatalization of the velars in the environment of front vowels. The appearance of /š/ resulted from palatalization and reduction of the cluster /sk/. Voiced fricatives developed from voiceless fricatives in intervocalic position and present-day English shows this alternation in forms such as *wife/wives*. In Middle English the voiceless velar fricative /x/ was modified in some words and disappeared in others, and the voiced palatal fricative /ž/ appears to represent both a direct borrowing from French, *eg*, *beige*, and the palatalization of /z/ before /y/ in words borrowed earlier, *eg*, *vision*.

The voiced fricative series which developed during the Middle English period corresponds to a period of strong French influence on English. The Norman French sounds, *eg*, /v/, /ð/ and /z/ may well have reinforced the evolving voiced fricatives through borrowings which acted as models for English speakers.

Phonological arrangements

The manner of presentation of phonemes may clarify or obscure the dynamic realities of a phonemic system. A phonemic inventory should clearly indicate the relationships which function within the phonological framework of the language in question. These relationships, based upon opposition of distinctive features, are in a functional-structural view essential for understanding the motivation behind change. The phonemes which are found among the major correlations in English, *ie*, voiced/voicelessness and occlusive/fricative, have been described schematically as follows overleaf.[28]

This description is based upon phonetic criteria, however, that obscure the phonemic facts. The whole notion of balance and economy within the system is virtually ignored. The chart contains more holes than phonemes, making it difficult to establish any meaningful equations extending throughout the entire paradigm.

The difficulty here is, first, that affrication – a phonetic feature – does not represent a minimal distinctive feature. The phonemes /č/ and /ǧ/ participate (as do the other phonemes in the above inventory)

		labial	labio- dental	apico- dental	apico- alveolar	frontal- palatal	dorso- velar
occlusive	vls vd	p b			t d		k g
affricate	vls vd				č ǧ		
fricative	vls vd		f v	θ ð			
sibilant	vls vd				s z	š ž	

in the major correlations of voice versus voiceless and occlusive versus fricative. They are opposed to the occlusives (*eg*, /t/ and /d/) by virtue of their distinctive place of articulation, *ie*, the palatal zone, and to the palatal fricatives (*eg*, /š/ and /ž/) by virtue of their manner of articulation, or occlusivity. An equation can now be drawn to express more realistically the equipollent nature of the phonemes, as well as their greater economy in terms of distinctive features.

$$p:b=t:d=č:ǧ=k:g$$

From a slightly different point of view, these proportions can be based on the existence of an archiphoneme and a minimal distinctive difference.

distinctive feature	p labial	t alveolar	č palatal	k velar
archiphoneme		voiceless non-nasal occlusive		

Second, and in a similar manner, the distinctive feature of /f/ and /v/ is not labiodentality but fricativity. They are phonemically labial fricatives opposed to the labial occlusives (*eg*, /p/ and /b/), by their fricative nature and not by their place of articulation (labiodental position). They oppose /θ/ and /ð/ by virtue of their labiality. The latter may represent the same relationship to /t/ and /d/ as /f/ and /v/ to /p/ and /b/. That is to say, they are not phonemically apicodentals but alveolars. Their place of articulation as apicodentals is a phonetic characteristic as is labiodentality for /f/ and /v/. The phonemic relationship of these consonants can be equated as follows:

$$p:b=f:v=t:d=\theta:\eth$$

The apicoalveolar sibilants /s/ and /z/ and the frontal-palatal sibilants /š/ and /ž/ can be divided into two palatal types – hissing and hushing – both of which are fricatives. Since the fricative counterparts of /t/ and /d/ are /θ/ and /ð/, and those of /č/ and /ǧ/ are /š/ and /ž/, the fricative phonemes /s/ and /z/ have no occlusive partnerships – that is, */ć/ and */ź/ do not exist. Similarly, there are no fricative partnerships for /k/ and /g/ since */x/ and */γ/ do not occur.

Diagrammed according to the above arrangements, the English phonemic inventory would appear as follows:[29]

		labial	dental	hissing	hushing	velar
occlusive	vls	p	t		č	k
	vd	b	d		ǧ	g
fricative	vls	f	θ	s	š	
	vd	v	ð	z	ž	

The four holes in the system reveal the lack of */ć/, */ź/, */x/, and */γ/. The phonemes extended throughout the major correlations in a close-knit unity of oppositions reveal an economy not evident in phonetic descriptions. The holes in the consonantal paradigm are potential centres of gravity around which phonological modifications are likely to revolve.[30]

Economy and redundancy

The relationship between phonological features and the number of phonemes is an important consideration in dealing with language modification. From a paradigmatic point of view, the most economical system entails a minimum number of features to express a maximum number of phonemes. This notion can perhaps be made clearer from another point of view. Based on a binary acoustic ap-

proach, four features will distinguish a maximum of sixteen phonemes, three features will distinguish a maximum of eight phonemes,
etc. Given x phonemes and all binary features, the fewest number of
features needed to distinguish x can be stated as Log_2^x. Conversely,
given x features, the maximum number of phonemes distinguished
will be 2^x.

Paradigmatic relationships between phonemes do not show maximum economy. Some redundant features are present to counteract
the effect of noise which may originate in the articulation of the
speaker or from external sources which affect the listener. These
redundant features may take the form of distinctive features if the
ordinary distinctive features are neutralized through noise, eg, the
loss of the feature voiceless/voiced in English, which distinguishes
/p-/ and /b-/ may be compensated for by aspiration of the /p-/, [pʰ-].
Given x phonemes the maximum number of features is $x - 1$. This
would be a highly redundant system. Conversely, given x features
the minimum number of phonemes would be $x + 1$. No language
shows maximum economy or maximum redundancy. If redundancy
is very high, speakers and listeners are doing more work than is necessary for intelligibility. If redundancy is very low some difficulties of
communication will arise through noise interference. Modification
of a phonological system must reflect these two contending pressures, maintaining a balance between them, so that the greater displacement from a neutral position will entail a greater restoring
force.

As redundancy increases speakers may become less careful in
articulation, giving rise to notions about laws of least effort, and
indolence.[31] When redundancy is too high, coalescence of phonologically similar units may easily occur. Utterances are then distinguished by fewer phonological units. This decreases the redundancy
to a point where channel noise becomes a problem and a correcting
force moves the system towards higher redundancy. To restore
balance there are many specific phonological adjustments.[32]

Notes

1 This and the generalizations following represent a view taken by Greenberg,
 Osgood and Saporta. They are stated in Osgood and Sebeok, p 148.
2 See Hoenigswald (1963), pp 44–45.
3 These statements imply probabilities and require much more statistical information to make them explicit.
4 See Martinet (1952) for a discussion of the role of function and structure in sound

change. For a description of paradigmatic and syntagmatic relations, see Lyons (1968), *pp* 70–81.

5 See Buck, *p* 78.

6 For a functional-structural treatment of diphthongs in early Romance, see Romeo.

7 Checked position acted as an inhibiting factor which generally prevented the diphthongization of stressed vowels except in Spanish.

8 For a detailed structural treatment of the shift from the Latin vocalic system to Vulgar Latin, see Haudricourt and Juilland. See also Spence and Romeo.

9 Margin of tolerance can perhaps be equated analogically with the molecular arrangements of physical matter. Sounds, like air molecules, maintain a certain distance between them. If air is compressed or rarefied, all the molecules adjust to the situation. Unlike air molecules, sounds sometimes merge. In both cases, however, space is important to maintain identity. See Denes and Pinson. For measurements of the relative distance between vowels in the front and back series, see Haudricourt and Juilland, *p* 22 and Romeo, *pp* 67–76.

10 For syntagmatic environments effecting phonological modification, see Pope, *pp* 236–255.

11 The following words from the Romance languages illustrate the general vocalic changes discussed above:

	Vulgar Latin	Italian	Spanish	Old French	Modern French	Portuguese	
ă	máre	mare	mar	mer	mer	mar	sea
ĕ	péde	piede	pie	piet	pied	pe	foot
æ	célo	cielo	cielo	ciel	ciel	ceu	sky
ĭ	féde	fede	fe	feit	foi	fe	faith
ē	mé	me	me	mei	moi	me	me
ī	víta	vita	vida	vide	vie	vida	life
ŏ	nóvu	nuovo	nuevo	nuef	neuf	novo	new
ō	óra	ora	hora	oure	heure	hora	hour
ū	dúru	duro	duro	dur	dur	duro	hard
au	aúru	oro	oro	or	or	ouro	gold
ŭ	gótta	gotta	gota	gota	goutte	gota	drop
ā	cláve	chiave	llave	clef	clef, clé	chave	key

See Boyd Bowman for more examples. For development in Modern French, see Pulgram (1967). For the basic vocalic system of these and other Romance languages, see Hammerström. Note that Italian /ε/ and /iε/, /ɔ/ and /uɔ/ appear to reflect dialectal mixing to the extent that the regularity of the changes /ĕ > iε/ etc is somewhat obscure.

12 See Jespersen (1949), *p* 232. Some variation may be the result of dialectal borrowings, *eg*, /ū/ did not always diphthongize in the northern dialects; Scotland and Northumberland show [hūs] for 'house'.

13 *Ibid*, *pp* 237–238.

14 Jespersen (1949), *pp* 232–233 takes the view that *i > ei* first. The vowel /a/ was the last to shift according to the description of a contemporary, Hart, in 1569. See Jespersen, *op cit*, *pp* 233, 245. For the concept of a *drag* chain, see Martinet (1952).

15 See Martinet (1955), *pp* 241–256 for this approach to the problem of the English vowel shift.

16 This process appears to have begun as early as AD 1000 in Old English. For a more comprehensive treatment of these notions underlying the great vowel shift, see Martinet (1955), *pp* 248–256. For a generative view of this change, see Chomsky and Halle, *pp* 249–289.

17 'H was weak and uncertain at all times in Latin, being doubtless little or nothing more than a breathed on-glide.' 'Grammarians say that H is not a letter but a mark of aspiration.' 'Latin H was surely very feeble and often silent during the Republic.' Grandgent, *p* 106. For the status of /gʷ/ in Latin see Palmer, *p* 227.

18 Both /kʷ/ and /gʷ/ became velars /k/ and /g/ in Latin. /gʷ/ > /g/ before /r/ and /l/ but in other cases became /u/ as in *venio*. The frontal allophone of /g/ appears to have palatalized first, suggesting that /gʷ/ was the first to reduce.

19 No exact chronologies have been established with regard to these changes, but Grandgent, *p* 135 states: 'The letter v was doubtless pronounced w; but, losing its velar element, the sound was reduced, probably early in the Empire, to the bilabial fricative β.' On *p* 109 he states: 'Before the front vowels e and i the velar stops k and g were drawn forward, early in the Empire or before, into a medio-palatal position. . . .'

20 The counterpart to /u/, *ie*, /i/ [y] in consonantal position, became /ź/.

21 The core system pertains to those phonemes that participate in the major phonemic oppositions. It has to be defined for each language. In English, for example, the oppositions of voiced/voiceless and occlusive/fricative contain the core phonemes as opposed to the non-core phonemes, *eg*, /l/, /r/, /h/, which participate in isolated oppositions. See Dorfman.

22 See Alarcos Llorach, *p* 262.

23 There is some question about the status of the sound [ǧ] in this arrangement; however, this problem need not interfere with the general theoretical framework. If [ǧ] had phonemic status or was simply an allophone of /ž/ the result was still /ǧ > ž > š/.

24 See Alarcos Llorach, *p* 266.

25 The brief sketch of the history of Spanish consonants was chosen to illustrate the theoretical notions contained in the structural-functional view of language change. For a more detailed and somewhat different account of structural events in the history of Spanish phonology, see Alarcos Llorach.

26 These concepts of allophonic range and variation and their value to historical studies were first put forth by Austin.

27 The above is only a general view of the forces at work in this change. For a feature analysis of this modification, see Harris.

28 Francis, *pp* 129–133. Gleason, *p* 24, presents the phonemes of English in a similar manner. He places the affricates, however, in an alveopalatal order.

29 For a contrary point of view, see Hughes, *p* 248.

30 There is some question, however, about the natural relationship of /t d/ to /θ ð/ or /s z/. Whether or not one or the other constitutes a homo-organic order would be relevant to the description. The hole for */ć/ however does appear to contain allophonic variants of /s/ occurring after nasals, *cf* [ts] in *mince, fence*, etc.

Studies of language change can help to answer this question which will again be considered in Chapter 11 under the Transformational Model.

31 For this suggestion and others, see Hockett (1966).

32 Hockett, *loc cit.*

Chapter 8

Morphological and syntactic change

As in phonological descriptions of change, there are a number of labels to distinguish the various types or processes of morphological change. A good deal of morphological modification appears to follow from phonological processes but this does not preclude the possibility that morphological considerations inhibit and direct phonological change.

The notion of morphology, however, is a structural concept and can supply only part of an explanation of the inception and nature of language change. Morphological structure appears partially responsible for events occurring among lower-level linguistic units; the causes of these events must be sought at the point of intersection between these levels. Included in this chapter are further considerations of change governed by morphological constraints (see also Chapter 6).

The structural details of morphological change relate to the particular language under consideration; nevertheless generalizations can be made which reflect the patterns of morphological processes as the following passage indicates:

Historical linguistics is full of cases in which a replacement (or generally a correspondence) relation exists between physically very dissimilar elements. French ('F') *le cheval* 'the horse' is one of the replacements for Latin ('Lat.') *equus*; the Indo-European phoneme sequence *#dw-* is replaced by Armenian #erk-; and so on. Nevertheless, some kind of affinity or resemblance often prevails, and, once the separate nature of the question is clearly understood, it is a matter of interest to investigate those affinities. The two chief criteria for the treatment of linguistic change are, then, (1) the REPLACEMENT PATTERN (*eg*, no replacement – as in amorphous change; one-to-one replacement; two-to-one replacement or merger; one-to-two replacement or split) and (2) the AFFINITY which exists between the phones and morphs figuring in the replacement process (*eg*, phonetic similarity in phones, phonemic identity in morphs, increase or decrease in the number of segments). This latter investigation leads frequently (3) to a consideration of the SOURCE for the replacement (*eg*, borrowing versus redistribution of available morphs or 'semantic change'). Finally, (4) there are those larger traits characteristic of changing languages and of speech communities affected by change which seem to have a bearing upon the PREDICTABILITY of change. All these factors also enter into the procedures used for reconstruction. Owing to the incompleteness of our knowledge of the small-scale processes involved, these various criteria tend to stand out against one another all too sharply; the replacement pattern and the affinities obtaining between replaced and replacing segments then appear as properties of the 'gross results' of change, seemingly amenable to formal statement, while the remainder may be open only to extrapolation from such observation as has been reported – not to mention the countless extralinguistic factors which are part of the picture.[1]

From a structural point of view, any of the influences in column A may lead to morphological processes in column B.

A	B
sound change	no split or merger
semantic change	split
analogy	merger
borrowing	
invention	

To column B can be added another process (a kind of amorphous change) in which the resultant morphological form is prompted by the physical and social environment. This relates to either borrowing or invention. A few examples will make clear the relationships between columns A and B. Sound change may lead to no split or merger: English /knɒt/ > /nɒt/ *knot*. On the other hand, morphological split may occur through sound change when doublets arise, *cf* English *person* and *parson* (see Chapter 9) while merger through sound change may result in a 'falling together' of once differentiated forms, *cf* Latin *porta* and *portam* > Spanish *puerta*. When Spanish *tío* replaced both Latin *patruus* and *avunculus*, morphemic merger occurred through borrowing.[2] If in some contexts a morpheme comes to mean one thing and something else in a different context, a case of morphological split has occurred prompted by semantic change. Such changes may be brought about by analogical creations leading to metaphors.

Certain factors govern the manner in which set A will occur. Part of the goal of historical linguistics is to determine the forces that give rise to the types of change listed in A while more specifically historical morphology is concerned with the affinities that exist between these changes and the morphological processes in B. These affinities are then to be explained in terms of some field of reference, *eg*, structural, social, psychological, etc. Over substantial periods of time morphological changes (as in column B) cluster around grammatical categories (nouns, verbs, articles, etc) and give to the language a certain directional bias.

Direction of change
Analysis

Continued change towards analysis results in the separation of linguistic signs into independent units. A trend in this direction presupposes an increase in the use of prepositions, articles, pronouns and auxiliaries, *cf* the analytic nature of English *we shall have loved* to the more synthetic construction of Latin *amāverimus*, ie, *amā-v-eri-mus*, and *I will love*, *amābō*, ie, *amā-b-ō*.

In Vulgar Latin analytic constructions arose through the use of auxiliary forms in conjunction with the infinitive to designate the future tense. The Latin future, for example, *amābō* was replaced by *amáre hábeo* employing the first person of the verb *habēre*.

Analytical developments are by no means confined to the Romance languages. The obligatory use of pronouns in English is an example of analysis resulting from the obliteration of person markers within the desinences or grammatical endings of the verbal system.

drīfan			
ic drīfe	'I drive'	wē drīfað	'we drive'
dū drīfst	'you drive'	gē drīfað	'you drive'
hē drīfð	'he drives'	hīe drīfað	'they drive'

Pronouns were used in Old English. The system was already showing ambiguity in the plural without them. That they were not needed
at an earlier period is evidenced by other Indo-European languages,
cf Latin:

amāre 'love'
amō   amāmus
amās   amātis
amat   amant

In French, pronouns are obligatory, for example, j'aime /žɛm/,
tu aimes /tüɛm/, *il aime* /ilɛm/, while the verbal paradigms (except
forms such as *nous aimons, vous aimez*) are in general not marked for
person. Spanish and Italian, on the other hand, maintain an optional
pronominal system in connection with verbal forms. The verbal
paradigms in both languages display person markers, *cf* Spanish
(*yo*) *amo, (tu) amas, (él) ama*; Italian (*io*) *amo, (tu) ami, (egli) ama.*
The obligatory use of subject pronouns in verbal constructions
seems to have been partly brought about by the loss or neutralization
of person markers in the verbal paradigm. In languages where subject pronouns are optional, they perform the function of resolving
ambiguity in cases where the context is not always apparent. In
Spanish, for example, the first and third persons of the verbs are
identical in the imperfect tense, (*yo*) *amaba, (él) amaba*. In such
cases subject pronouns may resolve potential difficulties in communication.

Further analytic developments in the Romance languages can be
seen in the history of nominal forms of French.

Latin singular
nominative mūrus   > mur(o)s > murs
accusative mūrum   > mur(o) > mur
genitive   mūrī   > mur(i)
dative   mūrō   > mur(o)
ablative   mūrō   > mur(o)

Latin plural
nominative mūrī   > mur(i) > mur
accusative mūrōs   > mur(o)s > murs
genitive   mūrōrum   > muroru
dative   mūrīs   > mur(i)s
ablative   mūrīs   > mur(i)s

Old French retained a two-case system as a reflex of the earlier Latin cases, *ie*, a nominative and a non-nominative or oblique case:

Old French
singular		*plural*
nominative	murs	mur
oblique	mur	murs

Italian forms generally come from the nominative, *mūrus > múros > muro*, in the singular and *muri* from Latin *mūri* in the plural. Spanish derives its forms from the accusative, *mūrum > muro* and *mūrōs > muros*. No ambiguity in these languages arises through the merger of morphological forms. Nevertheless, like French, these languages developed a definite article from the Latin demonstrative pronoun *ille*. The tendency to use *ille* in this manner, then, seems to go back in time to a common period of the languages in question, that is, to a period prior to differentiation.

In Old French the article is used to differentiate case and number, but it would be incorrect to assume that the article arose in Old French to distinguish these morphological oppositions after the ravages of phonological change led to an ambiguous situation, since it occurred in the other Romance languages also. Instead, the loss of final vowels which resulted in the two-case system could occur because no ambiguity would result; that is, another morphological signal made them redundant – the appearance of the article.

The strong stress habits of the Franks may well have precipitated the phonological events which led to the loss of unstressed vowels and obliterated case distinctions in this region of the Roman Empire, but there is reason to suspect that these events were guided by higher-level restraints in the linguistic system.

The definite article unfolded from the demonstrative pronoun in the following manner:

SINGULAR	masculine	*nominative*	ille	> (illi)[3]	> li
		accusative	illum	> illu	> lo/le
	feminine	*nominative*	illa	> illa	> la
		accusative	illam	> illa	> la
PLURAL	masculine	*nominative*	illī	> illi	> li
		accusative	illōs	> illos	> los/les
	feminine	*nominative*	illae	> ille	
		accusative	illās	> illas	> *las/les

This development gave rise to syntactic markers for nouns in Old French as well as paradigmatic signals which could carry relevant information to distinguish case and number, *eg*

	singular	*plural*
nominative	li murs	li mur
oblique	lo/le mur	los/les murs

The Modern French forms *le mur* /lə müʀ/ and *les murs* /le müʀ/ are the result of further reduction of the case system in which the nominative and oblique distinction was lost and final -*s* disappeared.

The notion that phonological change does not proceed in a manner entirely independent of higher-level considerations can be further

Vulgar Latin	*Spanish*			*French*		
	article	*object pronoun*	*subject pronoun*	*article*	*object pronoun*	*subject pronoun*
SINGULAR masculine ille				(Old		
nominative (illi)	el	le	él	French li)		il
accusative illum		lo		le	le	
feminine						
nominative illa	la		ella	la		elle
accusative illam		la			la	
PLURAL masculine				(Old		
nominative illī				French li)		il + s
accusative illōs	los	los	ellos	les	les	
feminine *nominative* illæ						
accusative illās	las	las	ellas	les	les	elles[4]

demonstrated by the behaviour of the Latin demonstrative pronoun with regard to its various reflexes. The form *ille* gave rise to the definite article, subject pronouns and object pronouns. As a third person subject pronoun the stress accent was retained on its original syllable; elsewhere it generally shifted to the second syllable, *cf* the reflexes of *ille* in Spanish and French.

In each case the unstressed portion of the demonstrative pronoun was lost but stress placement appears to have been governed by morphological and semantic considerations within the evolving analytic structures.

The change in morphological structure towards a more analytic-type language affected all the Latin grammatical categories in one way or another. Among the nouns the distinctions between subject and object and other categories formerly distinguished by case endings, were replaced by prepositions and more rigid word order. Apart from a few genitive survivals such as the names of the days of the week (*eg : martis* (diēs) > Spanish *martes*, French *mardi*) the five Latin nominal declensions were reduced to three terminations:

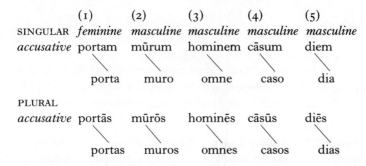

	(1)	(2)	(3)	(4)	(5)
SINGULAR	*feminine*	*masculine*	*masculine*	*masculine*	*masculine*
accusative	portam	mūrum	hominem	cāsum	diem
	porta	muro	omne	caso	dia
PLURAL					
accusative	portās	mūrōs	hominēs	cāsūs	diēs
	portas	muros	omnes	casos	dias

The Latin noun declensions retained the gender categories of masculine and feminine, with some shifts – for example, the masculine fifth declension noun *diem* moved to the first declension becoming feminine in form but retained the masculine article, for example, *el día* in Spanish. The neuter forms, however, mainly merged with the masculine types if they came from the singular, *eg, vinum > vino*, *vēlum > velo*, and with the feminine if they came from the plural, *eg, folia > hoja, vēla > vela*. Some neuter forms, *eg, corpora > cuerpos*, were remodelled by analogy with the masculine forms.

The grammatical category of number was preserved (in French mainly by devices other than the noun) and the accusative forms were generally the ones that persisted. The other five cases in Latin were either lost or they merged with the accusative.

Syntactic relations once described by case now were expressed by word order and prepositions, which in Vulgar Latin appear to have become generalized. In expressions such as *pro patriā mori* and *cum amicis deliberavi* the prepositions *pro* 'in the interest of ' and *cum* 'in the company of ' came to express the grammatical relationship that was previously carried by the noun case markers *-ā* and *-is*. The preposition *dē* took over the function of signalling genitive relationships in the Romance languages and through further generalization usurped the function of other prepositions, *eg*, *ā* or *ab* and *ex*. As case endings gave way to phonological modifications that tended to obscure their distinctive function, especially among the accusative and ablative singular, prepositions took on greater importance until all aspects of the declensional system were affected; compare, for examples, the same sentence in Latin and Spanish:[5]

Fīlium amicī in agrīs vidēmus
El hijo del amigo vemos en el campo

Synthesis
Linguistic forms become more synthetic in morphological structure as separate signs fuse into one linguistic unit. In Romance the synthetic future became analytic in construction and then synthetic once again. The combination of the infinitive with *habere* in Vulgar Latin developed into a fused unit through syncopation of unstressed vowels:

Latin	Vulgar Latin	Spanish	French	Italian
amabō	amáre hábeo >		j'aimerai	amerò
'I will love'	amar-ayo >	amaré	/žɛmɽe/	(< amarò)
dabō	dáre hábeo >		je donnerai	darò
'I will give'	dár-áyo >	daré	/žədɔnɽe/	

These new synthetic constructions for the future tense exist along with analytic constructions for the future:

French je vais aller
Spanish (yo) voy a ir   'I am going to go'
Italian (io) vado andare

In some Romance languages the conditional tense developed in a similar manner:

Vulgar Latin		Spanish	French
cantāre habēbam	>	cantaría	je chanterais

but in Italian

cantâre *hebuī (preterite of haber) > cantarei

The obligatory use of pronouns in French to distinguish person has led to some synthetic constructions in which first person pronoun and verb became one linguistic unit, eg, *j'aime, j'irai, j'ai*.

Drift
Modifications of a cyclic nature in language change are suggested by the available documentation. Languages pass from one general type to another as from a highly inflected type of language to an uninflected or analytic type. From an analytical structure they then tend towards a synthetic construction. Whether or not this is a natural or universal characteristic of language has not been established.[6] The consensus among linguists that no one language is a more effective instrument of communication than any other suggests that modification towards this or that type of system is not motivated by any abstract and ideal goal which reflects a more perfect language. The fact that both types of construction exist in the same language at the same time does not mean that eventually one will entirely replace the other. One may simply become predominant. The extent of dominance varies even in related languages with no necessary relationship to a time factor. Long term changes from synthetic to analytic constructions seem to follow parallel developments in different languages. In English, for example, particles, noun and verb morphology and syntactic relationships have evolved in much the same way as Romance structures. Old English possessed a fully inflected demonstrative paradigm surviving in Modern English as the definite article *the*, as a demonstrative *that*, and as a relative pronoun *that* :

	masculine	feminine	neuter	plural
nominative	sē	sēo	ðæt	ðā
genitive	ðæs	ðære	ðæs	ðāra
dative	ðǣm	ðære	ðǣm	ðǣm
accusative	ðone	ðā	ðæt	ðā[7]

The fact that these languages are related to a common source in the not too distant past presupposes some mutual restraints on their evolving structures. These restraints are at present not understood in relation to their underlying forms (see Chapter 11).

Within each language, however, certain specific characteristics prevail. Spoken French has favoured the use of the present perfect, *eg, j'ai vu* to express past action, disregarding the preterite *je vis*. The latter is confined to literary usage. Spanish, on the other hand, has maintained both tenses (*yo*) *he visto* and (*yo*) *ví* in ordinary speech. The allomorph /v/ in English which signals the perfect tense (*I've* versus *I have*) is often not heard in some forms of colloquial speech where the perfect and preterite tenses coalesce.

> I've walked
> ────────── > I walked
> I walked

but compare

> I've seen   > I seen
> I saw   > I saw

A continuation of this trend would lead to either the loss of the perfect or past tense, or to a new set of morphological relationships distinguishing the tenses at least in the irregular verbs. Note that the loss of /v/ does not occur in such constructions as *I've gone*. In German, another set of conditions tends to preserve the distinction:

> ich   sah
> ich   habe gesehen

The recorded histories of well-known languages such as the Indo-European languages are too brief to show any significant trends from synthetic constructions to analytic and back again.

Morphological differentiation
Phonological change may result in undifferentiated paradigmatic classes. Phonological levelling of this sort, however, may be offset by other phonological processes motivated by morphological differentiation:

Latin	Vulgar Latin[8]	Italian	Spanish	French
sum	soi (m)	sono	soy	je suis
es	es	sei (via seis)	eres	tu es
est	es(t)	è	es	il est

Differentiation of the second and third persons which fell together in some varieties of Vulgar Latin occurs in Spanish through borrowing *eres* from the Latin future tense. In French, differentiation is achieved by the general modification towards analysis resulting in the obligatory use of personal pronouns; and in Italian by analogy with the first person singular. The grammatical distinction between second and third persons in most other verbal paradigms was maintained and was in no danger of phonological levelling. Its obliteration in the verb *to be* then did not represent a general trend toward the elimination of this category. A good deal of ambiguity would have arisen in this high frequency verbal form, however, if differentiation had not occurred. In the following examples phonological environments may have been less relevant to the resulting forms than previously suspected.

Vulgar Latin	Spanish	French	Italian
cantáre hábeo	cantaré	je chanterai /žəšãtɼe/	cantarò
cantáre hábes	cantarás	tu chanteras /tüšãtɼa/	cantarai
cantáre hábet	cantará	il chantera /ilšãtɼa/	cantarà

A purely phonological interpretation of the resulting Romance forms from Vulgar Latin will not easily account for the differences among the languages nor for the differences in the paradigm of each language, *cf* Italian:

/ábeo/	> /ayo/ > /-o/
/ábes/	> /ays/ > /-ai/
/ábet/	> /ayt/ > /-a/[9]

Morphological differentiation of verbal endings in French was not a strong factor since the forms were distinguished by personal pronouns.

Analogy
Most examples of analogy occur once or perhaps several times in the speech of an individual and are then lost. Some cases of analogy persist, however, and diffuse throughout the speech community and become part of the language. Many analogical events can be considered sporadic insofar as their occurrence appears to be random, governed perhaps by individualistic psychological associations.[10]

Analogical restructurings may result from paradigmatic associations as in the example *sé > *sebo* ' *I know* '. The modification which sometimes occurs in Spanish among children may be influenced by the other forms in the paradigm (*sabes, sabe*). It may also be partially influenced by the subjunctive of the same verb *sepa, sepas, sepa*, etc or by association with another verbal paradigm, *tengo, tienes, tiene* – or all of these.

Form classes appear to be a factor influencing analogy but it is not always clear which particular lexical paradigms are involved or which are dominant, *cf* English:

help > help
holp > helped
holpen > helped

Such forms may have been remodelled on the basis of *walk, walked*.

Besides regularizing an existing pattern, new forms are sometimes created by analogy with forms already in the language, through back formation:

act:actor = sculpt:sculptor
write:writer = typewrite:typewriter

Analogical creations may sometimes originate a syntactic innovation, *eg, the king : the king's crown = the king of England : x*, where *x* becomes *the king of England's crown*.[11]

Analogy may result from anticipation of a following morphological marker in the syntagm. The plural ending /-e/ of German nouns may have been associated in some cases with the umlaut of the stem vowel, *eg, Gast* 'guest', *Gäste* 'guests', so that other lexical items without umlaut were influenced by this expectation habit and acquired it by analogy, *cf: Baum* 'tree', *Bäume* 'trees' from *Baume*.[12]

Analogical versus phonological pull

Phonologically regular developments result in irregular forms, while analogical regularizations result in phonologically irregular forms but regular paradigms.[13] Compare the following examples with respect to stressed and unstressed *a-*.

	Phonologically regular	Phonologically irregular
ámo	> aim	> aime
ámas	> aimes	> aimes
ámat	> aimet	> aime
amámus	> amons	> (aimons)
amátis	> amez	> (aimez)
ámant	> aiment	> aiment

In classical historical linguistics, sound change and analogical change are often regarded and sometimes even explicitly defined as opposing principles.[14]

Analogical extension occurs in several ways: a few forms – irregular in character – may show morphophonemic replacement in favour of the majority of regular forms; or a small number of morphemes may be extended over a much larger terrain and become the regular form. The Latin perfect /-u-/, as in *docuī, coluī, amāvī, audīvī, monuī, domuī*, while less frequent at an earlier period as a perfect marker, became the regular manner of forming this tense. The occurrence and subsequent spread of a morphological form replacing other more widely distributed forms must be governed by restrictions inherent in the particular language system.

The organization of the morphological system may to some extent condition the changes in morphological form. As the system expands or contracts on the semantic plane one would expect constant readjustments to occur on the phonological plane to maintain the formal differences that preserve the functional oppositions.[15]

In a language that expresses both tense and mood or tense and aspect, etc through grammatical signals, any new tense that develops in the language will theoretically conform to one axis or the other, depending on the formal relationships. The Latin morphological system is shown schematically as follows:

	ACTIVE		PASSIVE	
	indicative	*subjunctive*	*indicative*	*subjunctive*
present	amo	amem	amor	amer
imperfect	amabam	amarem	amabar	amarer
future	amabo	[ ]	amabor	[ ]
present perfect	amavi	amaverim	amatus sum	amatus sim
pluperfect	amaveram	amavissem	amatus eram	amatus essem
future perfect	amavero	[ ]	amatus ero	[ ]

The major formal paradigmatic characteristics of the system appear to lie along the vertical axis of tense, as indicated by the periphrastic constructions. As the system undergoes modification, and changes occur at the intersection of the two axes of tense and mood, the new emerging constructions would be modelled on the vertical axis. The evolution of the Romance languages seems to support these notions. New tenses and moods were shaped analogously by the overall pattern along the tense axis. Consider Spanish:

present	soy amado	'I am loved'	he amado	'I have loved'
past	era amado	'I was loved'	había amado	'I had loved'
future	seré amado	'I will be loved'	habré amado	'I will have loved'

Historical treatments of morphology have been primarily concerned with the origins, modification of phonological structure, and comparisons of morphological forms to other related languages. Attempts to account for the differences and similarities between forms in related languages necessarily led to concepts of change based upon notions of analogy, analysis, synthesis and the whole array of phonological factors. Implicit in these reasons for change is a relationship between various language elements, *ie*, that each language composes a system. The emphasis, however, has been on classifying and labelling the various types of change, first in phonology and then in morphology. A structural orientation toward morphological change demands some attention to the oppositions between morphological categories in both sound and meaning to determine the internal forces operating at any given time. How distinctions are identified phonetically seems little more important than how they function in relation to the overall morphological design.[16] In fact, there have been many probing investigations into the concepts concerned with economy of design and symmetry embedded in the phonological make-up of languages. The exploration of these principles extended to linguistic inquiries other than that of phonology (such as tense regulations, inflection, and syntax) have proved meagre indeed.[17]

In recent years there has been some attention to morphologically determined sound change. Changes in morphemic structure are no longer considered entirely the result of independent phonological processes. Motivation and direction of sound change appears to some extent to be governed by morphological conditions in a given language at a given time. Morphological categories, for example, may inhibit a sound change by checking or retarding it before it becomes general enough to affect all relevant morphemes. On the other hand, morphological relationships may also give impetus to changes in morphology which are carried out by phonological means. For example, in Gallo-Roman the present participle ending -*ant* of the first conjugation (< -*antem*, -*ando*) was generalized to the other conjugations, *eg*, Latin *vivent* > *vivant*. In Early Old French, *circa* tenth century, the association in assonance – sporadic at first, but gradually more frequent – of words other than present participles etymologically ending in *en* and *an* indicates that the change [ĕn] > [ãn], at first circumscribed to present participles, was being extended to the rest of the lexicon. That is to say, when the -*ant* type of present participle was generalized, there must have existed variants in -*ant* and -*ent* for the same stem, just as in Modern English certain speakers sometimes hesitate between *dove* and *dived*. Later the link was loosened between the category 'present participle' and the phonetic alternation [ĕn]/[ãn]; the change [ĕn] > [ãn] which had started within the verb paradigm but found favourable conditions in the phonological structure then spread to the remainder of the lexicon containing the relevant environments, *cf* Latin *tempus*, French *temps* [tã].[18]

How much phonological change is motivated by or, once begun, is inhibited by morphological considerations is a question of some magnitude. Further endeavours along these lines will reveal the various morphological conditions which affect phonological change but whether they play a major role or a somewhat minor role in the overall scheme of change is still an undecided issue. Linguistic structure on all levels (including the semantic, see Chapter 9), while a determinant of change, also interacts with features of the external environment. The extent and intensity of this interaction is at best difficult to pin down at any time let alone for periods of history in which many details can never be adequately recovered. Observations of language change in contemporary linguistic situations, however, help to determine the kinds of relations involved between linguistic structure and the external or social and cultural environment of the speakers.

Notes

1 From Hoenigswald (1960), *pp* 14–15.
2 For more examples as well as replacement patterns in morphological change, see Hoenigswald, *op cit, pp* 27–47.
3 About the second half of the sixth century, the masculine singular nominative *ille* was largely replaced by the form *illi*.
4 The above reflexes of the Latin demonstrative are simplified to the extent that

they do not represent stressed and unstressed syntactic object forms. The dative case which influenced French is not shown, etc. For details, see Elcock, *pp* 77–90.

5 For some syntactic changes from Latin to Spanish, taking into account Greek influence on Latin as well as spontaneous changes in Latin based upon redundancy rules and deep structure, see Lakoff, especially *pp* 218–235.

6 For a study of this problem in Indo-European languages, see Cowgill. Changes toward analysis in language structure have been known for some time. In the first decade of the nineteenth century, Friedrich von Schlegel examined this trend which is well illustrated by the Romance languages.

Previous synthetic languages from which the analytic types were derived were considered to be closer in structure to the original languages of man. They were seen to recede into the unknown past but to have reached their expressive climax at the dawn of history in the literature of the classical languages. This gave rise to value judgments in which the modern languages were considered degenerate forms of tie synthetic structures.

7 See Baugh, *p* 69. The development of English articles and demonstratives is not entirely clear. See Stevick (1968), *pp* 149–154 for further comments.

8 For variations on this paradigm in Vulgar Latin see Väänänen, *p* 147.

9 These changes may be viewed from different phonological angles, none of which seems entirely satisfactory.

10 Even if all analogical change were to be considered as sporadic change, this would not imply that all sporadic change is analogical. This issue has been somewhat confused by Postal, *p* 234.

11 For this and many other examples of analogy especially relating to children's speech, see Sturtevant, (1947b), *pp* 96–109.

12 For a structural treatment of analogy, see Kuryłowicz, who arrives at several generalizations about analogy in that it usually proceeds from a base form, *sputnik*, to a derived form, *sputniks*. A new analogical form takes over the primary function of a contrast while the replaced form is used for secondary functions, as in *brother/brothers* while *brethren* is relegated to a secondary role. These and other analogical processes described by Kuryłowicz represent an attempt to arrive at some universals underlying this type of change with regard to environments and function. Surface structure considerations, however, may not be enough to give many answers to questions relating to analogy.

13 See Dorfman.

14 See Sturtevant, *op cit*, *p* 109. Hoenigswald (1963), *p* 40 finds fault with this type of thinking and says:

> It is said that (conditioned) sound change creates 'irregular paradigms,' that is, morphophonemes, whereas analogic change serves to eliminate morphophonemic alternation. This is a tribute to one admittedly typical role assumed by those two forms of linguistic change; but it is also an exceedingly oblique approach to analogic change. Analogic change is essentially a replacement of one allomorph by another within the morpheme; and it is that quite regardless of possible morphophonemic consequences.

For example, as *shoon* > *shoes*, /-en/ becomes more restricted distributionally, and /-z/ more extended. But it is not true that this type of operation will inevitably favour one allomorph or a selection of allomorphs over all others, thereby minimizing irregular alternation and 'levelling' the paradigm. Analogical change has been known to create new allomorphs and to extend irregular (grammatically conditioned) allomorphs at the expense of their regular, phonemically conditioned competitors. English plurals /s/, /z/, /iz/ may have the advantage, but newly imported names of fish, *eg, muskellunge* are likely to receive the zero alternate seen in *trout*, *bass*, and *fish*.

Nor does sound change always increase alternation. If a sound change merges two alternating phonemes, reduction not increase in morphophonemic complexity will occur. The above paradigm, however, represents allomorphemic alternation between two stems,

$$\left\{ \text{aim-} \right\} \quad \begin{array}{l} \text{/am-/} \\ \text{/aim-/} \end{array}$$

which are the result of phonological change due to stress patterns. The replacement of /a/ by /ai/ is not a morphophonemic replacement but simply a phonemic replacement.

15 See Diver.
16 A study of content then is concerned only with the distinctions between morphological forms without regard to the particular phonetic means by which these distinctions are maintained. The more traditional approach was concerned primarily with the plane of expression. A third view (Diver, *pp* 43–44) is a synthesis of the two approaches.
17 See Malkiel, *p* 24.
18 For this view see Rochet. A counter view maintains that nasal vowels 'naturally' open, *ie*, lower for better perception (see Haudricourt, *p* 43). No such lowering has occurred in Portuguese, however, which maintains /ĩ ẽ ã õ ũ/ and has done so for many centuries (see Williams, *p* 70).

Chapter 9

Social and cultural influence on language change

The structure of a language appears to be continually influenced through the mechanism of imitation and hypercorrection. The intensity and geographical distribution of these mechanisms are related to social pressures both within and outside the speech community. They revolve around economic situations as well as prestige considerations based on non-economic values. When it is possible to assign a single social meaning to a linguistic feature, the propagation of this feature throughout the speech community is reflected in its social value. Varying social values, then, superimposed upon language structure, are partly responsible for dialectal differentiation which may ultimately lead – through social or geographical isolation – to different languages.

The origins of social motivations for change may be found within the speech community reflecting internal social situations or they may originate in the external environment such as neighbouring languages and dialects (see Chapter 5). In a number of words /ž/ was borrowed into English from French. The borrowings appear to be due to the prestigious position of French in England after the Norman conquest. It is evident that there is more involved in such borrowings than just social factors, since while /ž/ was borrowed, /ü/ was not. Linguistic borrowing is not radically different from other types of cultural borrowing inasmuch as some items or objects are accepted and others rejected by the borrowing culture. Any broad view of human behaviour must ultimately account for the rejection of cultural transference as well as for the transference itself. The intensity of the role of structural factors in language change, both internal and external, cannot be clearly delimited until social aspects have been adequately understood. Much of the so-called irregular change in language may be motivated and limited by social considerations. Changes restricted to single lexical forms such as Latin *venēnum* > Italian *veleno*, Spanish *veneno*, where dissimilation occurs in Italian but not in Spanish may reflect social phenomena not yet understood.

Internal lexical change (*ie*, development of new terms from within the language as opposed to lexical borrowings from foreign sources) corresponds to some extent to changes in social values within the society. This type of change often revolves around loss and addition of vocabulary items. Technical advancements in a society demand new designatory terms, many of which can be found in linguistics such as *hypercorrection, phoneme, allomorph,* etc. Changes in social outlook and manner of behaviour call for new terms such as *beatnik, peacenik, hippie*. Even new culinary arrangements demand new labels and in English they have come forth in the form of *cheeseburger, chiliburger, tomatoburger, mushroomburger,* etc. Apart from the designation *nik*, the new words are formed from existing forms within the language through a process of suffixation.[1]

As far as linguistic and cultural change can be shown to react to similar social pressures and psychological considerations both on an individual and collective basis, there is no reason to support the view that language change occurs at a constant rate even over long periods of time. A number of cultures have been (*eg* Japanese) or are (*eg* Masai) very conservative and even the smallest cultural changes are slow in coming. Others have undergone rapid cultural transformations.[2]

A recent study on the island of Martha's Vineyard investigated the frequency and distribution of phonetic variants of /ai/ and /au/ based upon regions of the island, age level, occupation, and ethnic group. The objectives were to correlate the linguistic pattern with parallel differences in social structure and thus to isolate the social factors that bear upon linguistic processes.[3]

Interaction of linguistic and social patterns

A poor economy on Martha's Vineyard causes some young people to leave the island for the mainland, and they model their speech habits on those of the mainland. Those people intending to remain conform to a centralization of /ai/ and /au/, which is most marked among the staunch defenders of the island's way of life who take pride in their differences of speech traits compared with those of outsiders. They once had a distinct whaling vocabulary which served this purpose, but now they rely upon phonetic differences. Parallel developments are found among residents who share their views and cut across ethnic differences, even though the various ethnic groups are not on good terms.

One group, then, has set the pattern; others who share their ideas imitate them. Those who are leaving, find their models elsewhere. The imitation of centralization appears to be a conscious event by an individual who has returned to the island and intends to remain.

In late Middle English the first element of the diphthong proceeding from the long vowel /i/ was a schwa, ie, /əi/. When the island was settled in 1642 this was the sound in words such as *right, wife, wine*. The diphthong /ai/, however, became general in New England and on the island, as revealed in the Linguistic Atlas of New England records (1933) which show only a few informants of the older generation with moderate centralization. Commonly heard on the island now are the centralized versions which are differentiating island speech from that of New England.

Social isolation has long been considered a prerequisite for language diversification. This has usually been studied in dialectal investigations with a view to geographical dislocation or social isolation of a minority group within a larger socially stratified environment. Social and psychological factors, however, are also considerations which lead to linguistic diversity without the benefit of isolation; they reflect internal stresses of the community in the form of a member's attitudes, ie, desires to be different or to gain recognition. On the basis of psychological motivations and perhaps to some extent perceptive innovations, speakers continually take advantage of their ability to use language in a novel way. Some of these innovations may be diffused throughout segments of the community, restricted in a large part to the social level in which they began.[4]

Dissemination of variations

Social influence is not easily determined for historical periods and must be reconstructed for past stages of languages by deductions from present-day observations of social influence as a factor in change.

Variation in speech may be introduced by any number of processes relating to anticipation and giving rise to assimilation, dissimilation, umlaut, etc or by analogy, borrowing, merger, split, contamination, etc. These variations begin in a word used by an individual and while most are simply linguistic events that do not recur, some are repeated and are imitated by others. They spread to the point where the new forms are in opposition to the older forms and at some subsequent time, one of the two forms will prevail at the expense of the other. When this has happened, regularity of change has been achieved. Before a linguistic feature can spread in this way, it is generally necessary for one of the rival forms to acquire some sort of prestige. It is usually influence from the standard dialect that causes one feature to be preferred to another. A case in point is the Andalusian dialect of southern Spain, where the sound /θ/ found in Castilian is lacking. The local speakers often insert the /θ/ for prestige purposes, especially when talking to people from outside the dialectal area. Since /θ/ corresponds distributionally to Andalusian /s/ in many lexical items, eg /θínko/ /sínko/ cinco 'five', natives of the region tend to hypercorrect and use /θ/ in distributional positions in which Castilian also has /s/, eg /si/ > /θi/ sí 'yes', and /señór/ > /θeñór/ señor 'sir'. In the course of time, the social balance of dialects may change with a subsequent change in the trend of linguistic diffusion. Under circumstances such as these a number of rival forms may continue for long periods of time and ultimately, if other conditions present themselves, the once-more homogeneous dialects may widen the gap between them. Lexical items in English undergoing present variation of this kind may be seen in the forms of roof, eg, /ruwf/, /ruf/.[5]

Structural constraints on socially motivated modifications appear to have been operative in the history of Spanish. The loss of morpheme final /-e/ and sometimes /-o/, characteristic of the Spanish of the twelfth and thirteenth centuries, exposed many new consonants and consonant clusters in morpheme final position. The written records of the period indicate that this loss occurred among the upper classes but the subsequent reintroduction of these morpheme final vowels, except after /l r n d s ć/, completed by the fifteenth century suggests that apocope did not affect the entire social hierarchy of the society. For prestige reasons the change appears to have influenced the upper classes, perhaps having been introduced from French, but was inhibited among the lower classes who, without recourse to sophisticated social influences, unconsciously modified

their speech habits in conformity with the syntagmatic and paradigmatic dynamics of the language. To the extent that this is the case,
their pronunciation differed from that of the upper classes who
temporarily allowed social considerations to override normal internal structural modifications.[6]

Throughout the history of Spanish the distinctive feature of
voiceless/voiced in morpheme and syllable final position has been
neutralized, resulting in both a lack of opposition in these environments and orthographic variants for some lexical items, *eg, paret/
pared* after the loss of /-e/.[7] This analogous behaviour of consonants
in syllable final and morpheme final environments reflects the
environmental similarity of these two positions. In general, only
those consonants found in one position were also found in the other,
cf : pan and *can-to.*[8]

Theoretically, apocope would have occurred first in words of the
following types:

```
pane  > pan  -n
cole  > col  -l
mese > mes  -s
```

where the loss of /-e/ resulted in no new final consonants but simply
extended the distribution of final /n l s/ to more lexical items:

```
en      > en
mel     > miel
minus > menos
```

The retention of /n l s/ in morpheme final position as well as the
resultant sounds from apocope, represented compatible final consonants whose distribution corresponded to syllable final position

```
canto
salsa
estar
```

Apocope further exposed in morpheme final position new occlusives
which had no etymological antecedents in this environment. They
were nevertheless compatible in the distributional system by virtue
of their occurrence in syllable final position after syncope; compare
for example, syllable final /d/ in *cadnado* from Latin *cat(e)natu*, and
/ż/ in *diezmo* from Latin *dec(i)mus*. Syllable final /r/ was etymologically present in *parte* from *partem*. New morpheme final consonants

corresponding to existing syllable final consonants were thus rendered compatible:[9]

Vulgar Latin	*Old Spanish*
parete	> pared˜paret
pace	> paz˜*/pać/
mare	> mar

Vowels in Castilian were not restored after these final consonants, indicating that their loss was complete throughout this Spanish dialect. There may indeed have been a strong tendency to eliminate a final vowel in order to extend the distribution of these consonants to morpheme final position allowing them to become more thoroughly integrated.

Further extension of apocope, however, encountered inhibiting distributional factors by exposing final consonants which were not compatible to the phonotactic rules underlying the syllabic patterns of the language. The advent of these new consonants suggests external motivations based upon social considerations. Compare

noche	> noch	-č
dixe	> dix	-š
calle	> cal	-λ
duque	> duc	-k
Diago	> Diag	-g
princepe	> princep	-p
quiçabe	> quiçab	-b
nueve	> nuef	-f
como	> com	-m

New final -cc exposed by apocope also ran counter to the syllabic pattern. The cluster /-nt/ in *sant(e)*, for example, had no equivalent distribution in syllable final position as does final /-n/ which consists of syllable final /-n/ in *cantar*:

Franco	> Franc	-nk
parte	> part	-rt
esta	> est	-st
humilde	> humilt	-lt˜-ld
entonces	> entonz	-nź
sante	> sant	-nt
donde	> dond	-nt˜-nd
dulce	> dulz	-lź

During the period of the loss of /-e/ the use of new final consonants by the upper classes was reinforced by the introduction of a number of learned words or cultismos, cf : concepto /-pt-/, efecto /-kt-/, digno /-gn-/, which were either rendered compatible by the introduction of new morpheme final consonants after loss of /-e/, or which rendered the new final consonants compatible by introducing them in syllabic final position. With the restoration of /-e/ the clusters in these words and others like them tended to reduce: conceto, efeto, dinno.[10] In the eighteenth century, the Spanish Academy restored the earlier learned forms, which once again influenced the pronunciation of the educated classes.

During the period of apocope two alternate forms çibdat/ciudad from cīvitāte were used. It might be expected that the form çibdat, the direct result of sonorization and syncope, would have been retained primarily by the aristocracy since syllable final /b/ would have been rendered compatible to the system by the addition of /-b/ after apocope. Those segments of society retaining /-e/ and thus not exposing morpheme final /-b/ would tend to modify (in this case through vocalization) the incompatible syllable final consonant /b/, resulting in ciudad.[11] Compare also the alternate lexical forms debda/deuda in Old Spanish and deuda in Modern Spanish. Distributional factors seem to influence the direction of change by inhibiting certain modifications and by propagating others. The nature and degree of syntagmatic influence, however, is related to the social level of the speakers and hence to exposure to outside influences. A broad picture of the history of a language must consider both sociological and structural forces from the standpoint of their relative influence and interaction at any given period.

The extent of a change may refer to either the gradual installation of it in all applicable environments of a linguistic system, or to the geographical extent to which it is carried out, either intradialect or interdialect. In both cases, disruptive factors may curtail its diffusion. The gradual installation of a change can be disrupted by subsequent change inhibiting the previous one before it has become general in all applicable environments.

Changes in meaning

Semantic change has been viewed as changes due to cultural modifications whereby the object referred to changes in the course of time but the name remains the same (eg, a pen today is considerably dif-

ferent from the quill used in early times) and changes due to social
stratification and interrelationships, where words take on specialized
meanings among various social groups and these meanings may then
be disseminated throughout the speech community. A word such as
'house', for example, has taken on a very specialized meaning for
members of Congress and retains this restricted meaning in everyday language in expressions like 'the bill has passed the House'.[12]
These notions do not reflect causes for semantic change as much as
they indicate the conditions under which change takes place.
Attempts to understand the causes underlying semantic modifications, however, have been put forth based upon psychological
notions; for example, emotive processes are reputed to have a bearing on semantic change.[13] Strong feelings on a subject prompt one to
talk about it but frustration, resulting perhaps from an uninterested
listener, may lead to a transfer of the terms usually employed in a discussion of the subject itself to other subjects. An enthusiastic base-
ball player may interlace his everyday conversation with such
phrases as 'to get to first base', 'a steal', 'strike out', 'a real curve'.
Words may then be transferred to other subjects where they were
not usually employed and expansion has occurred. The change of
meaning of German *Kopf* from 'cup' to 'head' is ascribed to a
spirited way of referring to headsmashing in battle.[14]

Explanation of semantic change and of language change in general
can only be partially understood from the linguistic facts. Attempts
to go beyond facts and establish, for example, a psychological basis
for change, or an explanation for specific kinds of change, may not be
empirically justifiable but nevertheless it opens up new ways of
viewing change which may prove fruitful in the long run.

An important relationship exists between semantic change and
evolving cultural conditions. The exact nature of this relationship is
elusive, especially since diverse external influences are operative
among all languages. Cultural factors are partially responsible for
semantic change in the form of taboos.[15] In specific circumstances
the use of a word may be interdicted by the rules of society, or a segment of society. In some less sophisticated cultures, certain words
are believed to invite evil consequences such as to exasperate demons,
alienate the gods, or activate a calamitous meteorological phenomenon. In place of the forbidden words, it is necessary to use some kind
of figurative paraphrase or in some manner render the word in-
nocuous. A Zulu wife, for example, is not allowed to mention the

name of her father-in-law or the names of his brothers. To contravene this rule is to be guilty of sorcery. If a word occurs in the language which is similar to these names it also must be avoided.[16]

Resorting to different words with similar meanings to convey the meaning of the prohibited lexical item, or resorting to paraphrase for the same purpose, undoubtedly has some influence on semantic extension. In a situation of this sort different individuals are subject to different taboos and the total effect on semantic change within the entire speech community is probably not very great over short periods of time. Societies in which taboo words are accepted as such by all the members would result in rather abrupt semantic changes over short periods of time in which the taboos are introduced. This essentially relates to vocabulary loss and replacement in an abrupt manner. Recourse to euphemisms is not restricted to particular societies. In Western society taboo words may be considered as such on one social level while not on another. The interchange between social levels keeps them free from complete extermination on the level which has prohibited them. This interchange in socially stratified societies works both ways: while the so-called upper classes may frown upon certain words, at least in some circumstances, so certain segments of the lower classes might be rather reluctant to use words that they feel are out of character. The average dustman for example would be somewhat hesitant to use adjectives such as *divine, exquisite, gorgeous*, etc.

There is no complete complementation, however, between social levels or between the different sexes with regard to lexical items: hence, any taboo forms are only partially distributed throughout the speech community and even then they are often not replaced by euphemisms if the situation does not warrant it.

Taboos vary from culture to culture and their influence on semantic change will then vary from language to language.[17] Whether or not there are any universal taboos is a question of some magnitude. In general, they appear to vary with the culture and to be learned by each generation and passed on to the next. If there are universal taboos, however, they must stem from a common conceptual basis.[18]

Polysemy

The rapidity and extent of change over a given period is presumably dictated in part by cultural events. All languages, however, have built-in characteristics which allow changes in meaning to occur. Polysemy, for example, refers to a certain amount of redundancy in meaning. It is probably a linguistic universal[19] of an absolute nature, for without it each word in a language would have an exact meaning, resembling symbolic logic or a mathematical formula more than a natural human language. This property of language allows expansion of meaning or semantic widening and the opposite, *ie*, semantic narrowing. Without polysemy there would be no metaphors.

Metaphors arise in several ways; for example, the expression 'a galaxy of beauties' seems to be based on an artistic comparison with the natural beauty of the Milky Way. The extension of the sense of the human foot to the base of a mountain, *ie*, 'the foot of the mountain', appears motivated by other perhaps less artistic reasons. In both cases, however, expressions existed in English which were usurped by the new metaphoric phrases, or partially so.

Sometimes a new thing enters a culture for which there is no word. In such a case, a word or phrase is found for it by expanding the meaning of existing words, often in a metaphorical way. This may result in a new term as is the case with 'sky-scraper'. Its success as a metaphor is attested by its use in many languages, *cf* French *gratte-ciel*, Spanish *rascacielo*, Italian *grattacielo*, and German *Wolkenkratzer*.

Most semantic change revolves around the processes of widening or narrowing in distribution. The term *deer* used to mean an animal, *cf* German *Tier*, but has now come to mean a specific type of animal, indicating a case of semantic narrowing, just as Old English *mete* once meant 'food' in general but has now come to refer only to a specific type of food – flesh.[20] *Steorfan* 'to die' in Old English may still mean 'to die' but in a specific way, *ie*, to starve. The term *horn* on the other hand has been extended from the bony protrusions on the head of a bull and from the musical instruments made from them to musical instruments of diverse kinds, and by further extension to noisy devices on automobiles.

How far semantic extension may proceed towards a large number of meanings or referents for specific words is not known, but presumably there are limits governed by the amount of ambiguity that would arise. When two or more meanings of the same word are differentiated by formal characteristics or contextual information, no conflict will ensue. If, on the other hand, these safeguards are lost,

ambiguity will result and may lead to the loss of some of the meanings of even all of them, hence to loss of the word itself.[21]

Theoretically a word has an infinite number of meanings since the
number of referents are infinite. The referents, however, fall into
semantic classes and a single reference functions for the entire class.
If meanings are extended beyond the class while retaining the same
reference or name, homonyms result. While most homonyms are the
product of converging sound modifications, such as Latin *valeō,
valēs, valet, vitellum,* and *vostrum* with their Modern French equi-
valents *vaux* /vo/, *vaux* /vo/, *vaut* /vo/, *veau* /vo/, and *vos* /vo/, they
may also result from diverging reference changes. This is the case
with English *flower* and *flour*, which had a common origin but the different meanings of the same word moved so far from each other that
they came to be regarded as separate terms.[22] The potential development of homonyms may be a factor in directing semantic change
along certain pathways.

Synonyms

The extension or reduction of the reference in distributional frame-
works has a counterpart in the extension or reduction of the referent.
A word such as *chair* may extend its distribution to include the
notion of *professorship* and thereby give rise to a synonym in a
restricted environment, but at the same time the word *chair* has extended its referent. The extension of a reference will often result in
synonyms, because the extension partially replaces an existing word
in specific environments. Even metaphorical extensions may do this:
'the foot of the hill' is synonymous with 'the base of the hill'. If,
however, the extension fills a semantic gap in the vocabulary, no
synonym will arise, *cf: sky-scraper*.

Synonyms arise through various processes. The use of a word for
another with which its meaning is closely aligned, for example, *chair*
and *professorship*, is referred to as metonomy. The naming of a thing
for one of its parts, *ie,* synecdoche, generates expressions such as
hands for *labourers, blade* for *sword* or *wheels* for *car*. Abbreviations
create forms synonymous with their longer counterparts, *eg, light* for
electric light, burgundy for *burgundy wine*, and *green* as in 'cross on the
green [light]'.

The opposite is also true in the form of a pleonasm, or using more
words than necessary, perhaps for emphasis, such as 'consensus of
opinion'.[23]

Structural considerations

Two broad types of semantic change may be distinguished: changes due to linguistic conservatism and those due to linguistic innovation. A structural approach to semantic change must explain the changes through the associative machinery provided by synchronous networks, and hence is confined to the second category since no such machinery comes into play unless an innovation takes place.[24]

Conservative changes revolve around modification of the referent while the name or reference remains the same as does the context. A factual change in the referent, *eg*, *pen*, or a change in our knowledge of the referent, such as *electricity*, is not strictly speaking a structural problem. In situations where semantic innovations have occurred through contextual changes, etc, structural or structural-functional considerations are difficult to determine. A study of formal or relational meaning, for example, and an investigation of referential meaning, *ie*, the relations between sign and object, are rendered less effective by the lack of information concerning precise connotations carried by a word in past ages. Latin *pater*, for example, had a social rather than a biological connotation. Languages with scant documentation compound this problem.

Most words appear to label realms of concepts rather than physical items. This follows from the fact that words refer to open classes. New physical entities that satisfy certain perceptual criteria may be assigned a label such as *house*. Exactly what these criteria are is still undetermined. Since words are not the labels of concepts already completed and stored away to be used later but labels of a categorization process, referents of words can easily change. Categories are always open and meanings can be extended. 'Words tag the process by which the species deals cognitively with its environment.'[25]

Similarity between two objects may cause a transfer of the name from one to the other, *eg*, the American robin, although a different species, was named after the English robin, thus extending the meaning of *robin*. Similarity between names, *eg*, phonetic similarity, may also bring about a transfer of the reference; for instance, some English speakers confuse the terms *perpetuate* and *perpetrate*.

A structural approach to semantic change must account for changes through the associative mechanisms which relate to categorization processes. The exact nature and extent of these associative patterns is not entirely clear but their existence is discernible from the fact that a number of objects are associated with a particular generic nomenclature such as silverware (knives, forks, spoons of various types) and are then differentiated by another process.

Dissemination

The origin and diffusion of some semantic change throughout the speech community is made possible by the following circumstances:

> Man's cognition functions within biologically given limits. On the other hand, there is also freedom within these limits. Thus every individual may have highly idiosyncratic thoughts or conceptualize in a peculiar way or, in fact, may choose somewhat different modes of cognitive organization at different times faced with identical sensory stimuli. His vocabulary, which is much more limited and unchangeable than his capacity for conceptualizing, can be made to cover the novel conceptual processes, and other men, by virtue of having essentially the same cognitive capacities, can understand the semantics of his utterances, even though the words cover new or slightly different conceptualizations.[26]

The spread of semantic changes from speaker to speaker will offer few obstacles within certain limits.

Further mechanism of semantic change

Phonological changes may serve as a means by which new lexical forms arise. Whether or not those that come into existence in this way do so because of situations among socio-semantic relationships, or whether it is due to an accident, is not entirely clear. Doublets, for example English *person* and *parson* (<*persona*), appear to be the result of phonological changes that led to a split in some forms giving rise to two different lexical items in the same language:

	Spanish	*French*
fragilis >	fraile	frêle
	fragil	fragile
lēgālis >	leal	loyal
	legal	légal
pensāre >	pensar	penser
	pesar	peser

One form of each of the examples above is more conservative as to the extent of phonological changes it has undergone. The fact that it remains in the language points to a semantic use for it related to the social characteristics of the culture. The more conservative form may, however, be a later acquisition. The consonant cluster /-ns-/ was reduced early in the history of Romance (*cf : mensa > mesa*) suggesting that *pensar* entered the language at a later date in the form of a literary or learned term and from there was diffused throughout the speech community.

Borrowings

Borrowed words are generally incorporated into a language along with the physical objects or abstract notions which they represent. In some cases, however – usually in closely related languages – a word may be borrowed that resembles the native word but which has a difference in meaning. The borrowed word may then take on the meaning of the native word as well as retain its own meaning. In such cases, the borrowed word has extended its meaning. The converse may also occur, however, *eg*, where a native word may extend its meaning based on the model of a foreign but similar lexical item.

Borrowing among languages in contact occurs when a speaker, exposed to another language, feels that some of his semantic fields are insufficiently differentiated. Italian dialect speakers in Italy used *corona* to denote 'wreath' and 'crown'. In contact with German, they borrowed *Kranz* for 'wreath', maintaining *corona* for 'crown'.[27]

A number of reasons besides those already mentioned have been put forth at various times to explain semantic change. Such reasons are changes in morals or standards of a community, shifts in focus of interest, closeness of events causing one name to become associated with another, and influence of one form on another such as *obnoxious* from Latin 'liable to harm' or 'exposed to injury' confused with *noxious*, hence 'offensive' or 'objectionable'. The terms *aggravate* and *annoy* have undergone some such semantic blending. While there is undoubtedly some cause-and-effect relationship between these states of affairs and semantic change, they are best not taken as explanations of change but simply as situations in which change occurs. When the effect of change is linked to a stimulus, perhaps of an associative nature within the situation, explanation becomes more realistic.

Some semantic changes have been described in terms of amelioration; for example, the word *success* once meant 'result' but came to mean 'favourable result'. The words *enthusiasm, zeal* and *romantic* were pejorative as recently as the seventeenth century, relating to violence and crudity. Still other semantic changes have been considered in the framework of deterioration, such as the form *lust* which once meant *desire* but has now taken on unflattering overtones. As meanings are extended to cover new situations, they may entail a loss of emotional intensity. The word *hellish* may no longer refer to the damned but to a related situation such as a ride on the subway during the rush hour. New words and new meanings may enter a language simultaneously as in the case of deliberate creations where a hitherto undefined or unknown physical or imaginary property is given a name; compare, *gas, gene, schmo*. This may also be the case with borrowed and analogical creations. What has sometimes been termed popular etymology, indicating associations between the phonic structure of lexical items, appears to have an influence on semantic change; the modification of Old English *scam-faest* 'confirmed in shame', that is, 'to be modest', became in early Modern English *shame-fast* and has now become *shame-faced*.[28]

Generalizations about vocabulary as a structural set must take into account that semantic mapping of the environment appears in general to be arbitrary, and the semantic map of each language is different from all others. Parallels between languages are not easy to formulate and quantify. Many of the outstanding semanticists have been optimistic about finding some kind of regularity behind semantic processes. Others have objected to the notion of semantic regularity for various reasons. Influenced by the notion of laws in sound change and laws within the natural sciences, some semanticists have sought parallels in their own discipline through analogous reasoning, while others have rejected all such analogies and considerations as not relatable to the area of semantics.

In semantic change, as well as phonological change, the motivating factors may be structural, cultural, social and psychological. Phonological convergence may induce semantic changes, while semantic structure, for example, homonyms, may direct or in some way inhibit phonological modifications. Words may be borrowed, invented or analogically formed to tag new cultural entities subject to cultural constraints but their phonic shape will depend on existing phonotactic rules. New meaning may arise through non-identical

conceptualization capacities of individuals and be diffused throughout the speech community, but they will reflect structural constraints.
These are just a few of the ways in which external and internal
linguistic forces interact. More specifically, internal linguistic considerations appear to be responsible for the preservation of certain
environmental conditions in French which keep apart potential
homonyms; *cf : les zéros* and *les héros*.[29] Phonological change on the
other hand has prompted semantic innovations, *cf* Old English
letten 'hinder', and *lǣtan* 'let'. When *letten* became homonymous
with *let* 'permit', it could no longer be used effectively, since an
utterance such as *let him* would have opposite meanings.[30]

The study of meaning has occupied the attention of philosophers,
psychologists, linguists and anthropologists. Some of the older views
on semantics that often hindered developments such as the idea that
meaning cannot be observed directly and its study is *a priori* unscientific, or that semantics is simply a by-product of syntactic
studies, are fading away.

An attempt to place the study of meaning within the confines of a
general structural framework was begun this century. It is characterized by the notion of semantic fields in which words and their
meanings cluster in groups (fields). The words in each field are
related to each other in the manner by which they divide up conceptual space. Terms in a field can easily be extended to other areas
of discourse but maintain their relative position. For example, the
adjectives *hard* and *soft* take on new meanings when extended to *a
hard teacher* and *a soft teacher*. The antonymy of *hard* and *soft* is
maintained in the new meanings which relate to something like
difficult and *easy* or *unsympathetic* and *sympathetic*.[31]

The idea of assigning specific semantic features to words (com-
ponential analysis) to determine their relationship to each other
relies on semantic field theory inasmuch as words are compared
which have semantic properties in common but differ in meaning by
other features. The use of + and − notations to indicate semantic
features is widely used in current approaches. The nouns *man* and
woman can be characterized thus:

man	*woman*
+ animate	+ animate
+ human	+ human
+ adult	+ adult
+ male	− male

The search for a comprehensive theory of semantics to be integrated into linguistic studies is in part a search for semantic universals. While one general approach views semantic structure as somewhat relative in nature, reflecting the cultural make-up of different societies, another stresses the universality of human cognitive parameters reflecting basic semantic agreement in interpretation of the universe.[32]

Notes

1 See Langacker, *p* 183 for these and other examples. The morpheme *nik* entered English as part of the Russian word *sputnik*. Like *burger*, an older borrowing from German in the form of *Hamburg > hamburger*, the morpheme *nik* is steadily broadening its distribution; *cf* also *Vietnik*.
2 For some parallels between language change and social change, see Capell, *pp* 51–62.
3 For this study see Labov (1963). For a similar but much more comprehensive and complex study as well as bibliography relating to social/psychological factors in language change, see Labov (1966). For more general comments and bibliography, see Capell.
4 Social motivations underlying language change have for a long time been considered as crucial factors. Even more explicit concepts such as occupation, education, income, attitudes, social aspirations, etc, have figured in discussions on language histories. Labov, however, has put them to the test with results that fully show the significance of social factors. His selection of linguistic variables is based upon their frequency, their immunity from conscious suppression, their relationship to larger units, and their responsiveness to quantification on a linear scale. See Labov (1964), *pp* 164–196. It has been suggested that such stylistic changes may yield a grammar that is not optimal through the addition of rules which in turn bring about changes towards a more optimal state in the language of the children. See Postal, *pp* 283–285.
5 See Sturtevant, (1947b), *p* 81.
6 The period of apocope corresponds to a time of strong French influence in Spain. This influence affected primarily the upper classes and the clergy. The upper classes, then as now, were somewhat conservative in their speech habits and did not respond readily to language change which occurred among the common people. They would react, however, to more prestigious forms of speech than their own — in this case French — where the final vowels had been lost for several centuries. The fact that apocope did occur among the aristocracy and clergy, who were the literate portion of the society, is evidenced by the written forms. The extent of French influence in Spain during this period was great, revolving around territorial possessions (Navarre), the reinforcement of French ideas through the Monks of Cluny who represented a strong force in Spain, French crusaders, etc. It appears no accident that, as Menéndez Pidal (*p* 169) states: 'Con todas estas apócopes el español de los siglos XII y XIII se asemejaba mucho al frances. . . .'

7 For neutralization of this type in Modern Spanish see Alarcos Llorach, *p* 185. For earlier periods see Anderson (1965).

8 The distributional pattern of specific consonants in syllable final position, regardless of syllabic position within the morpheme, characterizes Spanish phonotactics throughout its history. It is suspected that a good deal of phonological change occurs under the inhibiting influence of this arrangement – that phonological processes are directed by it. An investigation of this distribution may reveal that sooner or later all divergent phonological change conforms to the underlying relationship between syllable final and morpheme final consonants. Primarily external influences disrupt this relationship from time to time in the form of borrowed or learned words, but even this eventually adjusts to the pattern. The disruptions come mainly from social motivations, *cf*: *diño* replaced by *digno* where syllable final /g/ does not correspond to morpheme final /-g/. The learned form was imposed upon the language by the Spanish Academy and accepted by cultured speakers. From there it spread to other social levels.

9 For a treatment of the relationship of syllable and morpheme final consonants, see Saporta and Olson.

10 See Corominas; others modified in a different manner, *cf*: *absolver* /-bs-/ > *ensolver*.

11 Morpheme final /-x/ in Spanish does not have a syllable final counterpart. This sound occurs in the word *relój* which was borrowed early from Catalan *relotge* < *horologium*. For many speakers of Spanish, however, this incompatible final sound has been lost resulting in the pronunciation /reló/. See Corominas and Menéndez Pidal, *p* 170.

12 See Meillet (1921–1937), *pp* 230–271.

13 See Sperber.

14 See Lehmann (1962), *p* 200.

15 Structural considerations may have some bearing on change vis-à-vis taboos in that phonological change (and perhaps other levels) may be inhibited if the resultant phonic shape resembles a taboo form. What it means to resemble, however, is a difficult question.

16 See Jespersen (1922), *p* 239.

17 For examples of lexical distribution and loss in English due to undesirable connotation, see Bloomfield, *p* 396.

18 See Leach for a discussion of various types of taboos relating to such things as blasphemy and profanity, equating homo sapiens with other species and so-called dirty words referring to sex and excretion.

　　According to one view the physical and social environment of a child is conceived as a continuum and the child learns to impose upon this environment a kind of discrimination grid which serves to distinguish the world as being composed of a large number of separate things, each having a name. In English, bushes and trees are two different things. This is not apparent but taught. This is akin to an untrained observer looking at a forest in which he sees only a continuous blending of colours and shapes, whereas a botanist may see a number of distinct entities with which he associates specific names. For the child, learning to construct the environment in this manner, *ie*, by associating names with things, the basic discriminations must be unambiguous. There can be no overlap between the individual as an entity and those things in the environment as other entities. This perception is achieved by the use of language which labels things and the use of taboos which break up the continuum or inhibit recognition of parts of the continuum.

The child's first problem is to determine the initial boundary between itself and the environment. Semantically distinct verbal concepts arise as the boundary percepts that lie between them are repressed. There also appears to be a tendency to repress concepts that have some kind of semantic overlap causing interference.

Waste products are in a sense ambiguous as they are both part of oneself and not part of oneself: they do not fit into clear-cut categories. Consequently, various euphemisms are used to express these concepts since sometimes they have to be expressed. The word *urine*, for example, is more acceptable than the usual Anglo-Saxon word because as a borrowed form it has a loftier social connotation. There are a large number of taboo words to which these concepts can be applied, but the entire theoretical structure rests on the basic premise that a child views the universe as a continuum.

19 See Ullmann, *p* 232.

20 For this change, see Bloomfield, *pp* 426 and 430.

21 See Ullmann, *p* 234.

22 *Ibid*, *p* 235.

23 See Sturtevant *op cit*, *p* 140 for examples of pleonasms.

24 See Ullmann, *p* 211.

25 See Lenneberg (1967), *p* 334.

26 *Ibid*.

27 For this and other examples, see Weinreich (1953).

28 For examples, see Sturtevant, *op cit*, *p* 117.

29 See Ullmann, *p* 237. See also Schane (1968), *pp* 7–8 for the so-called 'H aspiré' words such as *le héro*, *les héros*, which phonetically contain an initial vowel but do not permit a preceding word to enter into liaison or cause elision with them, *ie*, (ləeɾo/ not /leɾo/, /le eɾo/ not /lezeɾo/.

30 See Bloomfield, *p* 398.

31 The notion of 'field' in semantics was first developed by Weisgerber and Trier and their associates as a reaction to the more traditional atomistic approach. For further discussion and bibliography, see Ullmann (1951) and Lyons (1968).

32 Present theories in semantic studies reflecting the two major approaches (*ie*, generative semantics and interpretative semantics) are still highly controversial and beyond our present purposes in discussing semantic change.

Chapter 10

Linguistic models

A model is not part of a system of language but, rather, is a hypothetical construction. It is essential therefore to consider the model as an abstract object which is not dependent either on the nature of linguistic elements, or on their linguistic interpretation. The interpretation consists of substituting something precise for the terms of the model. At different times, in relation to language change, certain of the various concepts in historical linguistics have been considered primary concepts from which further deductions have been made in terms defined by the primary notions. The desire to interpret language change has led students of historical linguistics to several re-evaluations of the basic assumptions underlying language relationships and language change, and to modify or establish new models when factual information could not be accounted for by the existing model.[1]

The genetic or kinship model

Various abstract configurations serving as models to represent language change have been presented over the past 150 years. Genetic concepts were first used in historical studies to relate languages to the family, establishing parent or mother languages (such as P I E) and daughter languages (such as Greek and Latin). In relation to each other, the latter then become sister languages. This terminology is still current. However, the notion of family reflecting a group of languages poses problems of interpretation. The varying degrees of difference between the numerous Indo-European languages do not lend themselves to the clear-cut distinctions necessary for family or genetic concepts. Indeed, even if kinship relationships were employed for these differences they would be cumbersome to the extreme: French, Spanish and other Romance languages are grand-daughters of PIE; dialects of recent origin of these languages are great-granddaughters; French is a niece of Greek, a sister of Italian, a daughter of Latin and a cousin of Hindi, and so on.

The family tree design

A more sophisticated kinship model developed by August Schleicher to represent the Indo-European group of languages was motivated by the prevailing views on evolution. His conception of the family tree permitted a clearer view of language relationship via smaller and smaller branches proceeding from a single source. (*Fig* 13)

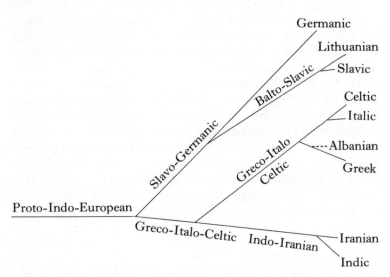

Fig 13: Earlier version of the Indo-European family tree.

The family tree notion has some evident shortcomings: it does not account for the influence one language has on another after they have branched off (usually in the form of substratum, adstratum or super-stratum – *cf* French and English or Frankish and Gallo-Roman). The criteria used to indicate relationships and divergences have been somewhat arbitrary and non-systematic. Various phonological and morphological features have been inconsistently applied to related languages, obscuring the nature and degree of relatedness rather than illuminating it, thus making interpretation of the model difficult.[2] Like the earlier kinship model, this model has also been objected to on the basis that it depicts a biological organism while languages are sets of conventions which do not have independent existence apart from the speakers.[3]

The Wave Theory

The tree system, in which each node may have a number of offshoots forming nodes with more offshoots but which indicates little about the relationships of one branch to another, was in part amended by the wave theory, first proposed by Johannes Schmidt in 1872. He inferred that the relationship among Indo-European languages was the result of a wave-like dissemination of dialectal peculiarities within Proto-Indo-European. Dialect waves spread out from different centres of innovation and spread in all directions crossing each other as they went. In this way, the common features shared by various branches could be explained.

Celtic, for example, shows dialectal traits diffusing outward and influencing the early Germanic and Italic dialects, but not to the same degree. Italic and Celtic showed more similarities than Celtic and Germanic. Some dialectal innovations were peculiarly Celtic. Crisscrossing of waves, for example those radiating from the Germanic group, would not only cross the Celtic waves but also those stemming from Balto-Slavic.

Dialectal waves originating in the Balto-Slavic dialect united Balto-Slavic with Indo-Iranian on the one hand and Germanic on the other. In this way a continuous relationship between the dialects would be established.[4] The fact that there is not a continuous transition within the Indo-European languages but well-defined boundaries between some of the branches was explained by the loss of many intermediate forms. In a continuous dialectal series of 1 through 10, dialect 5 may become prominent for social, political or other prestigious reasons and gradually submerge dialects 2, 3, and 4 as well as 6, 7, 8, and 9. In such an event, the remaining dialects 1, 5, and 10 would show a good deal of difference, perhaps even to the point of non-intelligibility. Extinct and little-known languages such as Venetic and Messapic in Italy seemed to fit the theory. The discovery of Tocharian and Hittite in the east with characteristics more akin to languages of the west (*centum* languages), however, seriously upset this position. The wave model interprets language relationships based on the spread and extent of dialectal isoglosses, but does not account for the origin of change or its regularity[5] (or lack of it) in each language.

The biological model

A biological model of language change suggests a construction that accounts for the evolution of language as a natural event within the framework of the species. It would have to account for such things as modification of language universals based upon changes in the central nervous system through genetic evolution; changes in underlying phonological, syntactic, and semantic properties based on evolutionary modifications in perception and conceptualization, and so on. In short, it would interpret the biological history of natural languages; but such a model is at present not available.[6]

The main deterrent to using a biological model for language change, however, has not been based primarily upon the above considerations, but on the seemingly inappropriate analogy between the genetic evolution of organisms on the one hand and the historical modification of a cultural phenomenon on the other. In short, rejection of a biological model of language change is not a rejection of such a model *per se* but a reaction against an equation between evolutionary biology and historical linguistics. In this framework, historical linguistics, then, has been primarily concerned with changes in linguistic systems and subsystems which affect linguistic rules, both paradigmatic and syntagmatic, and which reflect a common heritage or a common pool of sounds and rules among human beings. The biological antecedents of this heritage have traditionally not been a matter of concern for students of language change as they involve the study of the modification of organisms. It has been suggested that parallels between language change and evolutionary biology, based on a higher level than that of the reproducing organisms and individualization not found in language, can perhaps be fruitfully exploited to the advantage of historical language studies.[7] Both language and species continue, modify, and diversify. Hence both linguistics and biology distinguish variation and change. Variation is viewed synchronically and change diachronically. Both disciplines attempt to give an explanatory account of the processes of change and variation by describing the mechanisms and motivations that underlie them.

Variation in linguistics concerns degrees of precision in articulation, degrees of precision in perception, degrees of variation in timing, and degrees of phonological conditioning by the environment. These factors are limited by the particular system in which they are found.[8] The distribution of these variations appears random, yet phonological change can be considered systematic in process and generally regular in outcome. In language change, as in evolutionary biology, random variation combined with a selective factor produces order.

Phonological variations, for example, occurred in the inflectional suffixes of Old English nouns, resulting in loss of morphological markers which distinguished case desinences. In Old English gender was clearly distinguishable in most nouns. But as the unstressed vowels were levelled (/a o u/ > /e/) gender disappeared. Further levelling reduced /e/ > /ə/ > /ø/.[9] Out of all the variations and diverse causes of variations, Middle English nouns developed in a systematic fashion and on a new basis. Old English nouns with several paradigms for inflections indicating number, case and gender, became Middle English nouns inflected for number – that is, with a plural suffix. Compare:

	singular		*plural*	
nominative	stān		stānas	
genitive	stānes	} > stone	stāna	} > stones
dative	stāne		stānum	
accusative	stān		stānas	

Selective factors and their role in linguistics may revolve around expectation patterns which are highly inflexible. After five or six, a child has learned the patterns, and all after that age is simply variation. Features in unaccustomed combinations are discarded or selected out. A selective factor may help to account for the change observed in the transition from Old English to Middle English and can be thought of as a habit of expectation among English speakers, manifest in the overall morphological and syntactic patterns coupled with the meanings carried by the various suffixes. Grammatical relationships were also carried by word order and prepositional constructions, and even intonation (redundant and secondary devices). Gender had no semantic reference and no essential grammatical function except perhaps in pronouns of the third person *he*, 'he', *heo*, 'she', *hit*, 'it'. Number was expressed as singular and non-singular and was both grammatical and meaningful. It was further expressed in personal pronouns and verbs; compare *drifan* 'drive':

person	singular	plural
1	ic drīfe – e	wē drīfað – að
2	dū drīfst – st	gē drīfað – að
3	hē drīfð – ð	hīe drīfað – að

The deeply entrenched habit of singular-plural expressed by several devices, with correlates in experience outside language, continued as a well-reinforced linguistic feature.

The narrowing range of variation in shape and the frequent phonetic features of noun inflections came to be dealt with in line with expectation habits that were not satisfied in other aspects of utterances, *eg*, verbs were not inflected for gender and case. The persisting habit of specifying singular and plural, reinforced by pronouns and verbs, was the selective factor that produced the new order in place of random variation of inflectional noun suffixes. This view implies that language change occurs among the young – that is, prior to the establishment of firm phonotactic patterns. While this is only partially true, the analogical premises may still be maintained but perhaps should be broadened to include external stimuli which interfere with expectation habits and lead to new learning situations resulting in different expectations. For example, semantic and syntactic parameters influence a listener's ability to repeat an utterance; grammatical sentences are easier to remember than ungrammatical ones; grammatical but semantically anomalous sentences fall in between;[10] ambient noise competing with language signals forces the listener to rely on expectation of what was said based on what he heard; in ungrammatical sentences the listener's expectation habits hinder this ability to repeat. Once failure occurs, however, learning the new system begins and new habits emerge.

If analogy with biology stands up to the test of time and scrutiny then it can be carried further to include the concept of drift. Biological drift takes place among small populations which are isolated in some way from each other and where no interchange takes place. Variations occurring internally spread throughout the community meeting no counteractive force to negate the change (as would happen in larger populations). The selective forces are dictated by the internal environment. Drift from one type of linguistic system to another may be partially accounted for in terms of selection. In

Indo-European languages the category of plurality seems to be a persistent feature of language design. Even those languages of Latin origin which did not retain the plural marker /s/ from the accusative plural have compensated for it by other devices such as /i/ in Italian from the dative-ablative plural, *eg : arma, armi*, or /e/ from the nominative plural, *porta, porte*. A more open vowel quality in Andalusian (which accompanied the loss of syllable final /s/) serves to indicate plurality, *cf* /padre/, /padrɛ/.

Drift in language may be primarily governed by internal modification in which certain features become dominant and spread throughout the community. It can be thought of as '. . . constituted by the unconscious selection on the part of its speakers of those individual variations that are cumulative in some special direction.'[11]

Speakers of English often vacillate between the subjective and objective forms of the pronouns *who/whom*. The eventual loss of *whom* from the grammar appears inevitable when viewed within a larger framework. The form is structurally and perhaps psychologically isolated, representing a kind of fossil against a background of drift in a specific direction. Other interrogative and relative pronouns do not distinguish subject and object but display, along with interrogative adverbs, invariable forms:

What are you doing?
Where are you going?
Which did you give him?
When did he arrive?
Who(m) did you see?

Subject pronouns have counterparts in objective form such as *I/me*, *he/him*, etc but they do not pattern syntactically as do the interrogative *who/whom*. The object personal pronouns never precede the verb except perhaps in poetic speech, *eg, me the boy saw*, but are instead relegated to fixed syntactic positions.

I see the boy
The boy sees me

Whom, on the other hand, is never used in such a position; for example, *Did you see whom? Drift in English, then, would appear to be a slow but inexorable process in which certain characteristics of the language disappear as they become isolated from the linguistic pattern.[12]

The extent to which historical linguistics has relied on biological terms and theories is evident from the foregoing presentation. Evolution has been thought of as descent with modification brought about by natural selection, mutation, sampling error (drift), and migration. These notions have been applied to language change in an effort to understand it better. Besides processes of change, evolution has been viewed as changes in the morphology of organisms through time by examination of similarities and differences between ancestral and descendant populations. The study of language change must also establish the structural characteristics of different stages of one or more languages in order to determine their differences. When these differences are known, then attempts can be made to account for them. When organisms or languages are similar, the same kind of problem arises as to whether they represent a close phylogenetic relationship or the result of parallel development from a more remote ancestor. Close similarities in design or structure may also be the product of convergence even though the species or languages in question are not closely related.

The fact that evolution is irrevocable, in that once organisms have passed through various stages the processes are non-reversible, is also true for language change. Species and languages have many other interpretative characteristics in common with regard to change, as well as methodological procedures to arrive at these characteristics. In both cases, extinction occurs in two ways: either via a negative role of environmental selection in which organisms and languages die out, or by transformation into other species or languages. Modification in both may be examined from the point of view of changes in individual traits, changes in the entire structure, and changes in sets of related traits.

Methodological considerations extend to methods of dating. Of special importance to scholars concerned with evolution are the chronometric techniques currently in use for determining the age of a specimen. The methods are based on the precise measurement of the decay products of radioactive isotopes of fairly common elements such as potassium and carbon.[13] In historical linguistics an attempt has been made to determine the age of languages by analysis of vocabulary replacement (a type of decay) by establishing chronological periods that correspond to certain percentages of lexical loss.[14]

Efforts to formulate a biological or, more specifically, a genetic model of language change have not all been purely analogical in nature. Language is a tool used by man for a specific purpose, *ie*, communication and may, like other tools, have been subject to a process of improvement in efficiency since its inception. For those who have inquired into this notion, attempts to find a detectable influence of improvement in language sound systems have been of paramount importance. It is to the speakers themselves, however, that one must turn for answers as well as to the linguistic characteristics of language. Human beings (and presumably other forms of life) tend to conserve energy by channelling it along the most efficient pathways. This notion has been referred to as the principle of economy of effort. The principle of economy of effort has been expressed in several ways. Zipf has stated it as the principle of least effort which is found as a tendency in a wide range of human behaviour.[15] Speakers select those phonetic types which are easiest to articulate orally and to discriminate aurally. Since the physiological characteristics of the vocal apparatus are the same in speakers of different languages, there will tend to be substantial agreement in the selection of phonetic traits. When languages thus use similar sounds they will be employed with approximately the same frequency, since the sounds arising from least effort will be more readily used than those requiring more effort. Through sound change the frequency of occurrence of each sound in a given language is adjusted to its ranking position based on the effort needed in its production and perception. A sound that has become too frequent in relation to the effort needed (through lexical change, borrowings, etc) will be changed in at least some of its environments. There is no conclusive evidence, however, that indicates the general convergence of languages towards a particular phonological system which ideally represents the principle of least effort. Economy of effort as envisaged by Zipf does not appear as the prime mover of language change or at least does not seem to be a constant factor overriding all other factors. There are, in fact, a number of documented instances in which phonological change runs counter to the principle of least effort in the terms stated above. Old Spanish sibilants, for example, were voiced in voiced environments but during a subsequent stage became once again voiceless in the same environments, *eg*, $/\text{-s-}/ > /\text{-z-}/ > /\text{-s-}/$.

It has been proposed that genes control vocal preference, much as they do hair, eye or skin colour among population groups. The sound complement of a natural language is an expression of this preference which is directed towards economy or ease of vocal effort.[16] Differing from Zipf's point of view, this hypothesis maintains that anatomical characteristics of the vocal tract, due to genetic differences, vary among populations (mating groups) and vocal preference varies accordingly. Support for this hypothesis comes primarily from the present geographical distribution of certain sounds and their historical displacement in relation to population migrations.[17] The interdental fricative /θ/, for example, is presently confined to peripheral areas of Europe, *ie*, Scandinavia, the British Isles, the Balkans and the Iberian peninsula. In recorded history /θ/ extended towards the east as far as Russia. Further still to the east there is no record of it. Thus it appears that /θ/ has been steadily migrating westward or at least receding in geographical distribution in the direction from east to west. It cannot be correlated with genealogically related linguistic groups, since it is found in Germanic, Albanian, Basque and Lapp. The genetic interpretation of these facts has suggested to some observers that the loss of /θ/ and variants is the result of the expression of average preferences based upon the vocal tract of the speakers who once had it. The preferences derive in part from genetic inheritance which gives rise to physiological differences in the vocal tract. The loss of /θ/ reflects a change in that inheritance. The actual genetic influence (through migration and mixture) on the peoples of Europe has been from east to west. In the west the genotypes who had a preference for this sound lost the preference through dilution and replacement by the eastern genotypes who lacked this preference. Genetic inheritance, which gives a particular character to the speech apparatus of each population and therefore helps determine the sound system of the language of that population, may be based on combinations of genetic traits as well as individual genes. The migration of /θ/ has been related to the blood group *O* gene which seems to have had a similar geographical distribution throughout European history.

This view of language change has not won many adherents since it was first proposed almost three decades ago. It lacks cogency especially with regard to the fundamental premise that there are anatomical differences relating to speech activity which are the result of the genetic make-up of mating groups. Much more work is needed to demonstrate the soundness of the hypothesis but such endeavours are still in their infancy and should not be ignored as an aspect of language change.

Other approaches to phonological change have not disregarded the notion of economy of articulation but view it as a system-oriented tendency related to the number of phonemes and the number of distinctive articulatory features. Systems, then, tend towards economy by extending their phonemic inventory throughout the major oppositions of distinctive features to arrive at the most symmetrical pattern possible. This is said to be curtailed, however, by the asymmetry of the speech organs and by constant external disruptions. These approaches to articulatory ease take as axiomatic the physiological identity of the vocal tract in all human beings.

The dynamic model

Much of the previous discussion concerning structural factors in language change centred around what might be called a dynamic model.[18] The phonological system of a language is viewed as comprising series and orders in which empty slots or *cases vides* may occur. These holes in the system characterize in part the degree of lability in the system. The phonological system at any given chronological stage is best represented by the design of orders, series and empty slots which have been arranged by considerations of proportional equations and the least articulatory redundancy within the framework of phonetically similar units. The system (or subsystems – consonants and vowels) shows various conditions of equilibrium characterized by degrees of phonological homogeneity. The tendency of the system is to move towards complete homogeneity or a uniform structure in which all phonemes participate in proportional equations. This movement leads to new phonemes and new holes in the pattern since any change affects in some manner all the phonemes of the system. The system remains in a constant state of perturbation where changes are carried out by the least number of operations. This model is purely linguistic and represents a generating paradigmatic model in that, from a given phonological system and conditions, new phonemes are generated which in turn represent a new system and new conditions.[19] Certain fundamental notions of a structural and functional nature influence the behaviour of phonological units within the framework of this model. These concepts have been dealt with in Chapter VII with regard to specific changes.

Internal factors alone do not account for all aspects of language change, however, since complex social motivations arising in the external environment influence the direction of language change. The dynamic model emphasizes the internal paradigmatic role of phonological units, neglecting the syntagmatic aspects of modification. It should also be noted that the model assumes all language change to be motivated by phonological considerations and consequently does not relate to morphologically or syntactically induced change.

Implicit in this model is the notion that there is an ideal system. For example, among the consonantal paradigms four orders and four series with no holes would reflect a perfectly symmetrical pattern of sixteen phonemes. A tendency on the part of human beings to organize linguistic units along these lines can neither be proved nor disproved at present. Language systems, in fact, support the notion that symmetry is an important consideration in change. It is not inconceivable to think that more knowledge of man's modes of conceptualization may ultimately justify such a position. The fact that languages seldom reach or long remain in such perfect balance, however, argues against the position. The asymmetrical nature of the speech organs has been put forward as a reason why this state of equilibrium is not maintained. This gives rise to a host of new questions about the relationship between asymmetrical physiological features and psychological facets of symmetry. It is conceivable from linguistic evidence to hold the position that the most harmonious system is that which most closely reflects the asymmetrical structure of the speech organs. It can be maintained, however, that the relationships of the various phonological subsystems, coupled with external linguistic and social stimuli coming to bear on language, continually disrupt potential symmetrical arrangements or at least trends towards these arrangements. This model is nevertheless adapted to account for language change as opposed to simply describing it.[20]

Part of the problem concerning the acceptance of some linguistic models of language change by students of historical linguistics has often been their scepticism of the implicit teleological basis of such models. In view of the preceding remarks concerning the search for an adequate model of language change, consider the following statements:

Life is conceived as 'a process of looking forward' (in J. Bronowski's formulation), and the ensuing notions of purposiveness and goal-directedness, 'foreign to physics but lending themselves so readily to the description of organic phenomena' (Niels Bohr), actually take deep root in today's biology. These views may serve to corroborate a consistent application of a means-end model to the language design, to its maintenance of integrity and equilibrium (homeostasis), as well as to its mutations.[21]

Yet if the comparative material stored enables science to speak about the goal-directed activities 'from tropisms up to the most complex form protists' up to mankind and especially in regard to human lifeways and institutions, the ineradicable superstitious fear of teleological attitudes which still torments some linguists proves to be indeed out of date.[22]

Notes

1 The assumptions concerning glottochronology have been considered in Chapter 4 and will not be taken up again here.
2 More recently, however, this objection is disappearing. See Grimes and Agard.
3 Schleicher's model has been reprinted on a number of occasions, *eg*, Pedersen, *p* 312, Lehmann (1962), *p* 139.
4 For comments on the Wave Theory, see Pedersen, *p* 315 and Lehmann, *op cit*, *p* 141.
5 For further criticisms of the Wave Theory, see Sturtevant (1917).
6 For some remarks on the biological foundations of the history of natural languages, see Lenneberg (1967), *pp* 380-395.
7 For these concepts and the following examples from English, see Stevick (1963).
8 In biology, variation in the form of genetic laws is governed by information contained in the genes of each species.
9 See Nist, *pp* 184-194 and Pyles, *pp* 154-156.
10 See Miller and Isard.
11 Sapir, *p* 155. He further states '. . . it is not likely to occur to us that our language has a 'slope', that the changes of the next few centuries are in a sense prefigured in certain obscure tendencies of the present and that these changes, when consummated, will be seen to be but continuations of changes that have been already effected.'
12 For further details of this change and others, as well as phonological factors involved in drift, see Sapir, *pp* 147-170.
13 See Buettner-Janisch, *p* 20 for a more precise statement.
14 See Chapter 4 for a discussion of this method.
15 See Zipf (1965).
16 See Darlington and Brosnahan.
17 For this and further examples equating language sounds with population areas and possible genetic affiliation, see Brosnahan.
18 This model has been proposed by Martinet (1955) and in his various linguistic papers.
19 See Revzin.
20 For a critical examination of some of the concepts of this model, see Hoenigswald (1957).
21 See R. Jakobson (1967), *pp* 6-7.
22 *Ibid.*

Chapter 11

Generative-transformational model

SECTION I
Diachronic phonology

Within the generative-transformational framework, human language is viewed as a rule-governed phenomenon. The grammar of a language is a set of rules which relates sounds and meanings. In particular, a transformational grammar is presently formulated as containing a syntactic (or syntacto-semantic) and a phonological component. The syntactic component consists of the *base*, which generates abstract underlying phrase-markers (deep structures) for sentences; the *lexicon*, which specifies phonological, syntactic and semantic information for lexical items; and the *transformations*, which convert the underlying phrase-markers into derived phrase-markers (surface structures). The surface structures serve as input to the phonological component. Phonological rules convert the underlying phonological shapes of items into their final (phonetic) forms. In addition, the phonological rules serve to insert all predictable phonological specifications (such as degree of aspiration, etc) which are not distinctive in the language.

The rules within each component of a grammar are motivated (synchronically) on the basis of economy and generality. A particular utterance is a sentence within a language if a speaker of that language is equipped with an internalized grammar which will characterize that particular utterance. To say that the string 'Bill ate a plum' is an English sentence, while 'plum a ate Bill' is not, is to claim that speakers of English have an internalized grammar (largely unconscious) which will characterize the first, but not the second, string.

One of the linguist's tasks is to construct explicit grammars which characterize the same utterances as does the internalized grammar of the native speaker.

The rules within each component of a grammar are constrained as to their form and type, as well as to ordering. The discussion immediately following deals only with the phonological rules of grammars. Such rules must be at least partially ordered with respect to each other. To illustrate such rules and ordering, let us consider the past tenses of some of the regular ('weak') verbs of English.[1]

	present tense	*past tense*
walk	wɔk	wɔkt
bake	beyk	beykt
beg	beg	begd
wag	wæg	wægd
seize	siyz	siyzd
dim	dim	dimd
drop	drɒp	drɒpt
judge	ǧʌǧ	ǧʌǧd
touch	tʌč	tʌčt
bait	beyt	beytid
rob	rɒb	rɒbd
pet	pet	petid
fade	feyd	feydid

If we take the present tense form to be the underlying stem of the verb, the past tense form can be represented as *stem + d*, where the '+' represents a morpheme boundary which has no phonetic shape. The underlying forms for 'robbed', 'seized', and 'dimmed' are then *rɒb + d*, *siyz + d*, and *dim + d*. Similarly, the underlying forms for 'faded', 'baited', and 'walked' are *feyd + d*, *beyt + d*, and *wɔk + d*. However, the underlying forms for the last three items do not represent the correct surface shapes. Two rules are needed to convert the underlying forms to their proper final forms. We first need the rule

$$\text{P1}: \text{nul} \rightarrow i/\{t, d\} + \underline{\quad} d$$

which inserts the vowel *i* only in the case where the stem ends in a *t* or *d*, and when a *d* follows. By the application of P1 to the underlying form *pet + d* we obtain *pet + id*. The second necessary rule is,

$$\text{P2}: d \rightarrow t/\text{voiceless consonant} + \underline{\quad}.$$

This rule devoices *d* to *t* if the preceding consonant is also voiceless. By application of P2 to *wɔk + d*, we obtain *wɔk + t*. Rule P1 does not apply to the underlying form *wɔk + d*, so the item simply passes through unaffected and is submitted to P2. We shall adopt the convention that if no further rules apply to a form the morpheme boundary is deleted. Thus, we have *pet + id→petid*, etc. The ordering of the two rules is crucial. P1 applies only to stems with a final *d* or *t* (and thus P1 does not apply to forms such as *wɔk, beg*, etc). If P2 were to be applied before P1, we would derive forms like *beyt + d→ *beyt + t*. That is, the rules must be applied in the order that they are numbered above.

If the irregular verbs are included in the scheme, such changes as *teyk + d→teyk + t→teykt* ('taked') would be derived. Thus, rules which account for the irregular forms must be ordered so as to apply before the general rules are applied. Such a rule might be *teyk + d→ tuk* 'took', and this must be ordered so it applies before P1.

As the example above indicates, phonological rules can be synchronically ordered. The order of the rules, however, does not necessarily reflect the order of historical changes in the language. Various studies have demonstrated that within a synchronic description of a language a particular set of rules in a certain order is necessary, but that the historical changes, while using the same rules, took place in an order different from that specified for the synchronic rules.[2] Within the method of internal reconstruction, arguments for relative chronology of changes hinge on the assumption that the output of one change serves as input for the next. That is to say, in the method of internal reconstruction, changes are viewed essentially as rule addition at the end of the grammar. Yet when such rules are made explicit, as within the framework of ordered rules, such changes are sometimes found not to recapitulate the known history of a language.

Diachronic phonological rules consist of rule additions to the grammar and rule simplification. The development of a prothetic vowel [e-] in Spanish before [s] plus a consonant, *cf* Latin *stare* and Spanish *estar*, was essentially a case of rule addition and can be formulated as follows:

ø→e/# − [s] [+ consonant]

The modification of Vulgar Latin [u] to Old French [ü] in which a high-back-rounded vowel became a high-front-rounded vowel, *eg*, *muru→mür*, represents the addition of the following rule to the grammar:

$$\begin{bmatrix} \text{vowel} \\ +\text{high} \end{bmatrix} \rightarrow [-\text{back}]$$

The feature 'rounded' remains constant and need not enter into the rule.

Several rules were added to the grammar of Old High German. Final voiced obstruents became voiceless between AD 900–1200 depending on the dialect, *ie*

$$[+\text{obstruent}] \rightarrow [-\text{voice}] \mathbin{/}\_\#$$

A second rule around AD 1400 lengthened vowels before voiced obstruents, *ie*

$$\text{vowel} \rightarrow [+\text{long}] \mathbin{/}\_\begin{bmatrix} +\text{obstruent} \\ +\text{voice} \end{bmatrix}$$

Rule simplification appears to take place in one of several ways: rules are simply lost, or they are reordered. Reordering is a form of simplification that has certain ramifications concerning the relationship between synchronic and diachronic rule ordering. In the preceding example from German where the historical events are documented, the diachronic order of modifications differs from the synchronic ordered rules, *ie*

(1) DIACHRONIC			(2) SYNCHRONIC	
	path	paths		
underlying form	veg	vegə	veg	vegə
final devoicing	vek	–	veːg	veːgə
vowel lengthening	–	veːgə	veːk	–
phonetic shape	vek	veːgə	veːk	veːgə

The final lexical shape [vek] (adverb) 'away' is not possible in the synchronic ordering of the rules. It is the result of the diachronic rules in which a split occurred between [e] and [eː] under different environmental conditions. The synchronic rules do not reflect this split, however, indicating that at some point in time after the vowel lengthening rule was added, the rules were reordered. The assumption underlying rule reordering is that rules tend to shift into the order that allows their fullest utilization, *ie*, their broadest generalization in the grammar. Vowel lengthening operates on a larger number of forms in (2) than in (1). More traditional modes of inquiry might rely on the concept of analogy to account for vowel lengthening before voiceless obstruents ([veːk]) modelled on the plural formation [veːgə]. In this case, however, analogy does not seem to have motivated the form [veːk] since [e]→[eː] before voiced obstruents after synchronic rule reordering.[3]

Rule addition may cause certain modifications in the sequential arrangements of sounds without introducing any new sounds into the language. In some varieties of Canadian English words such as *pattern* and *modern* undergo metathesis under certain extra-linguistic conditions and are pronounced as [pʰatʰrən] and [maːdrən]. In standard Canadian these words are [pʰæːdərn] and [maːdərn]. In the latter pronunciation the intervocalic *t* is voiced and a stressed vowel preceding a voiced consonant is lengthened. In the variant pronunciation a metathesis rule changes the endings of these words from *-ern* to *-ren*. This rule appears to have been added so that it is ordered before the intervocalic voicing rule and prevents its application by removing the voicing environment. The metathesis rule also removes the lengthening environment and supplies the environment for aspiration of *t* before *r*.

Relationships between rules have been characterized as feeding order and bleeding order.[4] The former converts rule A to which rule B does not apply into forms to which rule B can apply. In Finnish, for example, [γ]→[ø], *ie*, *teγe*→*tee* and *tee*→*tie* through diphthongization. Applied in the order

(1) γ→ø
(2) diphthongization

rule (1) supplies a new set of cases to which rule (2) can apply. This may help determine the direction in which rules are reordered, *ie*, to maximize feeding. If on the other hand the application of a lowering rule converts [o]→[ɔ] an umlaut rule could then apply, *ie*, [ɔ]→[ɔ̈]. If the umlaut rule preceded the lowering rule, *ie*, [o]→[ö], the lowering rule would then not apply. Reordering of rules may occur to minimize the bleeding rule in which one rule precludes another from operating.

Changes may occur through modifications to the underlying representations of lexical items. The representations contain semantic, morphological and phonological characteristics. The phonological information is specified in systematic phonemic features. If there are changes at this level then different rules may apply to a particular word from those that applied to it at a previous stage. There will then be a different phonetic form for the word without any phonetic changes in the rules.

In Russian, dentals and velars palatalized, *ie*

$$\begin{bmatrix} t, k \\ d, g \\ s, x \end{bmatrix} \rightarrow \begin{bmatrix} \check{c} \\ \check{g} \\ \check{s} \end{bmatrix}$$

A second spirantization rule converted [ǧ]→[ž] through loss of occlusion. In Ukrainian [ž], which was derived from underlying /d/, was reaffricated and became once again [ǧ]. The [ž] in Ukrainian from other sources (*eg*, Slavic /g/→Ukrainian [γ]→[ž]) did not regain affrication:

$$d \rightarrow \begin{cases} \check{g} \rightarrow \check{z} \rightarrow \check{g} \\ d \end{cases} \qquad\qquad \gamma \rightarrow \begin{cases} \check{z} \\ \gamma \end{cases} \qquad\qquad \check{z} \rightarrow \check{z}$$

Without recourse to underlying forms the split of [ž] into [ž] and [ǧ] appears unmotivated since environmental conditions do not account for it. The regularity of the change is borne out by the fact that [ž]→[ǧ] if there was an underlying /d/. Ukrainian, then, dropped the spirantization rule that converted [ǧ]→[ž] and restored occlusivity on the basis of the underlying occlusive /d/.

As the foregoing discussion indicates, rules convert the underlying abstract representations in the lexicon into representations on the phonetic level. A lexical entry, expressed in the notation + or − (*eg*, + consonantal, − vocalic, + obstruent, − voice, etc) serves as input to the phonological component. This component contains rules which interpret the input in terms of the actual pronunciation of the language. The lexical item *pin*, for example, can be specified in the deep structure as follows:

p	*i*	*n*
+ consonantal	− consonantal	+ consonantal
− vocalic	+ vocalic	− vocalic
− nasal	+ diffuse	+ nasal
+ grave	− grave	− grave
− continuant	− tense	
+ diffuse		
− voice		

Redundant or predictable features, however, can be indicated by o and the above phonological description can be reformulated as follows:

	p	*i*	*n*
consonantal	+	−	+
vocalic	−	+	−
nasal	−	o	+
continuant	−	o	o
grave	+	−	−
diffuse	+	+	o
tense	o	−	o
voice	−	o	o[5]

This representation for *pin* is called a feature matrix. Each of the features assigned the value o in this matrix can be predicted on the basis of the presence of other features in the matrix. In the second column, representing the vowel *i*, that the feature *nasal* is considered redundant is based on the fact that nasalized vowels in English do not oppose non-nasal vowels. Therefore if the feature *vocalic* is specified +, then the feature *nasal* is automatically specified − and there is no need to provide a specification for *nasal* in the underlying representation. Similarly vowels are redundant in relation to the specification *continuant*, *ie*, there are no non-continuant vowels etc. In the word *pin* a change in a redundant feature such as nasality could involve a phonological split whereby nasal vowels arise opposed to non-nasal vowels, while a modification of a distinctive feature specification might lead to a phonological merger, *eg*, [− voice]→[+ voice]. Since phonological change involves a change in feature specification, the sequence structure must be taken into account. The feature [+ vocalic] may well be distinctive in some environments but in others it is entirely predictable. Compare, for example, the environment after three initial consonants in English. It could be shown that the sound in the environment *skr-m* in *scream* is predictable as [+ vocalic].

Certain features are redundant then, when their position of occurrence is considered, hence the number of features of the same sound may be different in various lexical forms. The /s/ in *sit* contains more feature-specifications than /s/ in *spit* since in initial position before an obstruent the only consonant to occur is /s/. If, for example, the second segment in the lexical entry *spit* is marked

+ consonantal and − vocalic, *ie*, as a true consonant, *s* need not be marked for those features that distinguish it from other consonants in English such as *p*, *t* and *k*. No other consonant in English occurs in initial position before a true consonant. Before a vowel, however, the features that distinguish *s* from other consonants would have to be specified since they are in opposition: *sick, pick, kick, tick*, etc. Such systematic relationships between environments and feature-specifications are important factors in phonological change which have not been given enough emphasis in other linguistic approaches.

Modern Standard French provides an example of change in under-lying representations. Until recently, most (if not all) speakers of Standard French made a distinction between *patte* [pat] 'paw', and *pâte* [pɐt] 'paste'. The vowel in *patte* was low and front while in *pâte* the vowel was low and back.[6] Many speakers of Standard French (here referred to as Variety B) do not now make this distinction. *Patte* and *pâte* are homophonous forms for these speakers. Variety B is a linear descendant of Variety A which made a distinction between *a* and *ɒ*.[7]

In Variety B, the low vowels have merged and there is a single underlying vowel for both *patte* and *pâte*. The merger did not involve simply a replacement of one vowel (or representation) by the other. This is clear by comparing Variety B with a subdialect of Canadian French. The latter reflects an earlier stage of Standard French and can be designated Variety A.

An abbreviated version of the Variety B system appears as follows:

(1) i   u
     e   o
     ɛ   ɑ   ɔ

There are seven vowels with three distinctive degrees of aperture. ɑ is the only central vowel and is thus distinguished from ɛ and ɔ.

Variety A, with two underlying low vowels, appears as

(2) i   u
     e   o
     ɛ   ɔ
     a   ɐ

There are eight vowels pertaining to four distinctive levels of aperture. The merger of *a* and *ɒ* not only reduced the vocalic inventory by one, but involved the restructuring of the underlying system. The restructuring appears to have required a new set of features and not simply a readjustment of feature-specification.

Variety B, for example, can be characterized by two features, 'high' and 'low' to distinguish the three levels of aperture (see 1):

(3)   i   e   ε
    high   +   −   −
    low   −   −   +

The features 'high' and 'low', however are inadequate for a four-level system as Variety A, since there is no means of distinguishing the mid vowels:

(4)   i   e   ε   a
    high   +   −   −   −
    low   −   −   −   +

The features 'high' and 'mid' can appropriately distinguish a four-level system, however, as shown in 5 (cf 2),

(5)   i   e   ε   a
    high   +   +   −   −
    mid   −   +   +   −

It can now be argued that the shift from Variety A to B did not involve the introduction of a new feature (ie, 'low') in the sense that (5) became (3) but that there was a different set of underlying distinctions which gave rise to the distinctively central characteristic of the vowel in *patte* and *pâte*. No underlying vowels in Variety A are distinctively central.

Naturalness and language change

As a theoretical concept within generative grammar, markedness has been proposed for specifying the representation of phonological properties of items in the lexicon. It is concerned with providing a more abstract level of representation than that provided by the notions + and −. Lexical items are designated marked or unmarked in accordance with each phonological entity. Unmarked sounds are considered more natural to the human organism since they are the result of least physiological or perceptual effort. Marked sounds, on the other hand, require some further adjustment to the vocal mechanism or perceptual apparatus. Consonants, for example, may be unmarked or marked and the latter may pertain to such features as

voice, glottalization, palatalization etc. On this highly abstract level
marked values are less predictable than unmarked values (less
natural). They are converted into universal features, *eg*, + voice,
+ glottalized or + palatalized etc on a less abstract level. If sounds
are marked by the addition of some feature to their more natural or
unmarked counterparts, phonological systems would not be expected to display only marked values. This, in a sense, would be a
sort of unnatural system in which all the sounds needed some added
adjustment from a more natural condition.

From the point of view of language change, then, languages would
be expected to add a marked feature to an unmarked consonantal
series but they would not be expected to lose an unmarked series
while maintaining only their marked counterparts. A reconstructed
phonological system that contained only marked values would be
highly suspect inasmuch as it would appear to violate the naturalness
condition of language.[8]

If a dialect *w* split into two dialects *w* and *x* the loss or merger of the
marked series would be considered a normal course of events, *ie*

dialect w			*dialect x*		
p	t	k	p	t	k
px	tx	kx			

(where x = a marked value).

Dialect *y* splitting into two dialects *y* and *z* and giving rise to the
loss or merger of the unmarked series would be expected to occur
only rarely:

dialect y			*dialect z*		
p	t	k	px	tx	kx
px	tx	kx			

The theory of naturalness finds support in the fact that the unmarked member has a higher frequency of occurrence in natural
languages. There is some evidence suggesting that it is the first to
occur in the acquisition of languages and may be the most resistant
to loss through neurological disorders such as aphasia.[9] It is the unmarked member which often appears in neutralized environments.[10]
Finally, the use of marked and unmarked conventions in language
description reflects rules with the greatest generality, hence economy.[11] Further verification can be expected to come from investigations of language change in which modifications are inhibited by

the natural condition.[12] Considerations of markedness and natural-ness in language change arise from attempts to understand the nature of rule change within the external principle of simplicity or economy. If it is assumed that rule changes tend towards simplifications then there must be some specific internal factors which not only permit simplifications but in fact favour and encourage them. Markedness and naturalness are two interwoven concepts designed to pinpoint these features and how they work.

The phonological processes involved in morphophonemic alter-nations may themselves be governed by natural considerations which can be ranked in order of frequency to yield predictions about the type of changes imminent in any system. The order of modification of linguistic processes which occur in natural languages may re-present the relative strength of these processes. Such considerations lead to a relative scale of likelihood of occurrence based upon the strength or weakness of the process.[13]

A rule that voices phonological segments in voiced surroundings is very common among the world's languages, for example, [ata→ ada].

$$\begin{bmatrix} -\text{vocalic} \\ +\text{consonantal} \end{bmatrix} \rightarrow [+\text{voiced}]/ \begin{bmatrix} +\text{vocalic} \\ -\text{consonantal} \end{bmatrix} - \begin{bmatrix} +\text{vocalic} \\ -\text{consonantal} \end{bmatrix}$$

Less common, but equally simple in terms of number of features, is the devoicing of vowels in voiceless environments, *eg*

$$\begin{bmatrix} +\text{vocalic} \\ -\text{consonantal} \end{bmatrix} \rightarrow [-\text{voiced}] /$$

$$\begin{bmatrix} -\text{vocalic} \\ +\text{consonantal} \end{bmatrix} - \begin{bmatrix} -\text{vocalic} \\ +\text{consonantal} \end{bmatrix}$$

While it has been maintained within the generative-transfor-mational approach that language change comes about by the addition of rules, the view has also been taken that all changes in language reflect a change in a rule in which the precursor must be sought in an earlier rule, *eg*, the voicing of Latin s→z/v-v is general-ized in Spanish by the rule

$$\begin{Bmatrix} s \\ p \\ t \\ k \end{Bmatrix} \rightarrow \begin{Bmatrix} z \\ b \\ d \\ g \end{Bmatrix} \text{ /V-V or } + \text{consonant} \rightarrow + \text{voiced /v-v}$$

It has been stated that:

> . . . historical change does not result from the addition of rules to
> the grammar of the parent language, but rather from operations
> on rules already present in the parent language. Every putative
> innovation in a daughter language must have a source in the
> parent language. This follows from my contention that there is a
> universal set of phonological rules. These rules are manifestations
> of certain very basic fundamental laws, or archetypal rules. These
> archetypal rules are a part of the genetic constitution of every
> individual. Any cerebrate human possesses these archetypal rules,
> which have different manifestations in say, Latin and Spanish, so
> that although it might look as if a rule were being added, actually
> we would be concerned with a change in specification of an
> archetypal rule.[14]

A fundamental departure from earlier views within the generative-
transformational approach concerns the difference between abstract
levels of phonological representation on the one hand and phonetic
representation on the other. Phonological change may be motivated
by deep structure considerations, *ie*, at the most abstract phonological level where the formatives act as input to the first phonological
rules. The idea that phonetic change, *ie*, modification motivated by
the surface structure, depicts all phonological change (except by
analogy) is losing ground. Phonological processes of the kind mentioned in Chapter 6 thus may be inhibited by abstract configurations, giving the appearance of irregularity where actually none
exists.

Language change in the generative-transformational framework is
by no means restricted to the types of modifications discussed so far.
Changes may occur, for example, among the syntactic relationships
of the items in the lexicon.

SECTION II
Diachronic syntax

Treatments of syntactic change generally have not shown much insight into the nature of the processes at work on the syntactic level of
language. More often than not, investigators have recorded the syntactic constructions of various stages of a given language and

attempted to account for the modifications on the basis of phono-logical change. Compare the following:

Latin	*French*
Per dei amorem et per	Pour l'amour de Dieu et pour le
christiani populi et nostram	salut commun du peuple
communem salutem . . .	chrétien et le nôtre . . .

Phonological levelling of inflectional categories gave rise to new syn-tactic constructions in the Romance languages based on prepositions, articles, auxiliaries, etc. Some changes, however, are purely syn-tactic and are not brought about by phonological modifications. During an earlier period of English the negative particle *not* could follow any verb:

He likes not John
He sees not the house

Such sentences are no longer grammatical since *not* has become restricted in the position following a verb to certain modal or auxiliary forms, such as,

He ought not to come
She has not arrived

Inadequate theories of syntax have in the past hampered clear for-mulations of syntactic change. Within generative-transformational theory the syntactic component consists of the base component and the transformational component. Changes in syntax take the form of rule changes in the transformational component and consist of addi-tion, loss or reordering of rules. Consider the following examples from Spanish in which we find such sentences as

Esta casa es la casa mía	'This house is my house'
Esta casa es la mía	'This house is mine'
Esta casa es mi casa	'This house is my house'

An underlying structure can be posited for all three sentences:

Esta casa es la mía casa

Hence a rule deletes in one case the word *casa*, while in another the article is deleted and by still another rule a change in position has occurred:

la mía casa
la mía −
− mi casa
la casa mía

A phonological rule deletes the final vowel *mía→mi* in the syntactic position before a noun.[15]

The following section explores more fully recent developments in diachronic syntax within generative theory.[16]

* * *

Language change in generative theory is viewed as grammar change. Generative grammars consist of a base component, a transformational component and a phonological component. The base consists of two subcomponents: the categorial component and the lexicon. The categorial component is a system of rewrite rules which produce terminal strings of elements bearing specific linear and hierarchical relationships to each other.[17] The lexicon lists words which can be attached to the nodes in the strings. Transformations are processes which operate upon various subsets of these strings to modify the previously specified relationships in determinable ways. The results, or output of these transformations is the derived structure and is the level to which phonological rules apply. There are, then, three levels of structure in the grammar; (1) a base component; (2) a transformational component; and (3) a phonological component. The first two are often called the syntactic component. The semantic component, which provides the semantic information relevant to the items in the base component, is not taken up in this section. Semantic change is dealt with elsewhere in this book and will not be treated separately here.

It is reasonable to anticipate that language change could affect each of the three components without any direct effects on the operations of the other two components.[18] This does not mean that there is not interaction between the levels and the changes that occur in each level: it only means that there are specific categories of change and that different components will have different manifestations of changes. For example, one would not usually expect to find that a modification in relative clause structures would bring about a remodelling of the phonological rules which palatalize velars before front vowels.

If the first assumption of generative diachrony is that language change is grammar change, then there must be specific elements of grammars that change. We have just seen that grammars consist of three major levels and that each of these levels is composed of a set of rules. We can now go on to assume that grammar change takes place through rule change. If this is the case, then what kind of rule changes occur? A first anticipation would be that rules can undergo internal change in two specific ways: (1) they might change so that they apply to a new set of items, a set which is smaller or greater than at an earlier stage; or (2) they might be modified so that they produce new outputs. Secondly, changes in the number of rules might occur either through rule loss or through rule additions. A third possibility would be that grammars change through reordering of rules. This section is devoted to understanding this conception of language change as rule change applied to the syntactic component of grammars.

Diachrony and the base

It has not been demonstrated that dialects show differences in the order of application of the rewrite base rules. This has suggested to some observers that the base component is unordered.[19] It is, however, difficult to determine whether or not dialects actually do differ in the ordering of the base rules, because of the power of the transformational process.

It has been proposed that the underlying word order in German is subject-object-verb (SOV) and that a transformation changes this order to SVO in main clauses. Another view posits the underlying order SVO with a transformation which changes this order to SOV in subordinate clauses.[20] These two proposals are summarized in (1) below.

(1) a b
Underlying $[S_1O_1[S_2O_2V_2]V_1]$ $[S_1V_1O_1[S_2V_2O_2]]$
Surface $[S_1V_1O_1[S_2O_2V_2]]$ $[S_1V_1O_1[S_2O_2V_2]]$

Although the two analyses differ in their underlying syntactic representations, they produce the same surface structures. Sentence

(2) fits the surface description in (1) if the lexical items in (3) are attached to the appropriate nodes.

(2) Hans vergisst die Tatsache, dass Fritz Anna sieht.

(3) S_1 = Hans
  O_1 = die Tatsache
  V_1 = vergisst
  S_2 = Fritz
  O_2 = Anna
  V_2 = sieht

The *dass* of sentence (2) is inserted transformationally. Since sentence (2) is not ambiguous it should have only one underlying structure. It cannot, then, be the case that both analyses in (1) are correct. This dilemma in the analysis of German derives from the fact that transformational procedures can be invoked to produce any desired result. If equally viable but conflicting descriptions of the base structure exist for the same set of data and if it is impossible to value one analysis over the other, then, in general, it is difficult, if not impossible, to specify whether or not changes can occur in the base. Any putative changes in the base rules may have been changes in the transformations.

A second consideration at this point is the proposal that there is a universal base structure. Under this proposal all languages share a common base and only differ from each other in the way structures are derived from it. If the universal base hypothesis is correct there cannot be any language-particular diachronic changes in the base. There could only be species wide changes accompanying alterations in the cognitive capacities of human beings. That is, there would have to be a biological change in order for base structures to change.

Although there appear to be some specific correlations between evolutionary stages and some aspects of linguistic phenomena,[21] there have been no demonstrations linking current discussions of the base component to attested biological phenomena. Therefore the lack of dialect differentiation at this level is easy to understand. It is possible that dialects differ in their base structures, but present knowledge and orientations suggest that they do not. It is, however, possible to speculate on the nature of changes that could occur as they would be observed in generative linguistic theory. If the position is correct that the base is unordered, then rule reorderings would not be possible. Rules could, however, be lost or added, or new subcategories introduced. Similarly the status of previously existing categories could be altered.

Let us say that (4) represents part of the base component at a particular stage in a language.

(4) a   S→NP   VP
    b   VP→(NP)   V
    c   NP→NP   (S)
    d   V→(AUX) MV

During that stage a sentence (S) consisted of a noun phrase (NP) and a verb phrase (VP). This dominance relationship is indicated by the unidirectional 'rewrite' arrow. A verb phrase consisted of at least a verb (V). A verb could be preceded by a NP although the presence of a NP was not a necessary part of the VP. This optional status of the NP is indicated by enclosing it in parentheses. Any noun phrase consisted at least of a noun (N) with an optionally associated embedded S. Verbs contained at least a main verb (MV) together with an optional auxiliary (AUX). If, during the evolution of the language in (4) the status of the AUX is changed from optional to obligatory, then (5) will represent a subsequent stage of the same language and auxiliaries will appear in all sentences.

(5) a   S→NP   VP
    b   VP→(NP)   V
    c   NP→NP   (S)
    d   V→AUX   MV

Alternatively, there might develop a reflex of this language in which no auxiliaries occurred and for which there would be no reason to have the category *AUX* present at all. In this case the portion of the grammar in (4) would be represented as (6).

(6) a   S→NP   VP
    b   VP→(NP)   V
    c   NP→NP   (S)

Yet another possibility exists. We could imagine that (6) represented the proto language and that (4) and (5) were reflexes of (6). In this case there would be a new category introduced as well as a new rule added.[22]

The lexical subcomponent of the base inserts lexical items into the terminal strings generated by the rewrite rules or categorial component. Each entry in the lexicon, or dictionary, is made up of semantic and syntactic information and an underlying phonological form. The syntactic information appears as features which are sensitive to the environment specified in terminal strings.

The functional properties reflected by the notation S O V in (1) are derivatives of the interrelationships between the categorial sequence NP-NP-VP. The interpretation might arise from a convention such as: the first NP in a sequence is the subject (S), the second is object (O) and a VP is the verb (V). In order for the correct lexical insertion given in (2) to occur, the lexical items are paired with the nodes NP and VP. Since it must take an animate subject, *vergisst* will have a feature [+ [NP + animate]]. This feature says that the item to which it is attached can be inserted into a phrase marker if a preceding NP is [+ animate]. Similarly *die Tatsache* cannot be inserted into an NP in subject position if *vergisst* is the verb. Diachronic changes in these co-occurrence restrictions on lexical items should be possible but, since they are closely involved with semantic change, they are not directly relevant to the present discussion.

Diachrony and transformations

Changes in the transformational component are much easier to determine because they have a direct bearing on the observable data, the textual information on which a great deal of our analysis rests. Whenever there are clear systematic changes in the way syntactic elements relate to each other in sentences, the historical linguist can look for some specific change in the rules which generate the relevant sequences.

In Old French, a sentence or clause initial adverb or object pronoun entailed an inversion of the subject and verb. For example:

(7) Là est-il.
    'There is he.'
    'There he is.'

(8) Dont dist le dus au chevalier . . .
    'Then said the Duke to the knight . . .'
    'Then the Duke said to the knight . . .'

The structural description of the transformation which inverted the subject and verb in (7) and (8) must mention the presence of a sentence initial adverb. If the environment is met, then the inversion takes place. A simplified version of this transformation would have looked something like (9):

(9) *adverb*   inversion: OBLIGATORY
    structural description X   adverb   NP   VP   Y
                           1   2   3   4   5
    structural change   1   2   ø   4+3   5

This transformation operates upon all sentences (strings) which are described by its structural description and is hence given obligatory status. The transformation states that if a string has an initial adverb followed by a NP and a VP, together with the variables X and Y, the order of the elements will be changed to that specified in the structural change. Variables like X and Y may be empty, they may contain fully specified constituents such as NP, VP and so on, or they may merely designate the presence of a boundary.

In the Middle French period (fourteenth–sixteenth centuries) inversion following sentence initial adverbs was optional. That is, in some instances the inversion occurred and in some it did not. There were no conditions which differentiated the inverted environments from the uninverted ones. This change is reflected in the grammar by a redesignation of (9) from OBLIGATORY to OPTIONAL status. With this status the transformation applies randomly (but only to the environment specified in the structural description).

There is a transformation in Modern literary French which is a direct reflex of (9). However, it has been very much altered from its Middle French prototype. Whereas in Old and Middle French the environment of *2* in the structural description of (9) could be filled by any adverb, in Modern French there are only a few adverbs which bring about the application of an inversion transformation, *eg*, *à peine* 'hardly', *peut-être* 'maybe', *en vain* 'vainly', *aussi* 'therefore', *toujours* 'nevertheless'.

Sample sentences are:

(10) A peine l'avait-il quittée qu'elle . . .
           'Scarcely her had he left when she . . .'
           'He had scarcely left her when she . . .'

(11) Peut-être était-elle une de ces . . .
           'Maybe was she one of those . . .'
           'Maybe she was one of those . . .'

(12) Ils étaient grands, aussi trouvais-je . . .
　　　'They were big, so thought I . . .'
　　　'They were big, so I thought . . .'

Between Middle French and Modern French the information in the section labelled *2* in the structural description of (9) has changed. Instead of the category simply being *Adverb*, it now includes much more detail: it appears to contain a list of the adverbs *à peine* and so on. When one of these adverbs occurs in initial position, inversion is obligatory. The adverb-inversion transformation then looks like (13).

(13)　　　　　　　　　　adverb-inversion　OBLIGATORY

$$
\text{X} \left\{ \begin{array}{l} \textit{adverb} \\ \text{à peine} \\ \text{peut-être} \\ \text{aussi} \\ \text{toujours} \\ \text{en vain} \end{array} \right\} \quad \text{NP} \quad \text{VP} \quad \text{Y}
$$

structural description	1	2	3	4	5
structural change	1	2	ø	4+3	5

The internal restructuring represented by the change from (9) to (13) is a complication of the grammar.

In Modern popular French the adverb-inversion rule has been completely lost and sentences like (14) occur.

(14) Peut-être il va venir.
　　　'Maybe he will come.'

These data then show several types of change: alternation between optional and obligatory status of rules, internal restructuring, and rule loss.

　　　Certain French dialects, including some varieties of Canadian French, illustrate diachronic change through the addition of a rule. In most French dialects the basic process of question formation is inversion of pronominalized subjects and auxiliaries.[23] The declarative sentences in (15) have the interrogative counterparts (16) in Standard French

(15) *a* Il vient.
      'He is coming.'
  b Jean vient.
      'John is coming.'
  c Ma soeur part demain.
      'My sister is leaving tomorrow.'
  d Je vais à l'école aujourd'hui.
      'I am going to school today.'

(16) *a* Vient-il?
      'Is he coming?'
  b Jean vient-il?
      'Is John coming?'
  c Ma soeur part-elle demain?
      'Is my sister leaving tomorrow?'
  d Est-ce que je vais à l'école aujourd'hui?
      'Am I going to school today?'[24]

In some dialects there is another question formation process. It involves the attachment of the particle *ti* in post verbal position so that (15) has the counterpart (17).

(17) *a* Il vient ti?
  b Jean vient ti?
  c Ma soeur part ti demain?
  d Je vais ti à l'école aujourd'hui?

Since these dialects also have sentences like those in (16) the evolution of the *ti* attachment rule cannot be seen as a replacement of the inversion transformation but is rather the *addition* of a rule. When this rule was first added it applied only to third person forms. It was then generalized to apply to all persons.[25]

It has been shown that it is possible for dialects (and therefore historical stages) to differ according to the order in which transformations apply.[26] Each set of sentences in (18) to (21) represents a different dialect and successive stages in the evolution of some varieties of English.

(18) *a* *He* and *I* left.
  b *Whom* did he speak with?
  c It was *I*.

(19) *a* *He* and *I* left.
    b *Who* did he speak with?
    c It was *I*.

(20) *a* *He* and *I* left.
    b *Who* did he speak with?
    c It was *me*.

(21) *a* *Him* and *me* left.
    b ————————————
    c It was *me*.

Each set of sentences in this series differs from the adjacent set by one item. These differences can be expressed as the diachronic residue of modifications in the sequential order in which the relevant transformations apply. Sentence (18)*b* differs from (19)*b* and (20)*b* in having *whom* where the latter have *who*. *Whom* and *who* both derive from the same underlying source. Both words are derived by a transformation called *WH* attachment which attaches the morpheme *WH* to an indefinite NP. An additional transformation, case attachment, applies to the output of *WH* attachment to give *whom*.

The underlying syntactic sequence for (*b*) in (18) to (20) is (22).

(22) WH – he – spoke – with – someone

The *WH* in (22) is an interrogative morpheme which is transformationally attached to one of the NP's in the string – in this case to *someone*. *WH* attachment moves the NP so affected to sentence initial position, as in (23).

(23) WH + someone – he – spoke – with

Both *whom* and *who* are derived by this transformation. The difference between these two words arises from a case marking transformation which applies in (18)*b* but not in (19)*b* and (20)*b*. Case marking affixes an overt case marker -*m* to third person pronouns following prepositions. There is independent evidence that the dialect represented in (19) also has a similar case marking transformation.

It is clear that the complex *WH* + *someone* in (23) does not meet the requirements of case marking, so that regular morphological processes will derive (19)*b* and (20)*b* from (23). The order of rules to derive (19) and (20) then is:

1 WH attachment
2 Case marking

Sentence (18)*b* cannot be derived by this order of rules.

If case marking is applied to (22) before *WH* attachment, then as shown in (24), the proper derived string for (18)*b* will result.

(24) *a* WH – he – spoke – with – someone
    b Case marking
       WH – he – spoke – with – someone + CASE
    c WH attachment
       WH + someone + CASE – he – spoke – with
    d Other rules
       Whom did he speak with?

Since (18) represents a prior stage in the linear sequence of developments implied in (18) to (21), the difference between (18)*b* and (*b*) in (19) and (20) is due to a change in the order of application of transformations.

The *me* in (20)*c* and (21)*c* derives from a modified (extended) case marking transformation: all pronouns following *be* are marked for case. This new case marking transformation follows *WH* attachment, so that there is no ordering change in the transition from (19) to (21).

Him and *me* in (21)*a* are not the result of another extension of case marking but reflect instead a change in the underlying representation of the subject pronoun.[27] The data in (18) to (21), then, present three types of change: rule reordering, internal changes or extension of transformations, and modifications of underlying phonological shapes.

One other type of change, while not strictly a syntactic change in the same sense as the examples discussed so far, has been observed. It has been noted that while there seems to be a great difference in the conditions under which subjunctives occur in subordinate clauses in Latin and Spanish, careful analysis shows this not to be so.[28] The differences appear to be due merely to changes in the list of words which are specially marked to take complements containing subjunctive verbs. That is, in Latin a certain set of verbs in the main clauses of sentences was obligatorily followed by subordinate clauses with subjunctive verbs. The subordinate clauses could be optionally introduced by a variety of complementizing constructions. In Spanish the type of complement structure is not optional but is governed by certain characteristics of the whole sentence. The complementizer (and subjunctive) rules in Latin and Spanish are essentially the same rules. The superficial differences are due to changes in lexical redundancies. Lexical redundancies are features attached to words which indicate how rules are to apply to sequences containing these features. Changes in these redundancies do not necessitate changes in rule structure but will of course result in different surface structures.

It has often been asserted that language change is simplification.[29] It may well be better to consider that change is part of a dichotomy whose members are simplification and complication. These categories apply to internal changes in transformations. An instance of simplification examined here would be the extension of the dialectal *ti* particle from third person to all other verb forms. This is a simplification because the *ti* attachment transformation does not need to refer to anything other than the presence of an interrogative morpheme. In its earliest stages it had to refer to the number of the subject. The structural description therefore contained a great deal of specific information which it does not contain now. The change of the adverb-inversion rule from Middle to Modern French is a case of complication because the category mentioned by the rule in Old and Middle French was very general whereas it is highly restricted in Modern French. The changes accounting for the differences between the sentences in (18) to (21) may not appear in the hierarchy of simplification and complication. Reordering of rules may simplify the derivation in some sense but there is no clear internal simplification of the relevant rules. Lexical redundancy changes may also be outside the realm of simplicity considerations. If the changes come about so that all verbs possessing particular semantic features behave in the same way, then the redundancy changes are simplifications. Otherwise they may be neither complications nor simplifications.

The rule addition and rule loss represented by the initial introduction of the *ti* attachment and deletion of the adverb-inversion rule in French are both instances of change which are definitely outside the realm of the simplicity-complexity bifurcation. Although the *ti* attachment rule at its inception was internally complex, that does not affect the fact that the addition of a rule as a unitary process does not increase complexity of the grammar in the way that the restrictions on adverb-inversion do. Similarly, the only way to conceive of the loss of adverb-inversion as a simplification would be to say that an internally complex rule has been deleted. A distinction between changes in the number, order and status of rules on the one hand and internal changes within rules on the other must be made.

Summary

The types of syntactic change that occur are:

1 optional-obligatory status changes (Middle French adverb-inversion)
2 internal restructuring (adverb-inversion in Modern literary French)
3 rule loss (adverb-inversion in Modern popular French)
4 rule addition (*ti* attachment)
5 rule reordering (English pronouns)
6 redundancy changes (Latin-Spanish subjunctive)

These six types of change are tentative classifications of specific examples. Some of these types interact with a simplification-complication dichotomy. There is at present no unified theory of diachronic syntax beyond the general notion of rule change within generative grammars.

Notes

1 The notation for the data ignores many phonetic specifications (such as stress, vowel length and nasalization, etc) which are not relevant for the present discussion. In a full grammar of the language, all such specifications would be indicated by the application of rules. I am indebted to G. Prideaux for comments concerning this section.

2 For example see Postal Chapter 13, especially *pp* 279–280. Kiparsky (1968a) presents an interesting discussion on the general topic of rule ordering and historical changes, including a discussion of the changes in underlying forms over time.

3 See Kiparsky, *op cit*, and King (1969).

4 See Kiparsky, *op cit* for this and the following example.

5 See Harms (1968), *p* 14.

6 There was also a length feature involved: *patte* [pat], *pâte* [pɐːt].

7 There are several ways to account for the change. One could argue that a new rule was added to B which merged, underlying *a* and *v* at some stage in the synchronic derivation. Since, however, all reflexes of *a* and *v* have merged, there is no need to posit an underlying distinction at all.

8 For more detail concerning marked and unmarked, see Chomsky and Halle, *pp* 400–435, Schane (1968b), *pp* 709–716, and Postal, *pp* 153–207.

9 See Jakobson (1967).

10 See Schane, *op cit*.

11 See Chomsky and Halle, *pp* 400–435 and Harms, *op cit*.

12 See Postal, *p* 170.

13 For details of this approach, see Foley (1969).

14 *Ibid*, *p* 45.

15 See also Langacker (1968).

16 I am indebted to George W. Patterson, University of Alberta, for the next section as well as for helpful comments and examples throughout the chapter.

17 The following discussion is based on the 'standard theory' of generative grammars as outlined in Chomsky (1965). The ways in which the standard theory has been modified by Chomsky (1969) and others (see Chomsky (1969) for partial bibliography) do not materially affect the discussion.

18 This is of course an oversimplification. If a phonological rule is dependent upon some particular syntactic environment for its operation, it will be affected if the syntactic environment is not produced because of a change in the syntactic rules. This is an indirect influence. A direct influence would occur if a syntactic change necessarily entailed an internal phonological change, or vice versa.

19 See McCawley.

20 See Peters in reference to this discussion based on an analysis of German presented by Bach, Bierwisch and Ross.

21 See Lieberman and Crelin.

22 Closs has presented some specific instances of changes in the base rules which derived English auxiliary structures at various stages. Her results are interesting but since they were presented in the preuniversal base era and for the reasons outlined by Peters (see Note 20), her findings may be reflections of the ways in which transformations handle the categories generated by the base and of changes in restrictions on what elements can co-occur in particular structures rather than changes in the base itself.

23 This is highly simplified. For detail see Langacker (1965, 1971), Hirschbühler, Huddleston and Uren, Patterson (1971b), Kayne.

24 Most first person singular interrogatives are formed by the insertion of initial *est-ce que*. For diachronic detail see Patterson (1971b).

25 For a discussion of some of the problems relating to the inception of this rule and its interpretation in generative diachrony see Patterson (1971a, 1971b).

26 See Klima.

27 A more detailed summary of Klima's findings appears in King (1969, *pp* 143–149).

28 See Lakoff, Chapter VI.

29 See Kiparsky (1968a).

Conclusion

Nineteenth-century philologists devoted most of their energy to comparative and historical studies in an effort to note the similarities and divergencies of Indo-European languages. In this century, language has been viewed as a structural phenomenon in which various levels, for instance sound, grammar and syntax, interrelate and are governed by strict rules of concatenation. Phonetic factors underlying syntagmatic arrangements were generally held responsible for language change. Changes that appeared not to be motivated by the phonological environment came to be examined in terms of the function of the linguistic units involved in the change as well as their structure and in the social context in which the change took place. Analytical examination of language along structural lines, based upon empirical data and coupled with rational deductions concerning the function of linguistic units and their social relevance, has prompted more fundamental questions about the relationship of human language to the psychological and biological make-up of man.

Various aspects of language change have been explored in the foregoing chapters. The common objective was to present some insight into the principles and methods of historical linguistics which differ somewhat according to the approach. Each individual study of a diachronic linguistic problem will vary in its approach in relation to the depth the investigator wishes to achieve and the particular doctrine to which he or she subscribes. One may list historical changes without further comment or one may seek to explain the changes within one or another of the viable linguistic alternatives which go beyond the data in attempts to account for it. In any case, language data are the essential raw materials for any significant insight into language behaviour.

Historical studies of language behaviour are of paramount importance to linguistics. Only through studies of language change can we account for many social and cultural phenomena and arrive at a basis for a dichotomy of these and innate linguistic properties. The more we examine change, the more insight we gain into its specific manifestations and the motivations behind them. Primarily through investigations of change, we can obtain a glimpse into the psychological linguistic characteristics of man. Study of the various manifestations of linguistic systems at different periods in the history of a language will lead to a better understanding of human modes of conceptualization and their influence on language change; that is, further data along these lines and refined theoretical notions may pave the way for more precise statements about universal limitations of change and their relationship to cognitive parameters inherent in man. Subconscious aspects of language change such as the seemingly inherent tendency toward symmetry in linguistic patterns, the influence of deep structure on surface structure, and man's somewhat spontaneous creativity in modifying his own language will become more clearly defined.

The study of language change can be of great importance in determining areas of synchronic interest. It has been noted for example that certain sounds or sequences of sounds occur only at morpheme boundaries in many languages: in Classical Greek ἕξ *hex* is distinguished from ἐξ *ex* by 'rough breathing' which occurs only in word initial position. In French we find /õ/ + /m/ *on mange*, where a nasal vowel plus a nasal consonant occur at a morpheme boundary. (*On habite* is a possible exception.) In English, certain sequences of segmental phonemes consistently occur only at morpheme boundaries, eg, /-θs-/ *withstand, widths,* /-čs-/ *matchstick,* /-čl-/ *searchlight,* /-ğl-/ *largely,* /-šs-/ *washstand,* etc. The significance of such sounds in speech perception vis-à-vis their aid in morpheme identification has not been established. If it could be demonstrated that in some way they behave differently under conditions of change, that is, if to some degree they resist phonological change or inhibit its spread throughout the lexicon, even for a short period of time, we would no longer think of these sounds as simply corresponding to fortuitous arrangements in the distributional system. They would become targets of synchronic investigations in attempts to fathom their role among the various things a listener reacts to upon hearing a speech event.

In a broad context, language behaviour appears to be a vocal extension of communication in general. There is communication between the honey bee and the flower, between the distant hawk and the mouse in the field, between the brain and each living cell in the body. In each case the transference of information is essential for preservation and development of life. Human vocal expression seems to lie near one end of a spectrum of communication, measured perhaps by the physiological complexity of the sending and receiving mechanisms and by the structural complexity of the message. Near the other extreme is information transfer between minute particles of living cells. Perhaps even smaller sub-atomic particles in inanimate matter may one day be shown to participate in a hierarchy of communicative properties. One aspect of this continuum of communication concerns language change. Human language in its structural, social and biological complexity, as well as its relationship to other forms of communication, can only be fully understood when we know how it responds to certain stimuli.

There is an endless number of problems pressing for solutions in linguistic studies. Our curiosity about the wonder of language may never be entirely satisfied. Each step forward reveals a new panorama of the linguistic landscape crisscrossed by a myriad of pathways leading just over the hill to still new horizons.

Bibliography

ALARCOS LLORACH, E. *Fonología española.*[4] Madrid: Gredos, 1961
ALLEN, W. S. 'Relationship in Comparative Linguistics'. *Transactions of the Philological Society*, 1953, *pp* 52–108
ANDERSON, J. M. 'A Study of Syncope in Vulgar Latin,' *Word.* 21:1, 1965
– and J. A. CREORE (eds) *Readings in Romance Linguistics.* The Hague: Mouton, 1972
APPLEGATE, J. R. 'Shilha: Descriptive Grammar with Vocabulary and Texts,' (Microfilm) PHD Dissertation, New York: ACLS, 1958
ARNDT, W. et al (eds) *Studies in Historical Linguistics in Honor of George Sherman Lane.* Chapel Hill: The University of North Carolina Press, 1967
AUSTIN, W. M. 'Criteria for Phonetic Similarity,' *Language.* 33:4, 1957
BACH, E. 'The Order of Elements in a Transformational Grammar of German,' *Language.* 38, 1962
– and R. T. HARMS (eds) *Universals in Linguistic Theory.* New York: Holt, Rinehart and Winston, 1968
BAUGH, A. C. *A History of the English Language.* London: D. Appleton-Century, 1935
BENNETT, W. H. 'The Germanic Evidence for Bartholomae's Law,' *Language.* 42:4, 1966
– 'The Operation and Relative Chronology of Verner's Law,' *Language.* 44:2, 1968
BIERWISCH, M. *Grammatik des Deutschen Verbs.* Studia Grammatica, Berlin: Akademie-Verlag, 1963
BIRNBAUM, H. and J. PUHVEL (eds) *Ancient Indo-European Dialects.* Berkeley: University of California Press, 1966
BLOOMFIELD, L. *Language.* London: George Allen and Unwin, 1933

BLOOMFIELD, M. W. and L. NEWARK *A Linguistic Introduction to the History of English.* New York: Alfred A. Knopf, 1963

BOAS, F. *Introduction. Handbook of American Indian Languages.* Washington, D.C.: Government Printing Office, U.S. Bureau of Ethnology, 1911

BOURCIEZ, E. *Eléments de linguistique romane.* Paris: Klincksieck, 1930

BOYD-BOWMAN, P. *From Latin to Romance in Sound Charts.* New Haven: Yale University, 1954

BROOK, G. L. *A History of the English Language.* New York: W. W. Norton, 1958

BROSNAHAN, L. F. *The Sounds of Language.* Cambridge: W. Heffer, 1961

BRUGMANN, K. *Kurze Vergleichende Grammatik der Indogermanischen Sprachen.* Strasbourg: 1904

– and B. DELBRÜCK *Grundriss der Vergleichenden Grammatik der Indo-germanischen Sprachen.²* Vol 1, Einleitung und Lautlehre, Strasbourg: Trübner, 1897

BUCK, C. D. *Comparative Grammar of Greek and Latin.* Chicago: University of Chicago Press, 1933

BUETTNER-JANUSCH, J. *Origins of Man.* New York: John Wiley and Sons, 1966

BURROW, T. *The Sanskrit Language.* London: Faber and Faber, 1955

BURSILL-HALL, G. L. 'Frequency of Consonant Clusters in French,' *Journal of the Canadian Linguistic Association.* 2, 1956

CAPELL, A. *Studies in Socio-Linguistics.* The Hague: Mouton, 1966

CARDONA, G. *On Haplology in Indo-European.* Philadelphia: University of Pennsylvania Press, 1968

CARRINGTON, R. *A Million Years of Man.* London: Weidenfeld and Nicolson, 1963

CARROLL, J. 'The Assessment of Phoneme Cluster Frequencies,' *Language.* 34:2, 1958

CATALAN, D. (ed) *Miscelánea homenaje a André Martinet.* Universidad de la Laguna, Canarias: Biblioteca Filológica, 1958

CAWS, P. *The Philosophy of Science.* Princeton, New Jersey: D. Van Nostrand, 1965

CHADWICK, J. *The Decipherment of Linear B.* London: Cambridge University Press, 1958

CHASE, R. A. 'Evolutionary Aspects of Language Development and Function,' *The Genesis of Language,* eds. F. Smith and G. A. Miller. Cambridge, Mass: The M.I.T. Press, 1966

CHILDE, V. G. *The Aryans.* New York: Alfred A. Knopf, 1926

CHOMSKY, N. *Aspects of the Theory of Syntax.* Cambridge, Mass: The M.I.T. Press, 1965

– 'Deep Structure, Surface Structure and Semantic Interpretation,' MSS Indiana University Linguistics Club, 1969

– and M. HALLE *The Sound Pattern of English*. New York: Harper and Row, 1968

CHRÉTIEN, C. D. 'The Mathematical Models of Glottochronology,' *Language*. 38:1, 1962

CLARK, J. G. D. *The Mesolithic Settlement of Northern Europe*. London: Cambridge University Press, 1936

CLOSS, E. 'Diachronic Syntax and Generative Grammar,' *Language*. 41, 1965. Reprinted in Reibel and Schane (eds) *Modern Studies in English*. pp 395–408

COON, C. S. *The Origin of Races*. New York: Alfred A. Knopf, 1962

COROMINAS, J. *Diccionario crítico etimológico de la lengua castellana*. Madrid: Gredos, 1954

COSERIU, E. 'Critique de la glottochronologie appliquée aux langages romanes,' *Linguistique et Philologie Romanes*. Xe Congrès International de Linguistique et Philologie Romanes. Paris: Klincksieck, 1965

COWGILL, W. 'A Search for Universals in Indo-European Diachronic Morphology,' *Universals of Language*, ed J. Greenberg. Cambridge, Mass: The M.I.T. Press, 1963

DARLINGTON, C. D. 'The Genetic Component of Language,' *Heredity*. I, 1947

DE LACOUPERIE *Beginnings of Writing*. Osnabrück: Otto Zeller, 1965. Reprint of 1894 edition

DE LAGUNA, G. A. *Speech, Its Function and Development*. Bloomington: Indiana University Press, 1963

DENES, P. B. and E. N. PINSON *The Speech Chain*. Bell Telephone Laboratories, 1963

DE SAUSSURE, F. *Course in General Linguistics*, eds C. Bally and A. Sechehaye. New York: Philosophical Library, 1959

DIEZ, F. *Grammatik der Romanischen Sprachen*. Bonn: Eduard Webers Verlag, 1882

DINES, A. M. *Honeybees from Close Up*. New York: Thomas Y. Crowell, 1968

DINNEEN, F. P. *An Introduction to General Linguistics*. New York: Holt, Rinehart and Winston, 1967

DIVER, W. 'On the Diachronic Role of the Morphological System,' *Miscelánea Homenaje a André Martinet*, ed Diego Catalan. Universidad de la Laguna, Canarias: Biblioteca Filológica, 1958

DOBLEHOFER, E. *Voices in Stone*, M. Savill (trans). London: Souvenir Press, 1961

DORFMAN, E. 'Correlation and Core-Relation in Diachronic Phonology,' *Readings in Romance Linguistics*, eds J. M. Anderson and J. A. Creore. The Hague: Mouton, 1972

ELCOCK, W. D. *The Romance Languages*. New York: The Macmillan Company, 1960

ENTWISTLE, W. J. *The Spanish Language*. London: Faber and Faber,
    1936
ESTRICH, R. M. and H. SPERBER *Three Keys to Language*. New York:
    Rinehart and Co, 1952
EWERT, A. *The French Language*. London: Faber and Faber, 1933
FARB, P. *Man's Rise to Civilization*. New York: E. P. Dutton, 1968
FLINT, R. F. *Glacial Geology and the Pleistocene Epoch*. New York: John
    Wiley and Sons, 1947
FODOR, I. *The Rate of Linguistic Change*. The Hague: Mouton, 1965
FOLEY, J. 'Rule Precursors and Phonological Change by Meta-rule,'
    UCLA. To appear in *Proceedings of the Conference on Historical
    Change from the Perspective of Transformational Grammar*, 1969
 – 'Morphological Investigations II.' (Unpublished manuscript)
FRANCIS, W. N. *The Structure of American English*. New York: The
    Ronald Press, 1958
FRIEDRICH, J. *Extinct Languages*, F. Gaynor (trans). New York:
    Philosophical Library, 1957
 – *Hethitisches Elementarbuch*. Heidelberg: C. Winter, 1967
GARDNER, R. A. and B. T. GARDNER *Training Through 103 Weeks'
    Report*. Washoe's Diary Abstract. Reno: University of Nevada, 1968
GARN, S. M. *Symposium on Culture and the Direction of Human Evolution
    Philadelphia 1962*. Detroit: Wayne State University Press, 1964
GELB, I. J. *A Study of Writing*. Chicago: The University of Chicago
    Press, 1952
GESCHWIND, N. 'Linguistics and Speech Behavior,' *Languages and
    Linguistics*, ed C. I. J. M. Stuart. Washington, DC: Georgetown
    University Press, 1964
GLEASON, H. A. *An Introduction to Descriptive Linguistics*. Rev edn New
    York: Holt, Rinehart and Winston, 1955
GRANDGENT, C. H. *Vulgar Latin*. New York: Hafner, 1962
GREENBERG, J. H. *Essays in Linguistics*. Chicago: University of Chicago
    Press, 1957
 – (ed) *Universals of Language*. Cambridge, Mass: The M.I.T. Press,
    1963
 – *The Languages of Africa*. The Hague: Mouton, 1966
GRIMES, J. E. and F. B. AGARD 'Linguistic Divergence in Romance,'
    Language. 35:4, 1959
GUDSCHINSKY, S. C. 'The ABC's of Lexicostatistics (Glottochronology),'
    Word. 12:2, 1956
GUISASOLA, F. C. *El enigma del vascuence ante las lenguas indeuropas*.
    Madrid: S. Aguirre, 1944
GUMPERZ, J. J. and D. HYMES (eds) *American Anthropologist*. 66:2, 1964
GURNEY, O. R. *The Hittites*.[2] Middlesex, England: Penguin Books Ltd,
    1954

HALL, R. A. JR 'Reconstruction of Proto-Romance,' *Language*. 26:1, 1950
- *Pidgin and Creole Languages*. Ithaca, NY: Cornell University Press, 1966
HALLE, M. *The Sound Patterns of Russian*. The Hague: Mouton, 1959
- 'Phonology in Generative Grammar,' *Word*. 18, 1962. Reprinted in *The Structure of Language*, eds J. A. Fodor and J. J. Katz, *pp* 334–352, 1964
- and S. J. KEYSER, 'Review of Bror Danielsson (ed): John Hart's works on English orthography, 1551, 1569, 1570': Part II, *Phonology*. Uppsala: Almqvist and Wiksell, 1963. *Language*. 43, 1967
HAMMERSTRÖM, G. 'The Romance Languages,' *Manual of Phonetics*, ed L. Kaiser. Amsterdam: North Holland Publishing Company, 1957
HARMS, R. T. 'The Measurement of Phonological Economy,' *Language*. 42:3, 1966
- *Introduction to Phonological Theory*. New Jersey: Prentice-Hall, 1968
HARRIS, J. W. *Spanish Phonology*. Cambridge, Mass: The M.I.T. Press, 1969
HAUDRICOURT, A. 'EN/AN en français,' *Word*. 3, 1947
- and A. JUILLAND *Essai pour une histoire structurale du phonétisme français*. Paris: Klincksieck, 1949
HENCKEN, H. 'Indo-European Languages and Archaeology'. *American Anthropologist*, American Anthropological Association, Vol 57, No 6, Part 3, December 1955
HILL, A. *Introduction to Linguistic Structures*. New York: Harcourt, Brace and World, 1958
HIRSCHBÜHLER, P. 'Traitement transformationnel de l'interrogation et de quelques problèmes connexes en français.' (Unpublished Dissertation) Université Libre de Bruxelles, 1970
HOCKETT, C. F. 'Time-Perspective and its Anthropological Uses,' IJAL. 19, 1953
- *A Course in Modern Linguistics*. New York: The Macmillan Company, 1958
- 'The Problem of Universals in Language,' *Universals of Language*, ed J. Greenberg. Cambridge, Mass: The M.I.T. Press, 1963
- 'Sound Change,' *Language*. 41:2, 1965
- *The Quantification of Functional Load*. Santa Monica, California: Rand Corporation, 1966
- and R. ASCHER 'The Human Revolution,' *Current Anthropology*. 5:3, 1964
HOENIGSWALD, H. H. 'Sound Change and Linguistic Structure,' *Language*. 22:2, 1946
- Review of 'Economie des Changements Phonétiques,' *Language*. 33:4, 1957

– *Language Change and Linguistic Reconstruction*. Chicago: University of Chicago Press, 1960
– 'Are there Universals of Linguistic Change?' *Universals of Language*, ed J. Greenberg. Cambridge, Mass: The M.I.T. Press, 1963
HUDDLESTON, R. and O. UREN 'Declarative, Interrogative, and Imperative in French,' *Lingua*. 22, 1969
HUDSON-WILLIAMS, T. *A Short Introduction to the Study of Comparative Grammar (Indo-European)*. Cardiff: University of Wales Press, 1951
HUGHES, J. P. *The Science of Language*. New York: Random House, 1962
HULTZEN, L. S. 'Consonant Clusters in English,' *American Speech*. XL: 1, 1965
HYMES, D. H. (ed) *Language in Culture and Society; A Reader in Linguistics and Anthropology*. New York: Harper and Row, 1964
IBAÑEZ, E. *Diccionario Rifeño-Español*. Madrid: Instituto de Estudios Africanos, 1949
IVIĆ, P. 'On the Structure of Dialectal Differentiation,' *Word*. 18: 1–2, 1962
JAKOBSON, R. *Linguistics and Adjacent Sciences*. II *Natural Sciences*. Bucarest: Xème Congrès International des Linguistes, 1967
– *Child Language. Aphasia and Phonological Universals*. The Hague: Mouton, 1968
JANKOWSKY, K. R. *The Neogrammarians*. Pre-publication edition. Washington, DC: Georgetown University, 1968
JESPERSEN, O. *Language*.[11] London: George Allen and Unwin, 1922
– *A Modern English Grammar*. London: George Allen and Unwin, 1949
JONES, L. G. 'English Consonantal Distribution,' *For Roman Jakobson*. Compiled by M. Halle, H. G. Lunt, H. McLean, C. H. Van Schoone-veld. The Hague: Mouton, 1956, *pp* 245–253
JOOS, M. *Readings in Linguistics*. New York: ACLS, 1958
JUNGEMANN, F. *La teoría del sustrato y los dialectos hispano-romances y gascones*. Madrid: Gredos, 1955
KAISER, L. (ed) *Manual of Phonetics*. Amsterdam: North-Holland Publishing Co, 1957
KATZ, J. J. and P. M. POSTAL *An Integrated Theory of Linguistic Description*. Cambridge, Mass: The M.I.T. Press, 1964
KAYNE, R. S. 'The Evolution of French Interrogatives,' to appear in *Proceedings of the Linguistic Symposium on Romance Languages*. Gainesville, Florida: University of Florida, 1971
KING, R. D. 'Functional Load and Sound Change,' *Language*. 43: 4, 1967
– *Historical Linguistics and Generative Grammar*. New Jersey: Prentice-Hall, 1969. Reviewed by W. N. Norman, *Language Sciences* 9: February 1970, *pp* 18–19
KIPARSKY, R. P. V. *Phonological Change*, M.I.T. dissertation, 1965

– 'Linguistic Universals and Linguistic Change,' *Universals in Linguistic Theory*, eds E. Bach and T. Harms. New York: Holt, Rinehart and Winston, 1968a

– 'Tense and Mood in Indo-European Syntax,' *Foundations of Language*, 4, 1968b

KLIMA, E. S. 'Relatedness between Grammatical Systems,' *Language*. 40 1964. Reprinted in D. A. Reibel and S. A. Schane, eds *Modern Studies in English*

– *Studies in Diachronic Transformational Syntax*, Unpublished Dissertation, Harvard University, 1965

KURYŁOWICZ, J. *Esquisses Linguistiques*. Wrocław-Kraków: Zakład Narodowy Imienia Ossolinskich Wydawnictwo Polskiej Akademii Nauk, 1960

LABOV, W. 'The Social Motivation of Sound Change,' *Word*. 19:3, 1963

– 'Phonological Correlates of Social Stratification,' *The Ethnography of Communication*, eds J. J. Gumperz and D. Hymes. Menasha, Wisconsin: American Anthropological Association, 1964

– 'On the Mechanisms of Linguistic Change,' *Report of the Sixteenth Annual Round Table Meeting on Linguistics and Language Studies,* ed C. W. Kreidler. Washington, DC: Georgetown University Press, 1965

– *The Social Stratification of English in New York City*. Washington, DC: Center for Applied Linguistics, 1966

LAFON, R. 'Concordances morphologiques entre le Basque et les langues caucasiques,' *Word*. 8:1, 1952

LAKOFF, R. T. *Abstract Syntax and Latin Complementation*. Cambridge, Mass: The M.I.T. Press, 1968

LANDAR, H. *Language and Culture*. Oxford University Press, 1966

LANGACKER, R. W. 'French Interrogatives: A Transformational Description,' *Language*. 41, 1965

– *Language and Its Structure*. New York: Harcourt, Brace and World, 1968

– 'French Interrogatives Revisited,' to appear in *Proceedings of the Linguistic Symposium on Romance Languages*. Gainesville, Florida: University of Florida, 1971

LAPESA, R. *Historia de la lengua española*. Madrid: Escelicer, 1959

LASS, R. (ed) *Approaches to English Historical Linguistics*. New York: Holt, Rinehart and Winston, 1969

LEACH, E. 'Anthropological Aspects of Language,' *New Directions in the Study of Language*, ed. E. H. Lenneberg. Cambridge, Mass: The M.I.T. Press, 1964

LE GROS CLARK, SIR W. E. *Man-Apes or Ape-Men?* New York, London: Holt, Rinehart and Winston, 1967

LEHMANN, W. P. *Proto-Indo-European Phonology*. Austin: University of Texas Press, 1955

– *Historical Linguistics : An Introduction.* New York: Holt, Rinehart and
Winston, 1962
– and Y. Malkiel (eds) *Directions for Historical Linguistics.* Austin:
University of Texas Press, 1968
LENNEBERG, E. H. (ed) *New Directions in the Study of Language.*
Cambridge, Mass: The M.I.T. Press, 1964
– *Biological Foundations of Language.* New York: John Wiley and Sons,
1967
LEROY, M. *Main Trends in Modern Linguistics,* G. Prince (trans)
Berkeley: University of California Press, 1967
LIEBERMAN, P. and E. S. CRELIN 'On the Speech of Neanderthal Man,'
Linguistic Inquiry. 2:203–222, 1971
LOCKWOOD, W. B. *Indo-European Philology.* London: Hutchinson, 1969
LYONS, J. 'Review of Katz and Postal, 1964.' *Journal of Linguistics.* 2:1,
1966
– *Introduction to Theoretical Linguistics.* London: Cambridge University
Press, 1968
MACKENDRICK, P. *The Mute Stones Speak.* New York: St Martin's
Press, 1960
MALKIEL, Y. 'The Inflectional Paradigm as an Occasional Determinant
of Sound Change,' *Directions for Historical Linguistics,* eds W. P.
Lehmann and Y. Malkiel. Austin: University of Texas Press, 1968
MALMBERG, B. *Notas sobre la fonética del español en el Paraguay.*
Vetenskaps Societeten: Lund, Arsbok, 1947
MARTIN, P. S. and H. E. WRIGHT (eds) *Pleistocene Extinctions.* London:
Yale University Press, 1967
– 'Function, Structure, and Sound Change,' *Word.* 8:1, 1952
– 'On the Preservation of Useful Sound Features,' *Word.* 9:1, 1953
MARTINET, A. *Economie des changements phonétiques.* Berne: A. Francke,
1955
– 'Phonetics and Linguistic Evolution,' *Manual of Phonetics,* ed
L. Kaiser. Amsterdam: North-Holland Publishing Co, 1957
– *A Functional View of Language.* Oxford: The Clarendon Press, 1962
MATTOSO CÁMARA, J., JR *The History of Linguistics.* (Unpublished notes)
MCCAWLEY, J. D. 'Concerning the Base Component of a Transforma-
tional Grammar,' *Foundations of Language.* 4, 1968
MEILLET, A. 'Comment les mots changent de sens,' *Linguistique
Historique et Linguistique Générale.* Paris: Champion, 1921–1937,
pp 230–271
– *Introduction à l'étude comparative des langues Indo-Européennes.* Paris:
Hachette, 1922
– *La méthode comparative en linguistique historique.* Paris: Honoré
Champion, 1954. First printed by Aschehoug & Co: Oslo, 1924
– et M. COHEN *Les langues du monde.* Paris: CNRS, 1952

MENÉNDEZ PIDAL, R. *Manual de gramática histórica española.*⁹ Madrid: Espasa-Calpe, SA, 1952

MICHELENA, L. *Fonética histórica vasca.* San Sebastian: Publicaciones del Seminario Julio de Urquijo, 1961

MILLER, G. A. and S. ISARD 'Some Perceptual Consequences of Linguistic Rules,' *Journal of Verbal Learning and Verbal Behavior.* 2, 1963

MILLER, R. A. *The Japanese Language.* Chicago: University of Chicago Press, 1967

MOORHOUSE, A. C. *The Triumph of the Alphabet.* New York: Henry Schuman, 1953

MOULTON, W. G. 'Dialect Geography and the Concept of Phonological Space,' *Word.* 18: 1–2, 1962

MUKAROVSKY, H. G. 'Baskisch und Berberisch,' *Wiener Zeitschrift für die Kunde des Morgenlandes.* 59–60, 1963–4

NIDA, E. A. *Morphology.*² Ann Arbor: The University of Michigan Press, 1946

NIST, J. *A Structural History of English.* New York: St Martin's Press, 1966

OSGOOD, C. E. and T. A. SEBEOK *Psycholinguistics.*² Bloomington: Indiana University Press, 1965

PALMER, L. R. *The Latin Language.* London: Faber and Faber, 1954

PATTERSON, G. W. 'French Interrogatives: A Diachronic Problem,' to appear in *Proceedings of the Linguistic Symposium on Romance Languages.* Gainesville, Florida: University of Florida, 1971a

– 'French Interrogatives: Synchronic and Diachronic,' PHD Dissertation. Edmonton: The University of Alberta, 1971b

PAUL, H. *Principles of the History of Language*, H. A. Strong (trans) New York: Macmillan and Co, 1889

PEDERSEN, H. *The Discovery of Language*, J. W. Spargo (trans) Bloomington: Indiana University Press, 1931

PETERS, S. P. 'Why There Are Many "Universal" Bases,' *Papers in Linguistics.* 2, 1970

PIGGOTT, S. *Ancient Europe.* Edinburgh: The University Press, 1965

POLÁK, V. 'La position linguistique des langues caucasiennes,' *Studia Linguistica.* Année IV, 1950

POLOME, E. G. 'The Position of Illyrian and Venetic,' *Ancient Indo-European Dialects*, eds H. Birnbaum and J. Puhvel. Berkeley: University of California Press, 1966

POPE, M. K. *From Latin to Modern French.* Manchester: Manchester University Press, 1958

POSNER, R. *Consonantal Dissimilation in the Romance Languages.* Oxford: Blackwell, 1961

POSTAL, P. M. *Aspects of Phonological Theory.* New York: Harper and Row, 1968

POSTMAN, L. 'The Present Status of Interference Theory,' *Verbal Learning and Verbal Behavior*, ed C. Cofer. New York: McGraw-Hill, 1961

PROSMAN, P. W., JR 'Proto-Indo-Hittite *b* and the Allophones of Laryngeals,' *Language*. 33:1, 1957

PULGRAM, E. *The Tongues of Italy*. Cambridge, Mass: Harvard University Press, 1958

– 'Trends and Predictions,' *To Honor Roman Jakobson*, compiled by M. Halle, H. G. Lunt, H. McLean, C. H. Van Schooneveld. The Hague: Mouton, 1967

PYLES, T. *The Origins and Development of the English Language*. New York: Harcourt, Brace and World, 1964

REVZIN, I. *Models of Language*, N. F. C. Owen and A. S. C. Ross (trans) London: Methuen, 1962

ROBINS, R. H. *Ancient and Mediaeval Grammatical Theory in Europe*. London: G. Bell and Sons, 1951

ROCHET, B. 'Un processus analogique comme origine d'un changement phonétique,' to appear in *Canadian Journal of Linguistics*

ROMEO, L. *The Economy of Diphthongization in Early Romance*. The Hague: Mouton, 1968

ROSS, J. R. 'Gapping and the Order of Constituents.' Reproduced by the Linguistics Club, Indiana University, Bloomington, Indiana, 1968, in *Proceedings of the Xth International Congress of Linguists*, 1967

ROUDET, L. 'Sur la classification psychologique des changements sémantiques,' *Journal de Psychologie*. XVIII, 1921

SAPIR, E. *Language*. New York: Harcourt, Brace and World, 1921

SAPORTA, S. 'Frequency of Consonant Clusters,' *Language*. 31:1, 1955

– and D. OLSON 'Classification of Intervocalic Clusters,' *Language*. 34, 1958

SCHANE, S. *French Phonology and Morphology*. Cambridge, Mass: The M.I.T. Press, 1968a

– 'On the Non-Uniqueness of Phonological Representations,' *Language*. 44:4, 1968b

SCOTT, C. T. and J. L. ERICKSON (eds) *Readings for the History of the English Language*. Boston: Allyn and Bacon, 1968

SOMMERFELT, A. 'Some Remarks on the Importance of a Substratum in Linguistic Development,' *Miscelánea homenaje a André Martinet*, ed Diego Catalan. Universidad de la Laguna, Canarias: Biblioteca Filológica, 1958

– *Diachronic and Synchronic Aspects of Language*. The Hague: Mouton, 1962

SPENCE, N. C. W. 'Quantity and Quality in the Vowel-System of Vulgar Latin,' *Word*. 21:1, 1965

SPERBER, H. *Einführung in die Bedenkungslehre*.² Leipzig: 1930

STEVICK, R. D. 'The Biological Model and Historical Linguistics,' *Language*. 39:2, 1963
– *English and Its History*. Boston: Allyn and Bacon, 1968
STERN, P. VAN DOREN *Prehistoric Europe*. New York: W. W. Norton, 1969
STURTEVANT, E. H. *Linguistic Change*. Chicago: University of Chicago Press, 1917
– 'Hittite and Areal Linguistics,' *Language*. 23:4, 1947a
– *An Introduction to Linguistic Science*. New Haven: Yale University Press, 1947b
– *A Comparative Grammar of the Hittite Language*[2]. New Haven: Yale University Press, 1964
THIEME, P. *Die Heimat der Indogermanischen Gemeinsprache*. Wiesbaden: in Kommission bei F. Steiner, 1954
TOVAR, A. *The Ancient Languages of Spain and Portugal*. New York: S. F. Vanni, 1961
TROUBETZKOY, N. S. *Principes de Phonologie*, J. Cantineau (trans) Paris: Klincksieck, 1957
ULLMANN, S. *The Principles of Semantics*, Glasgow: Jackson, Son and Co, 1951
– 'Semantic Universals,' *Universals of Language*, ed J. Greenberg. Cambridge, Mass: The M.I.T. Press, 1963
VÄÄNÄNEN, V. *Introduction au latin vulgaire*. Paris: Klincksieck, 1963
VACHEK, J. *Brno Studies in English*. Opera Universitatis Purkynianae Brunensis, Facultas Philosophica, No 93, Vol 4, 1964
VOGT, H. 'Phoneme Classes and Phoneme Classification,' *Word*. X:1, 1954
VON FRISCH, K. *The Dancing Bees* (rev ed). London: Methuen, 1954
VON WARTBURG, W. *La fragmentación lingüística de la Romania*. Madrid: Gredos, 1952
VOYLES, J. B. 'Simplicity, Ordered Rules, and the First Sound Shift,' *Language*. 43:3, 1967
WEIDENREICH, F. 'The Human Brain in the Light of its Phylogenetic Development,' *Human Evolution*, eds N. Korn and F. Thompson. New York: Holt, Rinehart and Winston, 1967
WEINREICH, U. *Languages in Contact*. New York: Linguistic Circle of New York, 1953
– 'On the Semantic Structure of Language,' Universals of Language, ed J. Greenberg. Cambridge, Mass: The M.I.T. Press, 1963
– 'Is a Structural Dialectology Possible?' *Linguistics Today*, eds A. Martinet and U. Weinreich. New York: Linguistic Circle of New York, 1964
WEINREICH, U., W. LABOV, M. I. HERZOG 'Empirical Foundations for a Theory of Language Change,' *Directions for Historical Linguistics*, eds

W. P. Lehmann and Y. Malkiel. Austin: University of Texas Press, 1968

WEINSTOCK, J. 'Grimm's Law in Distinctive Features,' *Language.* 44:2, 1968

WENNER, A. M. 'Sound Communication in Honeybees,' *Psychobiology, The Biological Bases of Behavior.* San Francisco: W. H. Freeman, 1966

—, P. H. WELLS and D. L. JOHNSON. 'Honey Bee Recruitment to Food Sources: Olfaction or Language?' *Science.* 164:3875, April 1969

WHEELER, SIR M. *Civilizations of the Indus Valley and Beyond.* New York: McGraw-Hill, 1966

WHITNEY, W. D. *Sanskrit Grammar.* Cambridge, Mass: Harvard University Press, 1964

WHORF, B. L. *Language, Thought and Reality ; Selected Writings of Benjamin Lee Whorf,* ed J. B. Carroll. Cambridge: Technology Press, 1956

WILLIAMS, E. B. *From Latin to Portuguese.* Philadelphia: University of Pennsylvania Press, 1968

WYLD, H. C. *A Short History of English.* London: John Murray, 1914

ZIPF, G. K. *The Psycho-Biology of Language.* Cambridge, Mass: The M.I.T. Press, 1965

— *Human Behavior and the Principle of Least Effort.* New York: Hafner, 1965

Index